"1812." Napoleon I. in Russia. With an introduction by R. Whiteing. Illustrated from sketches and paintings by the author

Vasily Vasil'evich Vereshchagin, Richard Whiteing, Napoleon

"1812." Napoleon I. in Russia ... With an introduction by R. Whiteing. Illustrated from sketches and paintings by the author.
Vereshchagin, Vasily Vasil'evich
British Library, Historical Print Editions
British Library
Whiteing, Richard
Napoleon
1899
266 p. ; 8º.

"1812"

NAPOLEON I IN RUSSIA

Art

GAINSBOROUGH. By WALTER ARMSTRONG, Director of the National Gallery, Ireland. With 62 Photogravures and 10 Lithographs in Colour. £5 5*s.* net.

LEONARDO DA VINCI. From the French of EUGÈNE MÜNTZ. In 2 vols., with 20 Photogravures, 26 Coloured Plates, and about 200 Text Illustrations. £2 2*s.* net.

MEISSONIER. By VALLERY C. O. GREARD. From the French by LADY MARY LOYD and FLORENCE SIMMONDS. With 38 Full-page Plates, and 250 Text Illustrations. £1 16*s.* net.

CORREGGIO. By CORRADO RICCI. Translated by FLORENCE SIMMONDS. With 16 Photogravures, 21 Full-page Plates in Colour, and 160 Illustrations in Text. £2 2*s.* net.

REMBRANDT. By EMILE MICHEL. Edited by FREDERICK WEDMORE. With 76 Full-page Plates and 250 Text Illustrations. £2 2*s.* net.

NEW LETTERS OF NAPOLEON I. Omitted from the Edition published under the auspices of Napoleon III. Translated from the French by LADY MARY LOYD. 15*s.* net.

NAPOLEON AND THE FAIR SEX. From the French of FRÉDÉRIC MASSON. With a Portrait. 6*s.*

LONDON: WILLIAM HEINEMANN,
21 BEDFORD STREET, W.C.

V. Verestchagin

"1812"

NAPOLEON I IN RUSSIA

BY

VASSILI VERESTCHAGIN

WITH AN INTRODUCTION BY

R. WHITEING

Illustrated from Sketches and Paintings by the Author

LONDON
WILLIAM HEINEMANN
1899

CONTENTS

FULL-PAGE ILLUSTRATIONS

"1812"

NAPOLEON I IN RUSSIA

INTRODUCTION

THE following pages are not offered to the reader as a history of the invasion of Russia by Napoleon. They are but the statement of the basis of observation on which M. Verestchagin has founded his great series of pictures illustrative of the campaign. These pictures are now to be exhibited in this country, and the painter has naturally desired to show us from what point of view he has approached the study of his subject—one of the greatest subjects in the whole range of history—especially for a Russian artist. The point of view is—inevitably in his case—that of the Realist; and this consideration gives unity to the conception of his whole career and endeavour. He has ever painted war as it is, and therefore in its horrors, as one of its effects, though not necessarily as an effect sought in and for itself. He has tried to be "true" in all his representations of the battle-field. His work may thus be said to constitute a powerful plea in support of the Tsar's Rescript to the Nations in favour of peace. My meaning will be best illustrated by a short sketch of M. Verestchagin and his work, as painter, as soldier, and as traveller.

He was born in the province of Novgorod, in 1842, of a well-to-do family of landowners. The son wished to be an artist; the father wished to make him an officer of marines. As the shortest way out of the difficulty, he became both. He passed his work-hours at the naval school, and his play-hours at a school of design, working at each so well that he left the naval school as first scholar, and eventually won a silver medal at the Academy of Fine Arts. He entered the service, but only for a short time, and he was still three years under twenty when he quitted it to devote himself wholly to art.

He was a hard-working student, though he always showed a strong disposition to insist on working in his own way. When Gérôme sent him to the antique, he was half the time slipping away to nature. He played truant from the Athenian marbles to flesh and blood. In the meantime he was true to the instinct—as yet you could hardly call it a principle—of wandering from the beaten track in search of subjects. Every vacation was passed, not at Asnières or Barbizon, but in the far east of Europe, or even in Persia, among those ragged races not yet set down in artistic black and white. He had been on the borders of a quite fresh field of observation in these journeys; and he was soon to enter it for a full harvest of new impressions. It was in 1867; Russia was sending an army into Central Asia, to punish the marauding Turkomans for the fiftieth time, and General Kauffman, who commanded it, invited the painter to accompany him as an art volunteer. He was not to fight, but simply to look on. It was the very thing; Verestchagin at once took service on these terms with the expedition, and in faithfully following its fortunes, with many an artistic reconnaissance on his own account, he saw Asia to its core.

He returned from a second Asiatic journey to settle at Munich for three years; and here he built his first "open-air studio." "If you are to paint out-door scenes," he says, "your models must sit in the open;" and so he fashioned a movable room on wheels, running on a circular tramway, and open to sun and air on the side nearest the centre of the circle, where the model stood. The artist, in fact, worked in a huge box with one side out, while the thing he saw was in the full glare of day; and by means of a simple mechanical contrivance he made his room follow the shifting light.

After a long rest at Munich, he was impatient for action once more, and in 1873 he set off for British India.

Verestchagin filled one entire exhibition with his Indian studies. They form a definite part of his collection, a section of his life-work. Amazing studies they are. The end of his sojourn coincided with the visit of the Prince of Wales, and he saw India both at its best and at its worst. In one immense canvas he has represented the royal entry into Jeypore, the Prince and his native entertainer on a richly-caparisoned elephant, and a long line of lesser magnates similarly mounted in the rear. A scene of prayer in a mosque is noble in feeling, and it exhibits an amazing mastery of technique. The Temple of Indra, the Caves of Ellora—all the great show-places—are there, with their furniture of priests, deities, monsters, and men-at-arms. He made a prodigious journey, from St. Petersburg by Constantinople to Egypt, Hindostan, the Himalayas, and Thibet.

On his return he saw a great national subject at last—the Russo-Turkish War. He followed the armies and saw it all, still as a civilian in name, but as a soldier in fact. He could not keep out of it, both from patriotism and from artistic conscientiousness. On one occasion his desire to study the effect of a gun-boat in the air nearly cost him his life. When the Russians were preparing to cross the Danube opposite Rustchuk, their engineers found it almost impossible to carry on their surveys for a bridge, owing to the proximity of the Turkish gun-boats. Some men were accordingly sent out to lay fixed torpedoes across the river to prevent the approach of the gun-boats. But they themselves required protection while engaged in the service, and a few torpedo-launches were accordingly ordered to patrol the river for that purpose. They were not to wait to be attacked, but to boldly assume the offensive, and sink or drive off the big gun-boats. It was a most dangerous duty, and when Verestchagin asked permission to serve in one of the launches the officer in command tried to deter him. "Russia has many hundreds of officers like me," he said, "but not two painters like you." Verestchagin, however, was allowed to have his way. The launch he chose was very swift; it went almost at the speed of a train. It soon came in sight of one of the gun-boats, to the great terror of the Turkish crew. They could be seen running about the deck shouting and shaking their fists at one another. The gun-boat turned tail at once, but the little torpedo-launch gained on it every moment. By this time the whole Turkish force had taken the alarm, and a fire was concentrated on the little launch both from the gun-boat and the banks of the river, under which it was evident she could not live. She pushed on, however, shoved the torpedo under the bows of the Turk, and—it hung fire. It touched her fairly, but the wire connecting with the fuse had been cut in half by shot. Having done this, or rather having failed to do it, the launch was carried away by the tide, and just as she got clear of the vessel the Turks renewed their awful fire from ship and shore. Verestchagin suddenly felt a sickening sensation, as if he had been roughly pushed, and putting his hand to the place found a wound that would admit his three fingers. At this moment the crew of the Russian launch saw another Turkish monitor coming towards them, and firing as she came, so that they stood a good chance of being caught between these two monsters—as they might fairly be called in relation to the size of the launch. However, the launch turned and ran, closely pursued by the nearest gun-boat, which she had amiably tried to destroy. The pursuer was fast gaining on them in their crippled condition, when, at a turn in the river, they saw a little creek. They made for it and were saved. The gun-boat could not follow for fear of going aground.

This incident nearly finished Verestchagin's artistic career. He lay between life and death for weeks, but a devoted Russian nurse brought him round. Of course he went back to work again as soon as he could move, and in one way or other saw and painted nearly all of the campaign, especially Shipka, and the final rush on Constantinople.

De Lonlay gives us a characteristic picture of Verestchagin at this time.

"On November 24, 1877," he says, "we were in Bulgaria, at the foot of the great Balkans. Our little expeditionary corps, commanded by the brave General Daudeville, had just taken possession of a city after an obstinate fight, and was still trembling with the excitement of the struggle. We ran through the deserted streets of the Turkish quarter, which had been abandoned by its inhabitants. Everywhere we saw the same lamentable signs of devastation—doors broken open, windows smashed; and within the houses, furniture in fragments, heaps of wearing apparel in rags, and a quantity of the stuffing of the ottomans strewed all about, the Bulgarian pillagers having cared only for the ornamental coverings. Amid all this confusion lay the bodies of three Redifs and an Arnaut. The marauders had already stripped them of their uniforms, leaving them nothing but a little underclothing. A little further on, a Redif, still dressed in his blue tunic, lay on the ground. Suddenly, there came clattering by a troop of Cossacks who had just been hunting the Turkish runaways. They were rough-looking fellows, these soldiers in their white linen, all in rags, and with their fur caps browned by the bivouac fires and half bare with the wear and tear of the campaign; but among them I remarked an elegant horseman who contrasted strongly with the rest of the troop. He was dressed half like a soldier and half like a tourist. He wore a high Circassian cap in Astrakan fur trimmed with silver. From his breast hung the officer's cross of the military order of St. George,[1] a high distinction justly envied in Russia. The handle and the scabbard of his poignard and sabre were in chiselled silver. I followed him a long time with my eyes, admiring his bearing. A little later on in the same day I found my unknown once more. He was sitting on a low camp-stool in a corner of the grand mosque, and making a study of the minaret. His aristocratic face, of a long oval, was ornamented with a beard of a chestnut colour, and it contrasted strangely with the olive complexion and high cheek-bones of the Mussulman-Cossacks who surrounded him and peeped curiously at the work he was

[1] The cross of St. George, the highest military distinction in Russia, is not given in the usual way on a mere order of the sovereign, but only after a special inquiry into the circumstances of each case by the Council of the Order.

doing. It reminded me of Salvator Rosa working in the midst of the bandits of the Abruzzi. At this point a common friend of both of us came on the scene and presented us to one another. I had before me the great Russian painter Basil Verestchagin, who had but just recovered from the serious wound received in the previous June. We talked for a long time of Paris and of the war. Verestchagin complained bitterly of not having been able to take part in the passage of the Danube, and see the winter campaign as he had seen the summer one. 'What good luck you had,' he said, 'to follow Gourko in his expedition beyond the great Balkans! What things you must have seen, the massacre at Shipka, and the burning of Eski Zara. If you only knew how it enraged me to be tied down to my bed in the ambulance while the army was going on!' Then he paid me a few compliments on the modest drawings which I was sending to the *Monde Illustré*, compliments which touched me very much as they were offered by such an eminent artist.

"A few days after, the branch of the Cossacks of the Don to which I was attached, and the regiment of the Grenadiers of the Guard, entered the pass of the Balkans by the route which leads to Statitza. At nightfall we halted on a plateau covered with snow, and where the temperature was below zero. We were therefore not at all disinclined to take refuge in an old Turkish block-house and to light up a good fire. There I found Verestchagin again, with Prince Tzerteleff, the former secretary of Ignatieff, and Prince Tchakowski, who were all following our columns as amateurs. Enveloped in our *bourkas*, we talked away for hours round this bivouac fire, Verestchagin telling us of his perilous expedition in Turkestan. I can still hear him talking in his soft and quiet voice of all those scenes of massacre and carnage which he had seen with his own eyes.

"A fortnight after, I was at Plevna, which had just fallen into the hands of the Russian army, and there I saw Verestchagin again. He was staying with General Skobeleff, governor of the city. The great artist was fresh from the terrible battles, and from the scenes of misery which he had seen in the camps of the Turkish prisoners, and he was projecting another series of pictures. He was therefore, with his usual passion for accuracy, taking pains to collect arms and uniforms of the enemy as models. He showed great joy when one of the officers present offered to conduct him to the place in which the spoils of the garrison of Osman Pacha were stored. By the light of a torch carried by a grenadier he rummaged a long time in this heap of Peabody-Martini rifles, covered with mud and dust, torn uniforms stained with blood, blue vests with red lacings of the Nizams, brass-buttoned tunics and red waistbands of the Redifs, etc. Next morning we separated. Verestchagin followed the column of Skobeleff in its march to Shipka; and I went to Orkanie to rejoin the corps of General Gourko."

As a war-painter Verestchagin is a great moralist, and he is a great moralist because he is quite sincere. He paints exactly what he sees on the battle-field, and he is far in advance of the French, who are the fathers of this species of composition, in his rendering of the truth, the whole truth, and nothing but the truth, about this bloody sport of kings. There was a whole wide world of difference in spirit between his little military gallery and the big one at Versailles. The earlier Frenchmen give us pretty uniforms, a monarch prancing on his steed in the moment of victory, an elegantly wounded warrior or two in the foreground, obviously in the act of crying, "Vive la France!" a host in picturesque flight, a host in picturesque pursuit, waving banners, and a great curtain of smoke to hide the general scene of butchery, with supplementary puffs for every disgusting detail. Verestchagin's manner, on the contrary, passing like a breeze of wholesome truthfulness, lifts this theatrical vapour, and shows us what is below—men writhing out their lives in every species of agony by shot and bayonet wounds, by the dry rot of fever, by the wet rot of cold and damp; and finding their last glance to heaven intercepted by the crows or the vultures, waiting for a meal. All this is very shocking, but looked at in the right way it is supremely moral.

His work is his biography. He has lived every one of his pictures, and he has often had to study at almost the cost of his life. All that he represents he has seen; all that he relates with his pencil he has lived. These pictures are just so many chapters detached from his history. They are the work of an artist of an exceptional nature; and are worthy of a book written on the critical method of Sainte-Beuve, a book wherein the man would occupy a place at least as considerable as the work itself; for the one and the other are inseparable. He is the first Russian painter who has given his countrymen a true impression of war—something besides those official pictures where victory is displayed and never defeat. Even when he paints victory he never separates it from its sadness, its ruin, its misery, its mourning beyond relief. I seem to have always before my eyes, as in a dream, that pyramid of piled-up skulls which he met with somewhere in his wanderings, and of which he has made one of his most striking pictures. He wrote underneath it, "Dedicated to the conquerors."

Verestchagin had done nothing but draw; painting

had frightened him. Gérôme and Bida in vain tried to persuade him to begin. When he returned from his second journey to the frontiers of Persia, among those nomadic tribes with changeless manners, who must have descended from Abraham, he showed his album and note-books to the two painters, and they pressed him all the more. Bida said, "No one draws like you," and he accepted a few sketches, one of which is to be found in his famous Bible.

After his Asiatic campaign he had three years' work at Munich, an enormous and improbable labour, so much so that his enemies insinuated that such a number and variety of pictures could not be the work of a single man, and that Verestchagin had been helped by German painters. The calumny reached St. Petersburg, where he was exhibiting at the time. At his request the Art Society of Munich opened a thorough inquiry into the matter. Models, porters, everybody that knew anything about it, testified on oath that no painter but Verestchagin had so much as entered the *atelier*. The report, covered all over with the best signatures of Munich, and with a postscript of the most flattering kind, was sent on to the Russian capital. When they gave Verestchagin the surname of the Horace Vernet of Russia, no doubt they thought they were saying something in his praise; but he certainly had a right to feel calumniated, for the general impression left by his work is not admiration for princes nor glorification of war. In telling the truth feelingly about the sufferings of the soldier, without distinction of nationality, with as much pity for the vanquished as for the victors, Verestchagin has shown himself essentially human. His pictures, with their poignant reality and elevated philosophy, are at the same time a terrible satire on ambitious despots. Verestchagin is a courtier of nothing but misfortune. A pupil of Gérôme, he seems to have travelled very much in search of himself. Sometimes he has drawn near to Meissonier, then there is something in him of Géricault and of Courbet, and again he is a true Impressionist in the best acceptation of the term.

As a traveller he saw Samarcand when the sight was almost as rare and strange as that from the famous "peak in Darien." "Samarcand," he says, "was occupied by the Russians. Our armies had taken it without assault, after having routed the troops of the Emir. On reaching the summit of the hill I stopped there, dazzled, and, so to speak, awed by astonishment and admiration. Samarcand was there under my eyes, bathed in verdure. Above its gardens and its houses were reared ancient and gigantic mosques, and I who had come from so far was going to enter the city, once so splendid, which was the capital of Tamerlane."

On that day, as Vambéry has told us, a new era opened for Central Asia. "The countries and cities once absolutely closed to the Western man are now opened before him. There where a European could not make a single step without danger of death, he now comes and goes as freely as he pleases, for a Christian army holds the land. At Tashkend, Khojend, and at Samarcand there are clubs, *cafés*, and churches. Tashkend has its Russian newspaper, and with the plaintive chant of the Muezzin is mingled the tinkling bell of the Greek Church, more terrible to the ear of the true believer than the thunder of cannonades. In the streets of Bokhara, where, but a few years ago, the author of these lines heard only Mussulman hymns, the Russian priest, the Russian soldier, and the Russian merchant are now walking together with the pride of the conqueror. A hospital and a storehouse occupy the once splendid palace where

Tamerlane used to command; the palace to which all the princes of the East came to do homage, to which the monarchs of Spain and the Indies sent an embassy to beg for the friendship of the great conqueror, and where the Turanians, humble and devout, knelt, to strike with their foreheads the green stone which forms the sacred pedestal of the throne of Timour. By the victory of the Russian eagles in Central Asia, Islam has received a most terrible wound. For the whole thousand years and more during which it has struggled with Christianity it has never been hit so full in the breast. In our time Western civilization acts vigorously on Mussulman Asia from Byzantium to India, and even Mecca and Medina have not escaped its influence. Central Asia alone had remained the sanctuary of Mahomedanism. The evil there had not been changed, and it was not Mecca but Bokhara which passed for the intellectual centre of Islam. The ascetic, the member of a religious order, the theologian, sighed for this sacred city, and the most zealous Mussulmans of the Ottoman Empire, of Egypt, of Fez, and of Morocco, came to cherish their fanaticism in its schools and in its mosques. Samarcand is incontestably the Maracanda of the Greeks, the capital of the ancient Sogdiana. It was the queen city of the basin of the Oxus. It lost its preponderance for a time, but recovered it, and under Tamerlane reached the height of its splendour. The Mahomedans had a thousand poetic expressions in praise of its wealth, its abundance of water, its innumerable canals fed from mountain torrents, and running in all directions through the plain."

When on the Himalayas Verestchagin ascended the highest mountain but one on the face of the globe—Kanchinga. Kanchinga is twenty-eight thousand odd feet above the level of the sea, and only Mount Everest in

Nepaul takes the palm of it with 29,000 feet. But Mount Everest is a peak, and no one can get up there; while Kanchinga is a huge mass of mountain that invites the climber. But Verestchagin was at Kanchinga in January, when the mountain was covered with ice and snow, so he could not get higher than 15,000 feet, and he was considered a madman for trying to do that. Some English officers in the neighbourhood, when first they heard of his project, did all they could to dissuade him from it. With his characteristic obstinacy he simply thanked them for their advice and went on with his preparations for the ascent. "At least," they said, "you will never take the lady?" Madame Verestchagin was with him, and had insisted on accompanying him. "That will depend upon her," said Verestchagin, and his wife went with him all the same. It was a frightful ascent. The coolies abandoned them when they had gone a very little way—these dark-skinned races cannot stand the cold—and at last they had only one man, who carried the colour-box and drawing-tools, the use of which was Verestchagin's main object in the journey. The painter wanted to go up there to study effects of snow and cloud. By and by even this man's courage failed him, it became so intensely cold. They were wading in snow up to the knees in some places and in others up to the waist. The ponies had been left below. There was no house or shelter of any kind. They called a halt, and the courier went back to get help, leaving Verestchagin and his wife on the mountain in the midst of the snow, with only a small wood fire between them and all but certain death, and with nothing but snow for meat and drink. They cowered over the fire till the falling snow put it out, and then for all that day and night till far into the next day they struggled as best they could for life. As a final and desperate effort, Verestchagin, taking leave of his wife, whom he never expected to see again, roused himself and dragged his almost frozen limbs down the mountain to look for help. When he had gone a long way he met the coolie who had last left them, coming back with food and aid, only just in time to save both the travellers' lives. Verestchagin was so exhausted that he had to be carried back to where his wife lay. As soon as he had recovered, he took out his colour-box and made some capital sketches of Himalayan effects.

In 1881, a memorable exhibition of Verestchagin's pictures was held in Vienna. Its success was probably without a parallel in the history of art exhibitions by a single painter. For a whole month the public poured into the rooms at an average rate of certainly not less than eight thousand a day (on the last day twenty thousand passed or tried to pass through the rooms), until, from the Emperor to his humblest subjects, the peasantry included, there was no class, and it may be added no nationality, within the Empire, which had not sent its representatives to the Künstlerhaus. An attempt, by some political papers, to make the enthusiasm of the Slavs for Verestchagin a means of exciting the hereditary jealousy between them and other races of the Empire was happily frustrated. It is literally true that the broad thoroughfare leading to the exhibition was often blocked by the immense crowd, and that the announcement, "The gallery is full to overflowing," had to be hung out to excuse the temporary closing of the building two or three times a day. The artist did not conceal from his friends that he was proud of the popular and even of the numerical element in his success, because it showed that his work had touched those it was above all meant to reach. He had painted for the people in the highest sense, and their response showed that he had not laboured in vain. *Du reste*, this and this only was his reward, for, beyond the payment of his bare expenses, he had no pecuniary interest in the exhibition.

I may now leave the painter to speak for himself in regard to his own guiding principles in art. The theory of them will be found in what he has written on Progress in Art, and on Realism. The practice, in so far as it relates to right methods of historic study for the painter, is, in all that follows relating to the Campaign of Moscow, his latest and his greatest series of works.

RICHARD WHITEING.

ON PROGRESS IN ART

WE artists always learn too little, and if we have recourse to books it is only cursorily, and without a system, as though we held a solid education to be quite unnecessary for the development of our talents. It must be allowed that herein lies one of the principal, if not the chief, reasons why art in its fuller and more complete development is checked, and has not yet succeeded in throwing off its hitherto thankless part of serving only as the pliable and pleasing companion to society, and in taking the lead, not merely in the æsthetic, but essentially also in the more important psychological development of mankind. While in all other regions of intellectual life it is admitted that new ideas arise, and with these the means of realizing and perfecting them, yet, in art, especially in sculpture and painting, and to a degree also in music, the old phrase still asserts itself—"The great masters have done thus, and therefore must we also do the same." In the handling of every subject, an advance in thought may be remarked. Our view of the world is far from being what it was a few centuries ago; our handiwork itself, in its execution, has changed and improved. Under such circumstances one would think that in the region of art—for instance in painting—either a new idea or a more truthful and natural style might be possible. But no! One is always met by the same assertion—that, "Not only in the perfect construction of their pictures, but also in the sublimity of conception, the old masters stand on an unapproachable height, and we can only strive after them."

The culture of the individual, as well as of society itself, has far overstepped its former level. On the one hand science and literature, on the other improved means of communication, have disclosed a new horizon, have presented new problems to artists. These ought also to have stimulated to some new efforts. But, again the same assertion blocks the way—"The old masters have done thus, and therefore . . . ."

* * * * * * *

In the art of painting, this excessive veneration and imitation show themselves to a certain degree in representations of the nude and in portraits, for both these branches of art reached a high stage of development among the old masters. But, even here, we are struck by the one-sidedness in the execution—the effect is always one and the same: a very bright light on a very dark and sometimes black ground—an effect often startling, but artificially produced, unnatural, and untrue.

Painters' studios were formerly, it is true, small and, owing to the costliness of gas, dimly lighted. But close to these studios there were courtyards, gardens, and fields, with a beautiful background, and an abundance and variety of light, which would have been as effective, and would have made the black tones clearer and less monotonous.

We know that the darkness of the ground in old portraits is only partly attributable to the influence of age, and that in most cases it is intentional. On studying a series of old portraits one can only regret that so much technical ability in representing the body, face, clothes, lace, jewels, etc., should have been harmonized, not with the light, airy shadows of a summer's day as we all sufficiently know and see it, but with a thick artificial black. Undoubtedly the new school of painters will render a service to art by taking men out of the darkness of attics and cellars into the clear light of gardens. It is indisputable that the monotonous early style, which showed everything in the same light of the studio, spares the artist many difficulties and embarrassments; but in art there ought to be even less hesitation than in anything else in the face of technical difficulties.

* * * * * * *

Turning to historical pictures, we are struck by the more thoroughly intellectual and characteristic handling of the subject at the present time. History is certainly still illustrated more or less by amusing anecdotes, and artists content themselves by depicting that which science has established, instead of contributing the results of their own researches; but even now there is a very marked advance on the usual adulation and the uncritical traditions, legends, and assertions of the old school.

If painters were to study history, not in a fragmentary way from this to that page, if they would understand that the imitation of dramatic exaggeration on canvas has become obsolete, they would begin to arouse the interest of society in the past quite in a different way from that which is possible by means of anecdote, picturesque costumes, and types that are for the most part fables of history. It is a fact, that hitherto the treatment of memorable events by artists has been of a nature to draw a smile from the educated. But by changing the sunny holiday of the historical picture into a more acceptable workday, truth and simplicity would certainly be the gainers.

It seems superfluous to mention the extraordinary advance made at the present day in landscape painting, an advance due to very many causes, but chiefly, of course, to the development of natural science. It is not too much to say that the landscapes of the old masters are mere childish essays, as compared with the works of the leading living artists in this field. And it is really difficult to understand how and in what direction landscape painting can be brought to greater perfection.

* * * * * * *

In the so-called religious painting, imitation of the old masters is nearly as great as in portraits. But this is fully explained by the gradual disappearance of religious perception, and the consequent preference for an old ideal, rather than the creation of a new one without the strong faith of olden times.

Nevertheless, the new school finds it not only possible, but even necessary, to reject inherited ideas, though hallowed by time and custom, when they evidently contradict the artistic eye and feeling of our time. First: the manner of placing God and the Saints on clouds, as though these were chairs and stools, and not substances whose physical condition is well known to us. Second: the custom of representing Christ and the holy men and women as a Roman patrician surrounded by his slaves. Third: the representation of God in the style of our kings, in robes of state, seated on a throne of gold, silver, and precious stones, with a crown on his head and a sceptre in his hand, all suspended in clouds. Fourth: the representation of the Virgin Mary in the costly robe of a lady of high rank covered with jewels. Possibly religious painting will not now rise to a second *renaissance*, but it may nevertheless be assumed that the advance in technical knowledge may even be useful in Church paintings, if the painter, in his representation of the Deity and the Saints in their manifestations in heaven or upon earth, would replace the dim, poor, and monotonous light of the studio by a brilliant, clear, sunny atmosphere, and delicate, transparent, airy shadows.

* * * * * * *

In order to explain our meaning, we will cite some of the famous religious works of the old masters as examples: for instance, the well-known pictures by Titian in Venice, and Rubens in Antwerp, representing the Assumption of the Virgin Mary. We are not going to speak of the great excellence of those two pictures, recognized all the world over, and by no means valued too highly. If it be also beyond doubt that these pictures have in course of time become darker, it must nevertheless be understood that they were executed within four walls, and produced by the traditional contrast of very strong light and very deep shadow. Now, we ask, whence could these black shadows have come? If the Assumption of the Virgin Mary had perchance taken place in a grotto, or in some dark, artificially-illumined space, these shadows would be intelligible, but in such case the strong lights would be inexplicable. Now it was accomplished in free air, and we may be allowed to suppose that a beautiful sunny day was chosen by God for so sublime and solemn an event. So much the brighter should the pictures have been painted, both on account of the direct and reflected sunlight. Whence then, we may ask, came these black tones? Well, they were simply due to the fact that the lights as well as the shadows were not derived from observation, but invented, as artists say, "by the head," and were therefore from beginning to end false. But, can it be supposed that great painters like Titian and Rubens should not themselves have recognized such defects? Of course this can be as little understood as that the great Leonardo da Vinci should not have remarked the false light in his celebrated picture of beauty, *La Joconde*, when he painted her in free air, with hard, metallic tones on the face, and an impossible landscape in the background. Had he, then, no presentiment of the wonderfully tender lights and half lights, shadows and half shadows, wafted over the face of a lovely woman by the air?—how everything out of doors has quite another appearance about it than within four walls?

We will not digress too far with our investigations, and only venture to ask whether it occurred to no one at that time to demand so much from the artist? No; they were not asked. But these niceties, are they not required in these days from the artist? Yes, they are. . . . Then the advance is evident.

In like manner, we cannot suppose that another shortcoming in the artistic conception of such masters could have escaped their acuteness. For instance, in the representations of the Apostles, whose personalities are so clear and convincing in the Gospels, we recognize in their forms, faces, and attitudes—particularly in Titian's pictures—not modest, humble fishermen, but fine Italian models of athletic appearance. This error was evidently acknowledged even then by the artists themselves, with their usual tact and good sense; and Rembrandt went so far as to introduce into his religious subjects Dutch market-figures. But there is still a long stride from this to the true rendering of the types and costumes recognized at the present day as indispensable. Is this not an advance? Certainly it is. We deny that study has ever yet created talent; but, on the other hand, we do not for a moment doubt that it stimulates it.

As regards time and place, the worshippers of the earlier style of painting go to such lengths in their imitation, that they not only work with the same colours and in the same manner as their adored masters, but also aim at lending to their pictures that peculiar tint which time has produced on the canvas. They cover their pictures with some dark shiny colour, in order to give an appearance of age, as if they were painted one, two, or three centuries ago. This tendency is even taught in many modern schools, and individual artists have gained great reputation as colourists merely because they can impart to their productions a resemblance to those of Rubens, Van Dyck, Rembrandt, or Velasquez. Let us hope that the new school will go to work with greater deliberation, not only as regards the conception of their subject, but also in colouring; for it is impossible to treat this aright by imitating, with a quantity of varnish, a canvas which has become yellowish or reddish through time. The young school will make it a strict rule to bring every event into harmony with the time, place, and light selected, in order to benefit by all the modern acquisitions of science, in relation to the characteristics, costumes, and every psychological and ethnographical detail.

A scene which takes place in heaven or on earth should positively not be painted within four walls, but in the true light of morning or mid-day, evening or night. The illusion and effect produced by the picture cannot but gain by this, and the language of painting will become more expressive and intelligible.

Perhaps the same might be said, with little variation, of sculpture, and even of music. All the arts are now, more than ever, brothers and sisters, and long ago should have been united in one temple of taste, intellect, and talent.

* * * * * * *

REALISM

I

An old Russian.

"REALISM — realism!" How very often do we hear this term, and yet how seldom does it appear to be applied understandingly.

"What do you take realism to be?" I asked a well-educated lady in Berlin, who had been talking a great deal about realism and the realists in art. The lady did not seem to be ready with an answer, for she could only reply that "A realist is he who represents subjects in a realistic manner."

I hold, though, that the art of representing subjects in a realistic manner does not entitle a person to the name of realist. And, in order to illustrate my meaning, I may present the following example—

When the war of the British with the Zulus came to an end, there could be found no man among the prominent English artists who would take upon himself the task of committing to canvas that epopee enacted between the whites and blacks, and so the English had to have recourse to a very talented French artist. They gave him money, and explained to him that such and such were the uniforms and the arms of the English soldiers, and such and such were the clothes, or what represents clothes, among the Zulus. Then, eye-witnesses to the military encounters told the Frenchman of what the background consisted in each case, probably supplementing their accounts with photographic views. Armed with this information the artist set to work, without having the least personal knowledge of the country he was going to reproduce, nor of the types, the peculiarities, nor the customs of Zululand. With much assurance the artist went on with his task, and turned out several lively pictures in which there are a great many men attacking an enemy—defending itself; a great number of dead and wounded; much blood; much gunpowder-smoke, and all that kind of thing; yet, with all this, there is total lack of the principal thing: there are no British nor Zulus to be found in the pictures. Instead of the former we behold Frenchmen dressed up in British uniforms, and instead of Zulus, the ordinary Parisian negro-models, reproduced in various more or less warlike attitudes.

Well, is that realism? No.

Most artists, besides, do not take sufficient pains to reproduce the true light under which the events they treat have really taken place. Thus, such scenes as are taken up in the just-mentioned pictures—scenes of battles under the intolerably torrid sun of Africa, are being painted by the greyish light of European studios. Of course the sunlight, and the numerous peculiar effects dependent on it, cannot prove successful in such a case, and the effect is lost.

Is that realism, then? Certainly not.

* * * * * * *

I go further, and assert that in cases where there exists but a bare representation of a fact or of an event without idea, without generalization, there can possibly be found some qualities of realistic execution, but of realism there would be none: of that intelligent realism, I mean, which is built on observation and on facts—in opposition to idealism, which is founded on impressions and affirmations, established *à priori*.

Now, can any one bring the reproach against me that there is no idea, no generalization in my works? Hardly.

Can any one say that I am careless about the types, about the costumes, about the landscape of the scenes represented by me? That I do not study out beforehand the personages, the surroundings figuring in my works? Hardly so.

Can any one say that, with me, any scene, taking place in reality in the broad sunlight, has been painted by studio light—that a scene, taking place under the frosty skies of the North, is reproduced in the warm enclosure of four walls? Hardly so.

Consequently, I can claim to be a representative of realism—such realism as requires the most severe manipulating of all the details of creation, and which not only does not exclude an idea, but implies it.

That I am not alone in such an estimate of my work, is proved by the following lines, from a correspondent to an American paper,[1] sent from Paris at the time of the last exhibition of my paintings in that city—

"The respect shown to certain pictured ideals—the ideals

[1] *Sunday Express*, Albany, July 22, 1888.

of a painter so foreign to Parisian conventions as Verestchagin—is noted as a pleasing indication of departure from the gross realism that was beginning to obtain in French art. Mr. Dargenty, of the *Courrier de l'Art*, does not consider Verestchagin as a 'seducing' painter, but concedes to him knowledge and talent, and declares that for his part he prefers the refinement of an idea to the 'brutal expression of vulgar realism.' He hopes for a reaction and believes that the crowd that 'precipitated' itself in the exposition of Mr. Verestchagin 'heralded' a running victory for the idea."

Still more notable was the judgment of the London *Christian* of December 2, 1887—a view having all the more interest to me because of the special character of the paper that published it—

"These paintings are the work of a Russian, Verestchagin, a painter equal to any of his contemporaries in artistic ability, and beyond any painter who ever lived in the grandeur of his moral aims and the application of his lessons to the consciences of all who take the least pains to understand him. . . .

"I will only say that he who misses seeing these paintings will miss the best opportunity he may ever have of understanding the age in which he lives ; for if ever the nineteenth century has had a prophet, it is the Russian painter, Verestchagin."

I repeat it : I cite this last passage expressed in consideration of its character, as an opinion emitted by a specially religious organ, an opinion made all the more significant in view of the attacks to which I had been submitted by people striving to prove themselves greater papists than the Pope.

* * * * * * *

Realism is not antagonistic to anything that is held dear by the contemporary man—it does not clash with common sense, with science, nor with religion. Can any one have anything but the deepest reverence for the teachings of Christ concerning the Father and Creator of all that exists —for the golden rule of Christian charity?

It is true that we are enemies of bigotry, of all ostentatious, assumed piety; but who is it that can blame us for this since Christ Himself has said—

"But when ye pray, use not vain repetitions, as the heathen do; for they think they shall be heard for their much speaking."[1]

As can be easily conceived, we have a different estimation of many things that were explained in another way some hundreds of years ago. The infancy of science and, consequently, of the entire conception of the universe can interest us now, but it can no more direct us. At the threshold of the twentieth century, we can no longer admit that the skies above are peopled by saints and by angels; that the interior of the earth is occupied by devils engaged in their task of roasting the sinners of the world. We refuse even to accept, in its literal sense, the ancient idea of rewards for good deeds, and that of torments in slow fires as punishment for evil deeds.

In our capacity of artists we do not deny the ideals of the past ages and of the ancient masters. On the contrary, we give them an honourable place in the history of art; but we refuse to imitate them, for the very simple reason that everything is good in its own time, and that the realism of one century already bears in itself the germs of the idealism of the next.

The very masters who are held to be great idealists

[1] St. Matthew vi. 7.

in art—have not they been great realists in their own time?

Who would risk the assertion that Raphael was not a realist in the age in which he lived: that his works did not scandalize many of his contemporaries, whose tastes were formed on the work of primitive masters?

And Rubens, who transgressed all limits of contemporary decency, and that, not only in his capacity of painter, but even as a thinker? I hope no one would be ready to question the fact that his powerful but one-sided genius has intermingled the types of the personalities of the Christian religion with those of the heathenish mythology; that his God the Father is the same as his Jupiter of Olympus; that they are portraits of the very same red-cheeked studio model; that his Virgin and his Hebe—one may even say his Venus—are all personalities of the same type, all alike red-cheeked, handsome, and self-satisfied! Who would deny that Rubens, having peopled the Christian heavens with heavy, buxom, healthy, and very immodest ladies and gentlemen, had reversed all traditions and thus had shown himself to be a talented, powerful realist in his time? Doubtlessly, he bewildered and scandalized a good many of his pious contemporaries.

And Rembrandt? and the rest of them, all of whom are now held to be idealists, more or less: was not each one of them a representative of realism in his time—realism that has been considerably smoothed down in our days by the hand of time on one side and the onward march of our self-consciousness on the other?

Who would think now-a-days of reproaching those painters for all that boldness, which certainly proved astounding to their contemporaries? And yet how many were the disputes concerning those painters, how many lances have been broken in their behalf! As we look back now all that seems strange to us. But is it not a sign of what awaits the noted works of our own time? These also were received inimically, were proclaimed to be too far-reaching, too bold, too realistic, yet will not they also in their turn acquire lasting strength under the influence of onward marching thought and technique? Will not the day come when they will also find themselves, unawares, in the archives of old ideals?

* * * * * * *

But we have to count with our irascible and exacting contemporaries. It is generally held to be unpardonable boldness—quite a scandalous proceeding in fact—to recede from formulas, recognized by successive generations, through centuries. Novelists, painters, sculptors, musicians, are all alike invited to make compromises with triviality and absurdity which invariably retard the development of the idea and of the technique.

Even such persons as grudgingly admit that we also are "men of thoughts," that we also are "men of well-developed technique," even they express their regrets that we should prove false to the traditions of the old masters; that we should not follow the tenets consecrated by great names.

Yes, it is true: we differ in many ways. We think differently, we are bolder in our generalization of the facts of the past, the present, and the future; we even work differently and transfer our impressions in a different manner.

Can we take it now in its literal sense—the generally-accepted conception of God, who had once assumed the form of man, and is now sitting on the right hand of the Father Almighty, with all the hosts of saints and angels gathered around Him? Can we admit as facts the idea of all those thrones that surpass in richness the celebrated thrones of the Great Moguls of India? Can we admit now the idea of all those splendid vestments, adorned with embroidery, with pearls and precious stones—and all that in the clouds? Can we sincerely and artlessly represent to ourselves the saints that are supposed to sit on those same clouds as on arm-chairs and sofas, likewise in the richest attire—saints who would thus be found amidst the luxurious surroundings that were so distasteful to them in their life on earth?

All those splendid garments, all those gilded surroundings, held out as everlasting rewards for virtue practised on earth—do they not appear to us quite childish now, not to say wholly inconsistent with good taste?

* * * * * * *

A good deal has been written about my works: many were the reproaches brought against my paintings, those treating of religious subjects as well as of military. And yet they were, all of them, painted without any preconceived idea,—were painted only because their subjects interested me. The moral in each case appeared afterwards, coming up of its own account, from the very truthfulness of impressions.

Now, for instance, I have seen the Emperor Alexander II. on five consecutive days, as he sat on a little knoll—the battle-field spreading out before him—watching, with field-glass in hand, first the bombardment, and then the storming of the enemy's positions. This surely was also the way in which the old German Emperor attended battles,—as well as his son, that admirable man, the late Frederick of Germany. Of this I have even been assured by eye-witnesses. Certainly, it would be ridiculous to suppose that an Emperor assisting at battles would canter about brandishing his sword as a young ensign, and yet the desire has been attributed to me to undermine by my picture the prestige of the sovereign in the eyes of the masses, who are prone to imagine their Emperor prancing on a fiery steed, in times of danger, in the very thick of the fight.

I have represented the bandaging and the transporting of the wounded exactly as I have seen it done, and have felt it in my own person when wounded, bandaged, and transported in the most primitive manner. And yet, that again has been declared to be a gross exaggeration, a calumny.

I observed during several days how prisoners were slowly freezing to death on a road extending over thirty miles. I called the attention of the American artist, Frank D. Millet, who was on the spot, to that scene; and when he afterwards saw my painting he declared it to be strikingly correct; yet for that painting I have been treated to such abuse as would not admit of repetition in print.

I have seen a priest performing the last religious rites on a battle-field over a mass of killed, plundered, mutilated soldiers, who had just given up their life in the defence of their country; and that scene again—a picture which I had painted, literally, with tears in my eyes—has been also proclaimed in high quarters to be the product of my imagination, a downright falsehood.

My lofty accusers did not deign to pay any attention to the fact that the lie was given them by that same priest who, disgusted with the accusations against me, declared—and that in the presence of the public standing before the picture—that it was he who had been performing those last rites over the massed bodies of the killed soldiers—had done it in the very surroundings reproduced in my picture. Yet, notwithstanding all this, my picture barely escaped being ejected from the exhibition, and when afterwards it was intended to publish all those pictures in coloured prints, the officials put their veto on the scheme, for fear lest they should find their way among the masses.

It should not be imagined, however, that that indignation prevailed exclusively in Russian high spheres. It was a very well known Prussian general who advised the Emperor Alexander II. to have all my military paintings burned as objects of a most pernicious kind.

* * * * * * *

There were still more inimical commentaries on those of my pictures which treat of religious subjects. Yet have I attacked the Christian morals? No—I hold these very highly. Have I attacked the idea of Christianity or its founder? No—I have the highest respect for them. Have I tried to detract from the significance of the Cross? No—this would be a sheer impossibility.

I have travelled all over the Holy Land with the book of the Gospels in my hand; I have visited all the places sanctified, centuries ago, by the presence of our Saviour in them. Consequently, I must have, and do have, my own ideas and conceptions as to the representation of many events and facts recorded in the Gospels. My ideas necessarily differ from the conceptions of artists who have never seen the scenery of the Holy Land, have not personally observed its population and their customs.

* * * * * * *

Here is my idea, for instance, of the fact of the Adoration of the Magi; a painting contemplated, but not yet executed:—

A clear, starry night; travellers are approaching Bethlehem—these are the Magi, men versed in science, having a knowledge of astrology. Proceeding on their way toward the city, the wise men notice a star standing over it—a star which they had never yet observed. Since, at that time, the idea was prevalent that every man had his own star, and, *vice versâ*, every star corresponded to some man on earth, so the Magi naturally conclude that this new star indicates the birth of a child somewhere in the neighbourhood, and that—the star being exceptionally brilliant—the new-born child must develop into a most prominent man.

Arriving at Bethlehem, the Magi put up at an inn. Soon after, the servant, who had been attending to the travellers' mules, comes in and tells the Magi that a poor woman had sought refuge in the place where their animals were kept, and there had given birth to a most beautiful child. Hearing this, the Magi exchange significant glances—the coming up of the star has been rightly interpreted by them.

"Let us go and see; it must be an extraordinary child," they say, and thereupon proceed to the grotto of the inn, where the horses, the cows, and the donkeys were kept, being followed by a few other travellers, who are likewise curious to see the new-born child.

In a corner of the grotto they observe a beautiful, pale young woman, sitting on a pile of straw and nursing her baby, whilst her husband, an elderly man, is seen in the distance, outside the grotto, preparing something for his family.

"What a beautiful child!" exclaimed the Magi, and, turning to the Virgin, say: "Remember our words, He will be a great man; we have seen His star."

Then, their pity being stirred by the poverty of the surroundings, one of the wise men would offer a gold coin as a gift to the child, while another would, perhaps, pour out a little of the precious myrrh from his travelling-flask. As the wise men get ready to leave the grotto, they turn once more to Mary and repeat their prediction concerning the great future of the child, and "Mary kept these things, and pondered them in her heart."

I firmly believe that such a realistic representation of the poverty and simplicity attending the nativity of Christ is incomparably loftier than the idealization of richness and other exaggerations to which the old masters had recourse. But such a treatment of the subject is new; therefore it appears strange, and very likely will excite comment. And only our descendants in a century or two will be able to decide which of these two opposing views was the correct one.

* * * * * * *

Among the paintings on exhibition will be noticed one portraying a not infrequent event in Palestine in the olden time—an event highly dramatic, yet retaining all its simplicity. I mean "A Crucifixion under the Romans."

The sky is overcast by heavy black clouds. Just outside the walls of Jerusalem, on a small rock, are erected three crosses, all of the same size, shape, and appearance. The figures of the crucified on the two sides are of a vulgar type and of coarse build, while the central figure is of a more refined form. His face is not seen; it is hidden by long auburn hair that hangs over it; long hair indicates that the crucified was a man who dedicated himself to God. The wounds on the hands and feet of the three crucified men bleed profusely (it being a well-known fact that physicians find it difficult to stop the flow of blood out of outstretched palms and feet). In front of the crosses stand two priests of high rank, and they seemingly argue about some matter, as if trying to prove something to a Roman in military attire; possibly they refer to the guilt of the man crucified on the middle cross, a guilt about which the military man seems to retain some doubts. Around the rock soldiers are forming a chain to restrain the crowd.

In the foreground of the painting are seen people of every description; some on foot, some on horseback; others mounted on camels or on donkeys. Those are country folks or nomads, who, returning home from market, stopped on their way for a moment in order to witness the event of the day—the execution of a man, the renown of whose deeds had reached even their huts and tents—a man whose arrest caused almost an insurrection in the city. Among others in the crowd can be noticed a few Hebrew merchants with their characteristic head-gear (which was discarded at a comparatively late date), and Pharisees with the letters of the Law written on the coverings of their heads. One of the Pharisees is discussing something with his neighbour concerning a woman who is seen weeping bitterly, in the corner of the picture, presumably the mother of one of the crucified men. Her face cannot be seen, but her sorrow must be great indeed, and none of the women surrounding her seem likely to be able to console her. Many a time, probably, had she tried to divert her son from his chosen course, but all in vain, and now his time has come.

By the side of the heart-broken mother stands a handsome young woman plunged into deep consternation at the sight of the executed man; the tears run down her cheek, but she is not conscious of it, so thoroughly absorbed is she by her terrible, unspeakable grief.

As soon as the authorities should retire and the crowd

thin out, there would be a chance for the mother, and those that surround her, to approach the crosses; then they would find it possible to say their last farewell. . . .

* * * * * * *

Further on, we have a representation of a contemporary execution, among other people and surroundings. Here we see a cold winter day in the North. A mass of people is crowding into one of the squares of St. Petersburg, pressing toward the gallows and being held back by mounted gendarmes. Close to the gallows only a select few are admitted, mostly the military, all representatives of the gilded youth of the city, who are in hopes of getting a piece of the cord used by the hangman: the superstition being very common that a piece of the cord on which a man is hanged is sure to bring luck at cards to its fortunate possessor.

The criminal, enveloped in a white shroud, with the cap drawn over his head, has just been hanged and is still whirling round on the cord, while the people stand in mute bewilderment before the instructive sight. There is but a single hoarse voice raised from among the crowd: "There now—serves him right, too!" But these words are immediately hushed by several women's voices crying out, "What are you saying? It is beyond us to condemn him now. Let God Almighty pass judgment on him!"

Meantime the snow continues to fall, the smoke is rising from the factories, work is going on as usual. . . .

* * * * * * *

It is worthy of notice that this last painting, while it did not please the Russians, pleased the English people very much indeed; on the other side the "Blowing from guns in India" is not at all liked by Englishmen, and yet the

Russians fancied it very much. Men who had seen much service in India assured me that I was mistaken in presenting such an execution as a typical, characteristic way of capital punishment in that country; they insisted that this mode of execution had been adopted but once—in the course of the last insurrection of the Sepoys—and even at that time it had been used only in a very few instances. But I maintain that this mode of execution—a comparatively humane one too—not only has been in constant use during the revolt referred to, when the Sepoys were blown from guns by the thousand, but that it was used by the British authorities in India for many years before and after the Sepoy revolt of 1858. More than that, I am quite positive that that particular mode of execution will have to be used in future times. The Hindoo does not fear any other kind of capital punishment received at the hands of the "heathenish, unclean Europeans." They hold that any one shot down or hanged by the European goes to swell the ranks of the martyrs who are entitled to a high reward in the future life. But an execution by means of a gun carries positive terror into the heart of a native, for such a shot tears the criminal's body in many parts, and thus prevents him from presenting himself in decent form in heaven. This bugbear was used by the British, and will be used by them as long as they fear to lose their Indian possessions.

In order to hold a population of 250,000,000 in political and economical submission by means of 60,000 bayonets, it is not enough to be brave and to be possessed of political tact—punishment and bloody reprisals cannot be avoided.

* * * * * * *

All this is so self-evident, that it seems really wonderful that, while we artists are required to observe and discriminate, people are still inclined to be astonished and indignant whenever we put those faculties of ours to use and transfer our impressions to canvas or paper.

The artists are on all hands pressed to give the public something new, something original, something that is not hackneyed by fashion and triviality; yet, when we make an effort to present something of the sort, we are accused of insolence.

And what are the results of such a state of things?

People get tired of books and gorge themselves on crude facts from real life as recorded in daily newspapers; people get tired of picture galleries and exhibitions, being certain to find in most of them the very same kind of pictures—all treating of the very same subjects, painted in an identical manner; people find it a dull task to go to the theatres where in nine plays out of ten they will find the very same conventional plot, invariably terminating in a wedding.

Well, what is now generally speaking the part of art?

Why, art is brought down to the level of a toy for such as can be and like to be amused by it; it is expected, as it were, to stimulate the public's digestive powers. Paintings, for instance, are considered simply as furniture: if there happens to remain an empty space on the wall between the door and the corner taken up, let us say, by a what-not surmounted by a vase—why then, that empty space is forthwith covered by a picture of light contents and of pleasant execution; such a one as would not distract too much attention from the other furniture and bric-à-brac, would not interfere with the *dolce far niente* of visitors.

And yet the influence and the resources of art are enormous. The majority of old-time painters were handicapped by their allegiance to power and riches; they were men who were not weighed down by any sense of serious civil responsibility, and yet, notwithstanding this, how powerful was the influence of art during whole centuries! It was felt in all the corners and hidden recesses of the life of nations!

What, then, is not to be expected from art in our time, when artists are inspired with their duties as citizens of their country—when they cease to dance attendance on the rich and powerful, who love to be called patrons of art—when artists have acquired independence, and have begun to realize that the first condition of a fruitful activity is to be a gentleman, not in the narrow meaning of caste, but in the wide acceptance of the term pertaining to the time we live in?

* * * * * * *

Armed with the confidence of the public, art will adhere more closely to society, will constitute itself its ally in the face of the serious danger that threatens society now-a-days —that kind of society which we all know, which we are all more or less prompted to love and to respect.

There is no gainsaying the fact that all the other questions of our time are paling before the question of socialism that advances on us, threateningly, like a tremendous thunder-cloud.

The masses that have been for centuries leading a life of expectancy while hanging on the very borders of starvation, are willing to wait no more. Their former hopes in the future are discarded; their appetites are whetted, and they are clamouring for arrears, which means now the division of all the riches, and so as to make the division more lasting, they are claiming that talents and capacities should be levelled down to one standard, all workers of progress and comfort alike drawing the same pay. They are striving to reconstruct society on new foundations, and in case of opposition to their aims, they threaten to apply the torch to all the monuments pertaining to an order that, according to them, has already outlived its usefulness; they threaten to blow up the public buildings, the churches, the art galleries, libraries and museums — a downright religion of despair!

* * * * * * *

II

A Russian Woman.

My friend, the late General Skobeleff, once asked me, "How do you understand the movement of the Socialists and the Anarchists?" He owned that he himself did not understand at all what they aimed at. "What do they want? What are they striving to attain?"

"First of all," I answered, "those people object to wars between nations; again, their appreciation of art is very limited, the art of painting not excluded. Thus, if they ever come into power, you, with your strategic combinations, and I, with my pictures, will both be shelved immediately. Do you understand this?"

"Yes, I understand this," rejoined Skobeleff, "and from this time forth I am determined to fight them."

There is no mistaking the fact that, as I have said before, society is seriously threatened at the hands of a large mass of people counting hundreds of millions. Those are the people, who, for generations, during entire centuries, have been on the brink of starvation, poorly clad, living in filthy and unhealthy quarters; paupers, and such people as have scarcely any property, or no property at all. Well, who is to blame for their poverty—are not they themselves to be blamed for it?

No, it would be unjust to lay all the blame at their door; it is more likely that society at large is more to blame for their condition than they are themselves.

Is there any way out of the situation?

Certainly there is. Christ, our Great Teacher, has long ago pointed out the way in which the rich and the powerful could remedy the situation without bringing things to a revolutionary pass, without any upheaval of the existing social order, if they would only seriously take care of the miserable; that certainly would have ensured them the undisturbed enjoyment of the bulk of their fortune. But there is little hope of a peaceful solution of the question now; it is certain that the well-to-do classes will still prefer to remain Christians in name only; they will still hope that palliative measures will be sufficient to remedy the situation; or else, believing the danger to be distant, they will not be disposed to give up much; while the paupers—though formerly they were ready for a compromise—may be soon found unwilling to take the pittance offered them.

What do they want, then?

Nothing less than the equalization of riches in the society to come. They claim the material as well as moral equalization of all rights, trades, all capacities and talents; as we have already said, they strive to undermine all the foundations of the existing state of society, and, in inaugurating a new order of things, they claim to be able to open a real era of liberty, equality, and fraternity, instead of the shadows of those lofty things, as existing now.

* * * * * * *

I do not mean to go into the discussion of the matter; I would not pretend to point out how much justice or injustice, how much soundness or unsoundness, there is in these claims; I state only the fact that there is a deep gulf between the former cries for bread and the sharply formulated claims of the present. It is evident that the appetite of the masses has grown within the past centuries, and the bill which they intend to present for payment will not be a small one.

Who will be required to pay this bill?

Society, most certainly.

Will it be done willingly?

Evidently not.

Consequently there will be complications, quarrels, civil wars.

Certainly there will be serious complications; they are already casting their shadows before them in the shape of disturbances of a socialistic character that are originating here and there. In America, most likely, those disturbances are lesser and less pointed; but in Europe, in France and Belgium, for instance, such disorders assume a very threatening aspect.

Who is likely to be victorious in this struggle?

Unless Napoleon I. was wrong in his assertion that victory will always remain with the *gros bataillons*, the "regulators" will win. Their numbers will be very great; whoever knows human nature will understand that all such as have not much to lose will, at the decisive moment, join the claims of those who have nothing to lose.

* * * * * * *

It is generally supposed that the danger is not so imminent yet; but, as far as I was able to judge, the imminence of the danger varies in different countries. France, for instance—that long-suffering country which is for ever experimenting on herself, whether it be in social or scientific questions, or in politics—is the nearest to a crisis; then follow Belgium and other countries.

It is very possible that even the present generation will witness a serious upheaval. As to the coming generations, there is no doubt that they will assist at a thorough reconstruction of the social structure in all countries.

The claims of socialists, and, particularly, the anarchists, as well as the disorders incited by them, generally produce a great sensation in society. But no sooner are the disorders suppressed, than society relapses again into its usual unconcern, and no one gives a thought to the fact that the frequency of these painful symptoms, recurring with so much persistency, is in itself a sign of disease.

Far-seeing people begin to realize that palliative measures are no longer of use; that a change of governments and of rulers will no longer avail; and that nothing is left but to await developments contingent on the attitude of the opposed parties—the energetic determination of the well-to-do classes, not to yield, and that of the proletariat, to keep their courage and persevere.

* * * * * * *

The only consolation remaining to the rich consists in the fact that the "regulators" have not had time as yet to organize their forces for a successful struggle with society. This is true to a certain extent. But, though they do it slowly, the "regulators" are steadily perfecting their organization; on the other hand, can we say that society is well enough organized not to stand in dread of attacks?

Who are the recognized and official defenders of society?

The Army and the Church.

A soldier, there is no doubt, is a good support, he represents a solid defence; the only trouble about him is that the soldier himself begins to get weary of his ungrateful part. It is likely that for many years to come the soldier will shoot with a light heart at such as are called his "enemies"; but the time is not far distant when he will refuse to shoot at his own people.

Who is a good soldier? Only one to whom you can point out his father, his mother, or his brother in the crowd, saying, "Those are enemies of society, kill them"—and who will obey.

I may remark here, in passing, that it occurred to me to refer to this idea in a conversation I had with the well-known French writer and thinker, Alexandre Dumas, *fils*, and with what success? Conceding the justice of the apprehension, he had no other comforting suggestion to offer than to say, "Oh, yes, the soldier will shoot yet!"

The other defender of society, the priest, has been less ill-used than the soldier, and consequently he is not so tired of his task; but, on the hand, people begin to tire of him, less heed is paid to his words, and there arises a doubt as to the truth of all that he preaches.

There was a time when it was possible to tell the people that there is but one sun in the heavens, as there is but one God-appointed king in the country. As stars of the first, second, third, and fourth magnitude are grouping themselves around the sun, so the powerful, the rich, the poor, and the miserable, surround the king on earth. And, as it all appeared plausible, people used to believe that such arrangements were as they ought to be. All was accepted, all went on smoothly: none of such things can be advanced now-a-days, however ; no one will be ready to believe in them.

* * * * * * *

Clearly, things assume a serious aspect. Suppose the day comes when the priests entirely lose their hold on the people, when the soldiers turn their guns' muzzles down—where will society look for bulwarks then? Is it possible that it has no more reliable defence?

Certainly, it has such a defence, and it is nothing else than *talent*, and its representatives, in science, literature, and art in all its ramifications.

Art must and will defend society. Its influence is less apparent and palpable, but it is very great; it might even be said that its influence over the minds, the hearts, and the actions of people is enormous, unsurpassed, unrivalled. Art must and will defend society with all the more care and earnestness, because its devotees know that the "regulators" are not disposed to give them the honourable, respectable position they occupy now—for, according to them, a good pair of boots is more useful than a good picture, a novel, or a statue. Those people declare that talent is luxury, that talent is aristocratic, and that, consequently, talent has to be brought down from its pedestal to the common level—a principle to which we shall never submit.

Let us not deceive ourselves; there will arise new talents, which will gradually adapt themselves to new conditions, if such will prevail, and their works may perhaps gain from it; but we shall not agree to the principle of general demolition and reconstruction, when this has no other foundation but the well-known thesis—"Let us destroy everything and clear the ground; as to the reconstruction—about that we shall see later on." We shall defend and advocate the improvement of the existing order by means of peaceful and gradual measures.

* * * * * * *

It goes without saying that we demand that society, on its side, should help us to fulfil our task; that it should trust us, give us all the freedom necessary for the development and exertion of talent.

There is the rub!

Well-fed, self-satisfied society quails at every change, at all blame, derision, and comment; it distrusts the foremost, daring representatives of science, literature, and art. Society strives jealously to retain the right not only to point out the road for talent, but even to regulate the measure, the degree of its development, and its manifestation.

In this society of ours anything that is common and conventional is shielded by all kinds of rights and privileges, while anything that is new and original is bound to awaken animosity and censure, has to go through a severe struggle under the pressure of wide-spread cant and hypocrisy.

Try to create anything ingenious in any of the regions of science and literature, try to present in graphic or plastic form the most original, striking conception, but only forget or refuse to surround it with the conventional layer of triviality and vulgarity so dear to the heart of society, you will be "done for," you will not even obtain a hearing, you will be called a charlatan, if nothing worse than that.

Why is that so? Was it society that has shown the way to all great discoveries? No; it has always delayed them, has always put brakes on them.

Has society, in its collective form, ever evoked any of the great manifestations of art or literature? No; society was always eager to worry, to persecute men of talent, though it erects monuments to them after their death.

How did society come to display such arrogance and presumption? It was tempted that way only by the unchristian conviction that "the aim justifies the means."

* * * * * * *

Can there be anything more exasperating than the conversation we hear sometimes—

"Have you been to the *Salon?*"

"No; we did not happen to go there this year, but last year we were there more than once."

There is irony here as well as truth, for in the majority of cases, you will find in the *Salon* the same number of pictures nearly of the same quality, treating on nearly the same subjects, and, most assuredly, painted nearly in the same style.

"Have you seen the new play of Sardou?"

"Just imagine, could not possibly get to see it yet, had to go to the country; but then to-morrow we go to the *Comédie Française* to see that new thing of Dumas'. They say both plays are very much alike in conception, as well as in plot." And this is perfectly true; they are doubtlessly more or less alike.

Whose fault is this, then, if not the authors'?

Ask the playwrights, whether they would dare to represent the action in such a way as it has been suggested to them by real life, with its logical conclusion, made unavoidable by the march of events, omitting, for once, the long-established, hackneyed, conventional termination?

"No," the authors would tell you, "such a thing is not to be thought of," and they will be in the right. Society, weighed down by cant, will not go to see such a play, however interesting it may be; so the author has to humour the public if he does not want to bring ruin on his manager and on himself.

The same is the case with artists, sculptors, even composers. How many favourites of the Muses have been driven into early graves by the animosity of the public against all new construction of poetical as well as musical ideas?

On one side we hear complaints of the dulness, the monotony, even the triviality, prevailing in art; people clamour for something inspired, something original; on the other hand, the same public arbitrarily chastises you for all that fails to come within the range of established, conventional ideas!

It is high time, it seems to me, to understand the necessity of treating art with tolerance and confidence, if we want it to fraternize with society, to become as one with it, to serve it faithfully and well in the present troubled times when the poet and the artist are soldiers at their posts.

* * * * * * *

"But, you representative of art," I might be asked, "what are the tidings that you are so eager to announce to us—what are your discoveries that would be so entirely new to society?"

Well, what we should say would, perhaps, not be news, yet certainly the idea of it has not yet penetrated the consciousness of the people. Armed with the rich, varied resources of art we should tell people some truths.

"Give up," we shall say to them, "give up enjoying yourselves amidst the illusions of the idealism which lulls your senses, of the idealism of high-sounding words and phrases. Look around you through the eye of sensible realism, and you will acquire the certitude of your mistake. You are not the Christians you assume yourselves to be. You are not representatives of Christian societies, of Christian countries."

Those who kill their kind by the hundred thousand are not Christians.

Those who are always moved, in private as well as in public life, by the principle of "eye for eye, and tooth for tooth," are not Christians.

Those who spend many hours of their lives in churches, yet who give nothing, or next to nothing, to the poor, are not Christians.

What have you done with the decree of the Saviour concerning Christian humility, and to help such as are in real need?

What is the stand taken now, let us ask, by those two great branches of the administration of Christ's Church, that call themselves the Roman Catholic and the Orthodox Churches, which have separated, thanks to their inability to agree as to whether the Holy Ghost proceeded from the Father and the Son or from the Father alone? Is it possible that they have not come yet to an understanding, and, blinded by mutual hatred, are neglecting the loftiness of their mission on earth?

What is the stand taken by those new Churches originated of late, comparatively speaking, on the plea of a more realistic understanding of the connection of life with its Originator? Is it possible that, having concluded the fight with their great adversary, those Churches have also drifted into a sweet nap over the existing order of things, and have also renounced taking a hand in any further reforms?

Well, if it be so, let men of talent shake the strong and

the powerful out of the somnolence into which they have fallen; a difficult task it will be, but a noble one. And if we are refused a hearing, or attempts are made to muzzle us, why, it will be the worse for society. Rouse itself it must; but it will be too late—the "Vandals will have burned Rome" once again. We may be assured that no churches, no bankers' offices will then be spared.

"If any man have ears to hear, let him hear."

I

NAPOLEON

Napoleon.

It is, no doubt, from the Dresden Conference that we must date Napoleon's open hostility towards Russia. After his unsuccessful endeavour to secure the hand of the Tsar's sister, it was rumoured in well-informed French Court circles that Napoleon had made up his mind once and for all to humble the pride of Russia. It was not, however, until the Dresden Conference that Napoleon threw off the mask. He then adopted a distinctly threatening attitude in the face of Alexander's refusal to reconsider his decision and humble himself in the eyes of Europe.

The Russian Emperor firmly refused to submit, and his defiant attitude was the more offensive to Napoleon inasmuch as it was open and undisguised. There was no question of concealing it or of receding from the position already adopted. "The bottle is opened—the wine must be drunk," was Napoleon's own expression.

It was, moreover, at the Dresden Conference that Napoleon attained the zenith of his power. At Dresden he was indeed a king of kings. The Emperor of Austria respectfully and repeatedly assured his august cousin that he might "fully rely upon Austria for the triumph of the common cause;" while the King of Prussia reassured him of his "unswerving fidelity."

The splendour and magnificence of the French Court at the time of the Dresden Conference, says an eye-witness, gave Napoleon the air of some legendary Grand Mogul. As at Tilsit, he showered magnificent presents on all sides. At his *levées* reigning princes danced attendance for hours in the hope of being honoured with an audience. This new order of would-be courtiers was so numerous that the Emperor's chamberlains and officials had constantly to give one another warning lest they should jostle a Royal Highness unawares.

Every country sent its contingent. There were no eyes but for Napoleon. The populace gathered in crowds outside the palace, following his every movement, and dogging his progress through the streets, in hourly expectation of some great event.

Never, probably, were such elaborate arrangements made as for this campaign. Besides the usual preparations for a war, engagements were made with tradesmen of all kinds—tin-workers, masons, watchmakers, and other skilled artisans. There was no word of explanation as to the place in which their services would be required, so that until the opening of the campaign the general public had no inkling of the object of all these preparations. It was even rumoured that Napoleon was about to aid Russia against the Turks.

The abrupt departure of the Russian military agent Tczernicheff from Paris, and the court-martial on certain persons who had treasonably supplied him with various documents, at last revealed the Emperor's plans, and it was then positively stated in the *salons* that the preparations were directed against Russia. The authorities, however, refused to confirm these reports, and went so far as to issue an order to the army, forbidding the officers and men to discuss the rumoured campaign.

The French army was at that moment in the most flourishing condition. It consisted of twelve infantry corps of 20,000 men each, three cavalry corps of the same strength, and with 40,000 men of the Guard, Artillery, Engineers, and Sappers, amounted to 400,000 men, including 300,000 Frenchmen. This enormous force possessed 1200 guns and more than 100,000 ammunition-wagons and caissons. Such a body of troops, accustomed to victory, proud of its traditions, full of confidence in its officers, and led by a commander with the prestige of twenty years' brilliant success, might well be deemed invincible.

Every subaltern regarded a campaign in Russia as a pleasant six months' outing. The whole army, fully assured of speedy success, looked forward to the war as a means of rapid promotion. All were eager to start. "We are off to Moscow," they cried to their friends, "*à bientôt!*"

It was said that Prussia would receive from the expected conquests full compensation for her former losses. Napoleon himself suggested this in his proclamation—"At the beginning of July we shall be in St. Petersburg; I shall be avenged on the Emperor Alexander, and the King of Prussia will be Emperor of the North."

There were prophets who declared that "if the Russians do not make their peace in time, Napoleon will divide their European territories into two parts—the Dukedom of Smolensk, and the Dukedom of St. Petersburg. The

Emperor Alexander, if Napoleon thinks it worth while to leave him his throne, will reign only in Asia."

The Comte de Narbonne, Napoleon's envoy to Vilna, was obliged to admit that the Emperor Alexander conducted himself with irreproachable dignity. He displayed neither fear nor arrogance. The answer with which Narbonne returned to his Imperial master at Dresden proved that the Russian Emperor was firmly resolved to offer no other terms than those which his Ambassador at Paris had already communicated. He had nothing to subtract from them, and nothing to add. An eye-witness describes the impression produced in Dresden, where everybody was eagerly waiting to learn the result of his mission, by the arrival of Comte Narbonne's travel-stained carriage, when he returned with the news that "the Emperor Alexander refused to alter his decision."

"Although," Alexander said, "no one tells me so to my face, I am well aware, and I am not ashamed to own it, that I am not so great a soldier as Napoleon, and that I have no generals who are a match for his. This assurance on my part should, I think, serve as the clearest proof of my sincere desire for the maintenance of peace."

Alexander was extremely indignant at Napoleon's subsequent high-handed proceeding in crossing the frontier without declaring war, for although the Russians were expecting hostilities, there were some, including Rumyantsef and other notables, who regarded it to the last as unlikely, firmly believing that the matter would end in a few threats and a compromise.

Nine years later, when Napoleon was at St. Helena, the Emperor Alexander caused him to be asked why he had refused the terms brought by Narbonne from Vilna. "Because by the terms of the offer," replied Napoleon, "a month was required before any definitive treaty could be arrived at, and such a delay might have involved the loss of the campaign, of all our stupendous preparations, and of the alliances that had been entered into, and which there was little prospect of renewing."

Napoleon loudly proclaimed that "Fate was leading Russia to her doom," and took upon himself the duty of executing the decree of destiny, by which the Russians, as enemies of European civilization, were to be driven into the wilds of Asia.

Napoleon's own baggage-train consisted of seventy wagons, each drawn by eight horses; twenty carriages, open and closed; forty pack-mules; and two hundred riding-horses. During his drives from place to place the Emperor was never idle. When darkness fell, a lamp fixed inside the carriage enabled him to work as comfortably as if he were sitting at home in his own room. Aides-de-camp and orderlies were always within call at the door of his carriage, and a number of riding-horses followed with the body-guard.

In this way Napoleon reached the Niemen on June 11/23, and mounted his horse at two o'clock at night. It is said that as he approached the bank of the river, his horse stumbled and threw him, and that some one cried out, "That's a bad omen; a Roman would have turned back;" but no one could distinguish whether it was the Emperor or one of his suite who uttered the words.

I extract from M. Bertin's book a characteristic account given by Count Soltyk, general of the Polish artillery. "On the arrival of the Emperor, several officers, together with myself and Suchorzewski, the major of the regiment, ran up. Napoleon quickly approached the major and asked for the colonel of the regiment. Suchorzewski, in no wise disconcerted at the absence of the colonel, who was still asleep, answered that he was filling his place, and was ready to receive any orders. Napoleon then asked him which was the road to the Niemen, and made inquiries regarding the outposts and the position of the Russians. Whilst asking these questions, he ordered a change of uniform, as it had been agreed, or rather ordered, that no French soldier should be seen by the Russians. He took off his coat, and the rest of us—the Prince of Neufchâtel, Suchorzewski, Colonel Pagowski, who had hurried to the spot, General Bruyères, and myself—followed his example. There were therefore five or six of us in our shirts in the middle of the bivouac surrounding the Emperor, each with his uniform in his hand. The Poles offered theirs to the French. Altogether the scene was most amusing. Of all our uniforms, Colonel Pagowski's coat and forage cap best fitted the Emperor. He had been offered a Lancer's head-dress, but refused it as being too heavy. All this took place in a few minutes. Berthier also put on a Polish uniform. The colonel's horses were at once led up. Napoleon mounted one of them; Berthier took the other, and Lieutenant Zrelski, whose company was on outpost duty, was ordered to accompany the Emperor as guide.

"They went as far as Alexota, a village about three miles distant, opposite Kovno, and within range of its guns. The Emperor alighted in the courtyard of a house belonging to a doctor, whose windows overlooked the Niemen, and from which one might easily survey the surrounding country. I had myself three days previously made a plan of Kovno from this very spot. From there Napoleon thoroughly reconnoitred the district without himself being seen. His horses were carefully concealed in the courtyard. After completing his survey he returned to the bivouac, and called for details as to the position of the enemy. The colonel having told him that I knew the neighbourhood thoroughly, he put several questions to me as to the fords that might be passable, the conformation and irregularities of the ground, and the position of the enemy. The Emperor questioned me searchingly as to where the Russians were massed, whether on the right or left bank of the Vilia. He evidently wished to ascertain whether the road along the Vilia was free, intending to march in that direction in heavy columns, so as to seize this centre of operations, and cut off the enemy's corps, which were spread along the whole length of the Niemen.

"When Napoleon returned we noticed a marked change of expression. He looked happy, even merry, being evidently satisfied with the idea of the surprise which he was preparing for the Russians on the following morning, and of which he had calculated the results beforehand. Some refreshments were brought to him, which he ate in our midst on the high-road. He seemed amused at his masquerade, and asked us twice if the Polish uniform suited him. After having breakfasted, he said laughing, 'Now we must return what does not belong to us.' He then took off the garments which he had borrowed, put on his uniform of Chasseur of the Guard, entered his carriage accompanied by Berthier, and rapidly drove away. That very day he inspected several other points on the Niemen, and chose Poniémon as the place of crossing. General Haxo accompanied him on this tour."

"This reconnaissance being finished," adds Ségur, "he issued an order that on the following evening three bridges should be thrown across the river. . . . Then he returned to his quarters, where he passed the day partly in his tent and partly in a Polish house, vainly seeking rest in the sultry heat that prevailed."

When the army began the passage next day, Napoleon took up a position near the bridge, and encouraged the soldiers by his presence, while they greeted him with the customary cries. But his impatience would not allow him to remain long on this spot. He crossed the bridge and galloped through the forest that stretches along the bank of the stream, careering along at full speed on his Arab, as though in pursuit of some invisible foe.

"What is to be said of an Emperor," remarks an eye-witness, "who dresses up in an outlandish disguise, rides off to his outposts, orders some one to bring him some water from the Niemen in a helmet, and tastes it with the air of a seer waiting for inspiration? It would have been better to keep these absurd tricks for the banks of the Nile, among the superstitious nations for whose behoof they were invented, rather than bring them over to Europe."

"Napoleon," says Boutourline, "was preparing to crush the First Army of the West with his Guards, Davout's, Oudinot's, and Ney's Army Corps, and Nansouty's, Montbrun's, and Grouchy's cavalry—250,000 men in all—by a sudden attack on the centre before the Second Army could come to its support. The King of Westphalia, with the corps of Junot, Poniatowski, and Renier, and Latour-Maubourg's cavalry, making a force of 80,000, was to execute the same manœuvre against the Second Army. The Viceroy of Italy, with an army of about the same strength, consisting of his own corps and that of St. Cyr, was to throw himself between the two Russian armies, and cut off all communication between them. On the left, Major Macdonald's division, some 30,000 strong, was to enter Courland and threaten St. Petersburg and the

Russian right. On the right, Schwarzenberg and the Austrians, also about 30,000 strong, were to hold Tormasof in check."

It was a well-conceived plan, and the movements of the French on Vilna were so swift and decisive that General Dokhturof's corps and Dorokhof's division were almost cut off.

This brilliant beginning was, however, followed by a number of mistakes. The execution of the plan was marred by the slowness of the King of Westphalia (who soon afterwards threw up his command and returned home), and by the Emperor's own irresolution. Napoleon appears to have lost sight of the fact that he should have taken the direct road from Vilna to Smolensk as his principal line of operations. If he had concentrated the whole weight of his army on this line he would have successfully outflanked Barclay on the left and Bagration on the right, and might then have fallen on either of them with the whole strength of his army, or, indeed, on both simultaneously. It was with the object of taking the Russians by surprise that Napoleon crossed the frontier without declaring war, and appeared at Vilna the day after the Emperor Alexander had left.

Mme. de Choiseul-Gouffier, in her reminiscences of Napoleon's stay in Vilna, describes among other events his visit to the church. "A herald shouted, '*L'Empereur!*' and I saw a short, stout little man in a green uniform with coat unbuttoned, and displaying a white waistcoat, surrounded by a crowd of marshals. He flew by like a bullet, and took up his place behind a *prie-dieu*. When mass was over he departed at the same lightning speed." She describes Napoleon's arrival at a ball—"At the first signal of his approach the dukes and marshals rushed off to meet him as quickly as they could hurry; and to tell the truth, their faces were a most amusing sight. We were hustled down the stairs almost on all fours. Napoleon's carriage drove up, with the Master of the Horse, M. Caulaincourt, galloping behind. They put down a footstool for the Emperor to alight on, as if the earth were unworthy of the honour of being trodden by his Imperial foot. He went up-stairs amid shouts of '*Vive l'Empereur!*' When he entered the *salon* he cried, as if giving an order, 'Ladies, be seated!'"

"Napoleon's face," says Madame de Choiseul-Gouffier, later on, "appeared to me as severe as an antique bust, and of the colour of yellow marble." And further—"Napoleon's expression when lighted up by his beautiful smile was pleasant, and even when seen closer his pallor was not remarkable. What is most noteworthy is that his countenance expresses more good-nature than genius. . . . He knew every bit of gossip."

The distance between the head-quarters of the two armies led Napoleon to express the belief that "in all probability, they are afraid of Alexander and myself meeting and coming to terms." However, when the opportunity of making terms did present itself, Napoleon let it pass. Balachef, the Russian general, presented himself at the French outposts demanding a parley. When they conducted him into Napoleon's presence at Vilna, he declared, in Alexander's name—"If there is war between Russia and France, it will be a long and bloody war, and before entering upon it the Russian Emperor solemnly proclaims that it is not he who is responsible for it. Though the Russian Ambassador has left Paris, war has not yet been declared; there is still time to come to terms; it is not yet too late."

Having been told that the messenger who had been

selected for the embassy was the Minister of Police, the French suspected that the sole object of his coming was to observe the position of the army and to gain time. They regarded his visit, therefore, as a sign of weakness in the Russian Government, and received his overtures with coldness. Besides, it would have cost Napoleon a great struggle, after refusing to listen to any explanations at Paris, to adopt a conciliatory tone in Vilna. What would Europe think of him? What possible explanation could there be of the enormous preparations, the vast movements of troops and expenditure of money? It would have been tantamount to a confession of defeat. Besides, he had gone so far in his utterances before the allies as to render retreat almost impossible. But this was not all. Napoleon lost control over himself, and broke out, as usual, into complaints and reproaches. He used insulting language in speaking of the Emperor Alexander to the Russian general. "Why did he ever come to Vilna? What does he want? Does he mean to match his strength with me? He, this carpet knight? Napoleon's only counsellor is himself; who will advise the Tsar? Whom does he mean to look to? Kutuzof is a Russian, he, therefore, will not be selected; six years ago Benigsen was old and useless—he is in his dotage now; Barclay, no doubt, is a man of courage and capacity—but he only displays it by retreating." Napoleon added spitefully—"You all imagine that you understand the art of war because you have read your Jomini, but if Jomini's book were enough to teach you generalship, do you think I should have allowed it to be printed?"

It is difficult to understand how, after sending such an insolent answer to his "friend and brother," Napoleon could bring himself to assure him later on of his unswerving devotion. On the other hand, it is easy to appreciate why his "friend and brother" after this message received all the French Emperor's subsequent blandishments in stony silence.

Napoleon began to be alarmed at the proclamations and manifestoes issued by the St. Petersburg Cabinet. He displayed a naïve astonishment at the expressions of hatred and anger which were levelled at his own person. What had happened to the Emperor Alexander, who had up to that time been so suave and gentle? It is said that Napoleon endeavoured to keep these vigorous proclamations from the knowledge of his army, and commanded that the Russians should be represented as disheartened and on the point of disbanding; the Russian Emperor as having actually left his troops and fled to St. Petersburg in order to implore assistance and mollify the wrath of the Senate, which was demanding an explanation of what had happened; the Russian generals as having lost their heads; and the people at large as ready to fling themselves in despair at Napoleon's feet.

Ségur has preserved to us the order of march of the French troops. The army advanced in column ready for instant battle, the Emperor on horseback in the centre. Rivers were crossed by fords which soon, however, became impassable, and the regiments in the rear crossed elsewhere, wherever they could; no one troubled his head about them. The staff neglected these details. No one remained behind to point out the dangers, if there were any, or the route, where several roads met. Each *corps d'armée* was left to shift for itself.

Duverger is yet more categorical—"The retreat has often been described, but the long and difficult march which preceded our misfortunes has never been sufficiently mentioned. Worn out by the rays of a tropical sun, we were reduced to drink foul stagnant water, to eat biscuits served out with a sparing hand. Famine and dysentery destroyed as many soldiers as did the war."

Labaume, another eye-witness, completes this picture—"This immense gathering of men on one spot increased the confusion and disorder that reigned on the high-roads. Stray soldiers sought their regiments in vain; orderlies with urgent despatches were unable to deliver them; while on the bridges and in the ravines a frightful tumult arose. Our soldiers, deprived of their rations, had to provide for themselves by pillage, and the result was the utmost disorder and paralysis of discipline, the usual forerunners of the approaching decay of an army."

The disorganization of the French army was thrown into stronger relief by the excellent order in which Barclay-de-Tolly drew off his men from position to position. There were no deserted wagons, no dead horses, not a single straggler or deserter.

The French troops moved, of course, not only along the high-road, but also by by-roads, and often by hardly perceptible footpaths, destroying everything they came across on their way, and feeding their horses on the standing corn. They camped at night in the midst of the crops, trampling and destroying them without scruple in the hope of getting some shelter, however slight, from the heat and rain. The soldiers, according to the account of French eye-witnesses, roamed the neighbourhood searching for food, ill-treated the inhabitants, and turned them out of their homes, looted the houses, carried off all the live stock, and indulged in excesses strangely at variance with their vaunted mission of civilization.

"The army at last approached Vitebsk," says de la

Fluse, who accompanied the expedition. "A number of cavalry and infantry regiments were extended in line, supported by strong bodies of artillery. Four strong columns of Foot Guards formed a square, in the centre of which were three tents—one for the Emperor, the other two for his suite. A squad of twenty Grenadiers, with an officer and a drummer, formed a guard outside the tents. The camp-fires were lighted, and the various regiments sent fatigue parties to fetch their rations. These were served out in a neighbouring field, where all the meat and corn had been collected.

"Around the Emperor's tent there was a great deal of bustle. Generals and aides-de-camps were constantly coming and going at full speed—for it was known that the enemy were not far off, and a decisive battle was expected.

"The Emperor left his camp two or three times with a telescope in his hand. Resting it on the shoulder of one of the officers or men, he inspected Vitebsk and the neighbouring hills. Beyond the town a broad plain was visible, on which Russian cavalry and infantry were performing some evolutions.

"Napoleon looked at them—'To-morrow they will be ours,' he said. Then he gave orders to prepare for battle. A proclamation was read before each regiment—'Soldiers, the day we have longed for has come at last. To-morrow we shall fight the battle for which we have waited so long. We must end the campaign with a single thunder-clap. Remember your victories at Austerlitz and Friedland; the enemy shall see to-morrow that we have not degenerated.'

"The proclamation was enthusiastically received; the troops were confident of victory; all hoped that this battle would end a war of which they had already had more than enough. Brandy was distributed, and after supper and the various preparations for the morrow they turned in, many thinking, no doubt, that this would be their last night.

"Next morning they were up by dawn, dressed in their smartest, as if for some festival. Every eye was turned to the quarter in which the enemy had been manœuvring on the previous day; but the plain was empty—as the sun rose it became clear that the Russian army had disappeared.

"The drum began to beat outside the Emperor's tent," continues the same writer. "This meant that the Grenadiers on guard were being relieved. I hurried up with my companions in order to ask the officer of the relief if he had heard any news, for, placed as he was close to the Emperor's tent, he might have heard something. He told us that Napoleon flew into a passion when he heard of the enemy's retreat. When Prince Poniatowski—who had instructions to cross the Dvina with the cavalry, sweep behind the Russians and cut off their retreat—entered the tent, the officers of the Guard heard what passed. The Prince came to report that it was absolutely impossible to cross the Dvina, as he could find no ford, and the water had risen in consequence of the recent storm. His horses, moreover, had had no fodder. Thereupon high words passed between the Emperor and Poniatowski, the former rating the Prince roundly for not carrying out his instructions, Poniatowski for his part being at no loss for a reply.

"'So you urge want of fodder as an excuse, Prince?' said Napoleon. 'I may tell you, sir, that when I was in Egypt it was not once nor twice that I had to make expeditions without fodder.'

"'Of course, your Majesty,' replied Poniatowski, unabashed, 'I do not know what you fed your horses on out there, but I do know this, that my horses cannot dispense with their hay, especially when there is no grazing, which is often the salvation of cavalry. Lacking fodder as I did, I ran the risk of finding myself in the position your Majesty was in at St. Jean d'Acre; for want of horses, if you recollect, you were unable to bring up your guns, and were obliged to raise the siege.'

"Then they both raised their voices and spoke at once. Some of the generals who were present joined in, and the din was so great that I could not make out a word of what they were saying. 'They are still at it,' he added; 'go close up to the tent, you will probably be able to hear something.'

"I and my companion approached the tent, as if we were just strolling by. We could indeed hear the voices of Napoleon and Poniatowski, but could gather nothing distinctly except the latter saying—'No, your Majesty. I know this country better than you do, and I assure you that that is out of the question here, quite out of the question!' The two sentries shouldered arms, which meant that the Emperor was just coming out; so we made off.

"On parade the Emperor turned to the group of officers and said—'Gentlemen, you are not maintaining proper discipline in your corps; there are too many stragglers. Officers seem to stop on the march whenever they please, in order to spend their time in country-houses. They are tired of camping out; but true courage does not fear rainy weather, nor will mud stain a soldier's honour. The men have no regard for discipline; under the pretext of foraging for provisions they desert from their regiments and wander about in disorder. Complaints reach me from every side of their lawless behaviour. This condition of things must be put a stop to, gentlemen; and those who absent themselves without leave shall be severely punished. In the event of an engagement with the enemy, our regiments would be greatly below their strength. The efficient force of our army is such as it might naturally have been after a battle, whereas we have not yet even seen the enemy. Marshals Oudinot and Macdonald have secured victories because they had their full complement of troops when they came to the banks of the Dvina and Drissa.'

"Then the Emperor called for Baron Larrey, but as he was not to be found, Dr. Paulet, the head of the Ambulance Corps, presented himself instead. Napoleon asked him—

"'For how many wounded have you bandages ready?'

"'Ten thousand,' replied the doctor.

"'And about how many days does it take to heal a wound?'

"'About thirty,' answered the doctor.

"'If that is so,' replied the Emperor, 'you cannot even give assistance to four hundred men! We shall want many more than that!'

"There was a low murmur in the crowd, and some one remarked, 'I wonder how many he thinks there will be killed?'

"Napoleon must have heard the remark, but he paid no attention. He continued his cross-examination of the doctor, and asked him, 'Where are the ambulance and medical stores?'

"'They were left at Vilna for want of means of transport.'

"'So the army is entirely unprovided with medicine,' cried Napoleon, 'and if I wanted physic I should have to go without it?'

"'Your Majesty has your own private medical stores,' replied the doctor.

"This made the Emperor very angry. 'I am the first soldier in the army,' he said, raising his voice, 'and I have a right to be attended to in the army hospital.' Then he asked where the chief dispenser was. He was told at Vilna.

"'What!' cried Napoleon. 'One of the chief medical officers absent from the army! Let him be sent back to Paris to peddle his drugs to the women of the Rue St. Honoré! Appoint some one else in his place, and let the whole medical service rejoin the army.'"

The army did not meet with the same enthusiastic reception at Vitebsk as at Vilna. The inhabitants treated the French not as liberators, but as conquerors. Evidently Lithuania was not particularly well pleased at the prospect of re-union with its native Poland, for the disposition of the inhabitants was by no means friendly.

Napoleon made great efforts to impress the Lithuanians. In a single audience he would discourse upon religion and the drama, war and the arts. He rode about at all hours of the day or night, giving orders to build a bridge here, and a bastion there, and on the eve of an engagement he would appear at a ball or a concert. He evidently did his best to astonish the natives by his versatility.

As the Russians had left Vilna and it was impossible to overtake them, Napoleon returned to this town on July 28.

According to Ségur, when he entered his head-quarters he took off his sword, threw it on the table, which was covered with maps and plans, and said in a loud voice, "Here I am, and here I shall stay! I shall look about me, complete my army, give it a rest, and organize Poland. The campaign of 1812 is at an end; that of 1813 will do the rest!" Orders were given to provision the army for thirty-six days, and extensive plans were announced. Napoleon did not neglect amusements; actors were to be brought from Paris to Vitebsk for a winter season, and as the town was empty the audience was to be drawn from Warsaw and Vilna.

"Murat," said the French Emperor, turning to the King of Naples, "the first Russian campaign is over. We will plant our standards here. Two broad rivers outline our position; we will build block-houses along this natural entrenchment, commanded by artillery in every direction. We will form a square with guns at the angles and on each front, and within this square we will build our barracks and magazines. The year 1813 will see us in Moscow; 1814 in St. Petersburg—the war with Russia shall be a three years' war!"

On the same day he turned to one of the principal civil officials attached to the army and said, "As for you, my dear sir, you must see that we are properly provisioned, for we must not repeat the mistake of Charles XII."

It was at this very time that Napoleon received news that peace had been concluded between Russia and the Porte. "The Turks," he said, "will pay dearly for their mistake. It is such a foolish one that I did not even foresee it."

Recognizing that the advance of the Russian army of Moldavia on his rear had now become both possible and probable, he began to think that perhaps it would be as well to destroy the two Russian armies in front of him, and that the sooner this was effected the better. These and other circumstances caused him to alter his views. He was no longer convinced that his wisest course was to stay at Vitebsk, and he became at once anxious and irresolute.

For a solution of his doubts he would appeal in broken phrases to intimates whom he met as he went about. "*Eh, bien*, what are we to do? eh? Shall we stay where we are, or go on? Is it right to stop half-way?" Then without waiting for an answer, he would go on as if looking for somebody or something that would settle the question for him. Brooding over these questions, not daring to make up his mind, he would fling himself on his bed in nothing but his shirt, overpowered by the heat and his anxiety.

In this way he passed the greater part of his time at Vitebsk. Meanwhile the advantages of a forward movement appealed to him more and more strongly.

"If we stay in Vitebsk," he argued, "we must make up our minds to die a lingering death of *ennui* during the seven long winter months! I, who have always been the first to attack, obliged to stand on the defensive! Shame and dishonour await me. All Europe will say, 'He stayed at Vitebsk because he *dared* not advance!' Am I to give Russia time to arm? And how long am I to put up with this uncertainty, which is undermining my reputation for invincibility, already shaken by the resistance of Spain? What will the world think when it learns that, what with the sick and those who have fallen behind or disappeared, I have lost a third of my army? I must dazzle the eyes of the nations with the glamour of a brilliant success—the laurels of victory will cover a multitude of losses."

Napoleon began to find at last that Vitebsk promised nothing but misfortune and loss, with all the discomforts and anxieties of standing on the defensive; while Moscow on the other hand offered the most signal advantages—provisions, money contributions, glory, and, last but not least, peace!

A Dispatch.

But the more resolutely the Emperor wished to act, the more obtrusive were the prevailing signs of discouragement and discontent. After two weeks of rest the soldiers began to complain that they had gone too far already, and that the prospects of war were gloomy. They abused everything that tended to prolong the campaign, and approved of everything that might possibly shorten it.

The Emperor, who wished at any cost to secure general approval of his plans, even from those who did not as a rule give expression to their views, called a council of the principal officers of the army, and his colleagues were invited—perhaps for the first time in their lives—to speak their minds freely.

"The more vigour the enemy displays," he said to the marshals and generals who surrounded him, "the less ought we to slacken in our attack. We must not give these Oriental fanatics time to gather together against us from their remotest wilds. How can we go into winter quarters in July? And what sense is there," he asked, "in breaking up a campaign like this into several parts?" forgetful of his own recent advocacy of the opposite view. "Be assured, gentlemen, that I have pondered deeply over the question. Our troops are always ready to advance, an offensive war is a war after their own hearts, whereas a long stay in one place is not acceptable to the French temperament. To shelter ourselves behind frozen rivers, sit in mud huts and endure privation and *ennui* for eight months, with daily manœuvres and never a step in advance—is that the style of warfare we are accustomed to? The winter has other terrors than its frosts. It may bring with it endless diplomatic intrigues. Is it safe, think you, to give all these allies—whom we have successfully won over to our side, but who feel strangely out of place, I doubt not, in our ranks—to give them time, I say, to realize how unnatural is their position?

"Why should we remain inactive for eight months when we can attain our end in twenty days? Let us forestall the winter! We run the risk of losing all if we do not strike a swift and decisive blow. If we are not in Moscow in twenty days, it is possible we shall never get there at all. If peace be signed at Moscow, I shall have won the best and most glorious of all my victories!"

It was, however, already too late in the year, and the marshals were of opinion that further advance was out of the question. Berthier, Prince of Neufchâtel, was so bold as to urge this fact upon the Emperor, and to explain his reasons. The Emperor gave him a very warm reception. "Begone!" he said. "I have no need of you, you are only a ——. Go back home! I will keep no one with me against his will."

Berthier, however, endeavoured to dissuade Napoleon from the decision he had arrived at, not by argument but by an appealing glance; there seemed almost to be tears in his eyes. Lobau and Caulaincourt tried to influence him by more open opposition, which took the form of bluntness with the former and persistence with the latter. The Emperor angrily swept all their opinions and advice on one side, and replied with the remark, aimed more particularly at Caulaincourt and Berthier, that he had made his generals too rich. "They can think of nothing but hunting and driving about Paris in expensive carriages—they are sick of the very name of war."

To Duroc, who also opposed him, the Emperor replied that he was perfectly well aware that the Russians were trying to lure him on, but he must get to Smolensk at any cost. There he would go into winter quarters, and in the spring of 1813, if Russia did not end the war, he would end Russia. "Smolensk," he said, "was the key to two roads, the road to St. Petersburg and the road to Moscow; and they must seize it because they would then be able to attack both capitals at once—to destroy the one and preserve the other." Caulaincourt remarked that peace would be no nearer at Smolensk or Moscow than it was at Vitebsk, and that to advance so far, relying upon the fidelity of the Prussians, was the height of rashness. When the Emperor asked Count Daru for his opinion, he replied that it was not a popular war, and that neither the importation of English goods nor the restoration of Poland was a sufficient justification for so distant a campaign. "Neither we nor our troops can see the necessity or object of it, and everything points to the advisability of stopping where we are."

"Great heavens!" cried the Emperor; "do they think that I am out of my mind? Do they imagine that this war gives me any pleasure? I have always said that the Spanish and Russian wars are the two sores that are sucking away the life of France, and that they are more than she can bear at once. I wish for peace, but in order to enter upon preliminaries there must be two sides, whereas there is but one at present—for Alexander has not vouchsafed two words as yet. What good can we expect from staying at Vitebsk? True, the position is bounded by two rivers, but in winter there are no rivers in this country; they will be merely imaginary lines. Here we shall want for everything, and shall have to buy whatever we need; whereas in Moscow there is plenty to be had for nothing. I might of course retire to Vilna, but even if provisions could more easily be obtained at Vilna, defence is more difficult, and for real safety we should have to retreat beyond the Niemen, which means the abandonment of Lithuania. On the other hand, if I advance to Smolensk I shall either secure a decisive victory or a strong position on the Dnieper.

"If we were always to wait for the most favourable combination of circumstances no enterprise would ever be undertaken. There can be no end without a beginning—there never was an enterprise in which everything fitted in perfectly, for chance plays a leading part in all the affairs of men. Obedience to rule does not ensure success, but success on the other hand furnishes a canon of conduct, and if this campaign be successful, these new triumphs will doubtless give new guidance for the future.

"No blood has as yet been spilled, but Russia is too great to yield without a struggle. Alexander could not come to terms, even if he would, except after a serious defeat. I will inflict that defeat, cost what it may, and if need be, I will follow it up by advancing to their sacred city. I am confident that peace awaits me at the gates of Moscow. Even if Alexander remains obdurate, I will win over the nobles and the inhabitants of the city to my side. They will know their own individual interest best, they will recognize the value of liberty." "Moscow," he added, "hates St. Petersburg, and I intend to avail myself of their rivalry—the consequences of their mutual jealousy may prove incalculable."

Such, according to Ségur, and others, was the line of reasoning adopted by Napoleon, who inclined more and more strongly to an immediate advance on Moscow. Sebastiani's disaster at Incova at last furnished him with a definite excuse for advancing. The Russian cavalry utterly routed the opposing French horse, and the dash and daring of the attack compelled the Emperor to seek some opportunity of retrieving the disaster by a decisive victory.

Napoleon's want of decision at this moment was, however, reflected in the movements of the French army, and the well-conceived plan of separating the two Russian armies and destroying each of them in detail was never carried out.

The great efforts of the Russians to effect a speedy junction helped to upset the invader's plans. Every man in Russia, from the Emperor to the last recruit, believed that if the armies were once united, not only would they cease their retrograde movement, but they would be able to fall upon the enemy, who had already over-reached himself by penetrating too far into the country. As a matter of fact the Russian Commander-in-chief had no intention of assuming the offensive against such overwhelming forces.

The account given by Dumas, General-Intendant of the French army, throws valuable light upon this point. He says that one of the officers spent three months in Memel on terms of intimacy with Barclay-de-Tolly, who was brought there after receiving a terrible wound at Eylau. The officer in question clearly recollected the details of the plan of "successive retreats" "by which the Russian general hoped to lure the formidable French army into the very heart of Russia, if possible beyond the Moskva; to wear it out, separate it as far as possible from its base of operations, and tempt it to waste its ammunition and provisions. At the same time he proposed carefully to nurse the Russian forces until the frosts came to their aid and the time was ripe for commencing offensive operations, and subjecting Napoleon to a second Pultava on the banks of the Volga. This grim programme was but too faithfully executed."

Napoleon was aware that he was being "lured on," as he called it; but, as we have already seen, he could not refrain from advancing, if not to Moscow, at any rate to Smolensk. He moved on, therefore, to the latter town, still adding to the list of so-called "victories" chronicled in his bulletins.

These bulletins were the more credible, inasmuch as the Russian plan of retreat lent them a sort of colour. The French were always advancing and the Russians always retreating; the inference was of course that the former were gaining a series of victories. Even Neverofsky's exploit is described in Bulletin XVII. as an "engagement in which the advantage rested with the French." The "engagement" really amounted to this—Neverofsky's division, while hurriedly withdrawing towards Smolensk, was overtaken by Murat and surrounded by thirty regiments of cavalry, together with Nansouty's and Grouchy's army corps and the Light Brigade. Finding himself in this dangerous position, the Russian general formed square, and continued his retreat in that order. The French cavalry, though they fell upon the little detachment on every side, found it impossible to break through, even after forty attacks.

The French surrounded the Russians so closely that they were able to exchange words with them, and Murat more than once called upon Neverofsky to surrender. He only managed, however, to capture seven Russian guns, and Napoleon greeted him with the remark, not unmerited, that he should have brought back "not only those wretched guns, but a whole Russian division as well."

At Smolensk Napoleon spent an evening in personally

Russian Grenadiers.

questioning prisoners, and in congratulating himself on the fact that he had at last come up with the Russian army. He attacked it, however, in front, instead of outflanking it and falling on its rear. He might have made a demonstration before the city with a strong detachment, and meanwhile sent the main body of the army to the right over the Dnieper to attack the left flank of the Russians defending the town, for Napoleon's army was so numerous that he could well afford to divide his forces. It is said that he did in fact intend to cut off Prince Bagration, but could not find the ford over the river.

The French censure Marshal Davout for the fearful losses sustained at Smolensk, holding that these sacrifices were due to his want of foresight. They blame Napoleon, moreover, almost unanimously, for failing to surround the Russians. "In storming the fortifications of Smolensk," says the author of the *Letters on the Russian Campaign of 1812*, "when he might have contented himself with surrounding the city and cannonading it, he committed a mistake. In allowing the Polish infantry to be cut to pieces so near their own country, he made a second mistake. In advancing into a huge and resourceless country at the beginning of winter, he fell into a third and far more serious error."

After the battle of Smolensk Napoleon was seen riding over the field and rubbing his hands with an air of glee. "Five Russians," he said, "for every Frenchman!" This, however, was not the fact, for the French lost not 8000 as they said, but nearer 20,000. Bourgeois admits a loss, besides 6000 killed, of 10,000 wounded, though according to the usual ratio the number of wounded would be still greater. He puts the Russian loss at the same number, not more. This is not surprising, in view of the fact that the Russians were fighting under cover, while the French were attacking in the open, and were several times repulsed.

Russian authorities, on the other hand, admit that our losses at Smolensk filled many of our countrymen with dismay, although they had hitherto looked upon the invasion with the utmost indifference. The scenes of terror and desolation presented by the interior of the town were fearful in the extreme. Some of the streets were literally burned to cinders, and the roadway filled with dead and dying, many of whom were half-consumed by the flames.

When Napoleon, from the old tower on the city walls, surveyed the position that had been occupied by the Russian army on the previous day, he perceived that Barclay-de-Tolly was no longer there — he had again escaped! Napoleon had failed in his endeavour to annihilate the Russian army, and the capture of a city in ashes did not represent the final paralyzing blow which could justify his losses in the eyes of Europe.

The French Emperor already appreciated the necessity of lowering his haughty Dresden tone, and took every opportunity of throwing oil on the troubled waters that threatened to engulf him. The letter sent by Marshal Berthier to Barclay-de-Tolly under the specious pretext of offering his sympathy and condolence, but serving as a matter of fact to cloak an attempt to open indirect overtures, contained the following passage—"The Emperor, to whom I have communicated the contents of this letter, desires me, Monsieur le Baron, to beg you to convey the assurance of his respect to the Emperor Alexander if he is still with the army. Pray tell him that the sentiment of esteem and friendship which the Emperor Napoleon entertains towards him will be impaired neither by the vicissitudes of warfare nor by any other circumstances."

These tentative approaches did not elicit any reply. Napoleon then availed himself of the first convenient opportunity that occurred to mention his peaceful inclinations and intentions to his prisoner, General Tutshkof, begging him to communicate them to his brother, another general in the Russian army. "It was not I that began the war," he said. "Why do the Russians retreat? Why have they abandoned Smolensk to me? There is nothing I desire so heartily as peace." He also begged Tutshkof to mention that the Commander-in-Chief was wrong in carrying all the civic functionaries away with him. He invited Tutshkof to constitute a sort of tribunal of arbitration to decide which of the contending parties had more chance of victory, and if that question was decided in favour of the Russians, to appoint a rendezvous for a battle; if for the French, then why shed blood in vain, and why not discuss terms and conclude peace? It was also through Berthier that he called upon the Emperor Alexander to instruct the governors not to leave their posts.

Such overtures could not of course be expected to have any result; their only justification is to be sought in the pitiable frame of mind to which Napoleon was then reduced. He began to realize how gigantic was the enterprise he had undertaken—an enterprise that grew in magnitude the further he advanced. He was now dealing with a nation in arms—with a second Spain, but more powerful, more remote, vaster in extent, and more unproductive. . . . . The name of Charles XII., we are told, was at this time always on his lips.

Murat was once heard to say to Napoleon, "If the Russians refuse to give battle it is not worth while to pursue them; it is time to stop." The Emperor answered him with some warmth; though what he said is not known.

It was, however, subsequently understood from the King of Naples' own lips that he went on his knees to his brother-in-law, and implored him to stop. Napoleon, however, would hear of no halt short of Moscow, which held everything that was dear to him—honour, glory, and repose. "Every one remarked," says Ségur, "that when Murat left Napoleon after his interview his face wore an expression of deep affliction, and his gestures were excited and abrupt—he repeatedly uttered the words, 'Oh, ce Moscou!'"

So soon as he made up his mind to advance, Napoleon again acquired complete command over himself. He became cheerful and tranquil, as was usual when he had definitely settled upon any project. After the battle of Zabolotye—or Valutina, as the French called it—he said: "We have come too far to retire; if I thought of glory alone I should return to Smolensk, plant my standard there, and treat the town as my own. The campaign would be ended, although not the war. Peace lies before us—we are only eight days' march from it. Shall we hesitate now that we are so near our goal? *En avant!* to Moscow!"

The best answer to this resolve was given in one of the Emperor Alexander's proclamations—"He threatens to march on Moscow—let him do so. Even if he is victorious he will still share the fate of Charles XII."

Napoleon himself was far from feeling the confidence which he endeavoured to inspire into others. For instance, in writing to Marshal Victor from Smolensk he said—"It may be that I shall not find peace where I seek it; in that case I shall be able to retire under cover of your reserves steadily and without precipitation."

If one compare the words of Napoleon at the beginning of the campaign, when his intention was to remain at Vitebsk, or even at Smolensk, with what he said when his decision to march on Moscow was irrevocable, one is struck with wonderment at the total change of ideas, and at the irresistible impulse of which he was the victim.

We have already mentioned the plan sketched out by Barclay-de-Tolly as to the best method of carrying on the war in Russia. Barclay was not the only person to recognize the weak spot in Napoleon's genius.

When the storm first began to gather, Tczernicheff, the military agent, pointed out with remarkable penetration both the French Emperor's probable course of procedure and the best way of replying to his intended moves.

"The preparations for the war are complete," he wrote to the Minister of War at St. Petersburg in 1811. "The Emperor Napoleon's animosity against us increases day by day, and if this autumn does not see us at war it will only be because the season is late, and Napoleon, taking a lesson from the Pultusk campaign, will perhaps be afraid of the marshes of Poland. They would of course hinder him in his plans, which are no doubt to end the campaign in one lightning stroke, as he has done in all preceding wars.

"Accepting the conclusion that hostilities are unavoidable, we must make every preparation, not only for withstanding the first shock, but for prolonging the war as much as possible. Experience tells us that this is the only method by which we can hope for success against Napoleon; and it also tells us that he has always been embarrassed and led into mistakes of strategy when he has met with prolonged resistance. This is the course which our Government should adopt, in this difficult and critical situation. It is the only course that offers any hope of final triumph over the world's oppressor.

"The proper way to conduct this war, in my opinion, is to avoid a general engagement and to conform as far as possible to the guerilla tactics adopted against the French troops in Spain, so as to gradually demoralize them, and reduce by starvation the enormous forces they will bring against us."

The advice given by Marshal Bernadotte, who was at that time King of Sweden, is also interesting:—"In the position in which Russia stands towards France, it is to her advantage to prolong the war, because it is in her power to do so, but not in Napoleon's. One ought to depend as little as possible upon chance. It is therefore essential to avoid big battles and endeavour to reduce the war to a series of petty skirmishes. You must have plenty of Cossacks. You must capture Napoleon's baggage and cut off his supplies. Even if you have to retire behind the Dvina, nay, behind the Neva, so long as you continue to offer a stubborn resistance everything will turn out well, and Napoleon will meet at the hands of Alexander with the fate meted out to Charles XII. by Peter the Great.

"Napoleon neglects nothing that can conduce to success; but his means are already exhausted, and he cannot stand a two years' war. He lacks men, money, and horses for such an undertaking; and the further he advances the worse he will fare. But of course it would be best if such extremities could be avoided, for the provinces will suffer severely, and the reverses that may be expected in the early part of the campaign will produce a bad impression."

In spite of these prudent counsels, we were all but hoist with our own petard at Drissa. Nevertheless, looking back, we may now say that it was a good thing for Russia that we were obliged to retire behind the Dvina, inasmuch as we should otherwise have had great difficulty in coping with our opponents.

Napoleon marched straight on Moscow. In passing through Viazma he came upon signs of want of discipline that made him furious. He rode into a crowd of soldiers; struck some of them, knocked others down with his horse, and ordered a canteen-keeper to be arrested, tried, and shot. But they allowed the poor wretch to kneel in the road, surrounded by a fictitious family group consisting of a woman and a few borrowed children, when the Emperor was passing by, and this stratagem saved his life. Fezensac mentions it—"In passing through the little town of Viazma, Napoleon came upon some soldiers who had looted a wine-cellar. He flew into an ungovernable passion, charged down upon them, and began abusing them and hitting right and left with his riding-whip. The impossibility of catching up the Russian army, and the devastations they had made on our line of march, angered him so much that he fell foul of everybody he came across."[1]

* * * * * * *

Prince Kutuzof had been appointed Commander-in-Chief of the Russian army, and Napoleon hastened to gather all possible information as to his new opponent. He was described to him as "an old man who had originally attracted notice by virtue of a most interesting and unusual wound." From that time he had made the most of his opportunities. Even the defeat which he had suffered at Austerlitz, and which he had foretold, served only to raise his reputation. But it was exalted still higher by the last campaign against the Turks. There was no doubt that he was a man of

[1] There seems to be no doubt about the incident in question. But though it would appear that the French plundered the houses in Viazma, Napoleon writes in Bulletin XVI.—"The Cossacks pillaged Viazma so completely before their departure that the inhabitants do not think there is much chance of the town ever renewing its allegiance to Russia."

parts, but he was accused of attending too closely to his own interest, and having an eye to some personal end in all his actions. He was, further, a man of phlegmatic and unforgiving character, and above all of great cunning—in fact a thorough Tartar—rather a courtier than a general, but redoubtable on account of his reputation. To the Russians his person, his conversation, his dress, and, last but not least, his superstitions and even his age, recalled Suvoroff and the Russia of the days of Catharine the Great—a fact that endeared him to his fellow-countrymen. In Moscow the popular enthusiasm aroused by his appointment was so great that the people exchanged congratulatory embraces in the streets. All were confident that the new Commander-in-Chief would, by hook or by crook, prove more than a match for Napoleon.

The arrival of Kutuzof at head-quarters created an excellent impression on the army, especially as the constant succession of retreats had undermined, not to say destroyed, confidence in their commanders. The person chiefly blamed for what was considered the cowardice of our strategy was of course the Commander-in-Chief, a man of great talent and intelligence, who, when once a plan of operations had been definitely adopted, was accustomed to carry it out to the bitter end. He was completely misunderstood by his contemporaries, including the Emperor Alexander, who, yielding to the pressure of his *entourage*, expressed signs of impatience, and demanded offensive tactics and immediate victories. The impulsive Prince Bagration, who was an especially strong advocate of the offensive, so far forgot himself as to make complaints to the Emperor against the Commander-in-Chief. He, however, had not the terrible responsibilities that devolved upon Barclay, and he practically admitted in private that a decisive battle might be disastrous to Russia. The Emperor Alexander's Council of War might decide upon an attack, but the Commander-in-Chief would inevitably defeat their intentions, although he would at first pretend to share their enthusiasm. This course of action rendered him extremely unpopular.

Kutuzof, the new Commander-in-Chief, was unwilling to endanger his enormous popularity, and decided to accept battle, although, as a prudent man, he was almost as strongly opposed to such a course as was his predecessor. It cannot be denied that the selection of the plain of Borodino for the great defensive battle was creditable both to Kutuzof and to Colonel Tol, the head of his staff.

"On two lines," says G. de Pimodan, "it is an extremely strong position, and still worthy of a visit from officers of the general staff, who may profitably study the scheme of the defences that were hastily constructed. Their only weakness was on the left flank."

The French army, which at the passage of the Niemen numbered 400,000 men, after comparatively insignificant losses in battle mustered no more than 160,000 when it reached the plain of Borodino. The question naturally arises: what had become of the 240,000 men who, even on the admission of Bulletin XVII., were missing? Moreover, where did all the Russian troops come from after being incessantly slaughtered by the French, tens of thousands at a time according to Napoleon's bulletins, for the space of ten weeks, and after the wholesale desertions which he chronicled?

On the day before the battle of Borodino, Napoleon, according to the evidence of his valet, was in a perfectly tranquil state of mind. He spoke of Russia as if it were a smiling province of France. From his conversation it might have been supposed that the neighbourhood was a vast granary ready-stored for the army, and offering all facilities for the establishment of winter quarters. The first step of the new administration which he was about to establish at Gjatsk would be the encouragement of agriculture. He was evidently enchanted by the vistas that opened up before him. Seldom had the Emperor appeared so much at ease or displayed such calmness in his conversation and demeanour.

It should be mentioned that the entrenchments at Borodino were very slight, partly on account of the haste in which they were constructed, and partly owing to the fact that the Second Army, which constituted the left flank, had no entrenching tools. Bayefsky's battery, therefore, and the entrenchments on the Semyonof heights, were far from formidable. Scarcely anything was done to Tutshkof's position at Utitsa owing to want of appliances.[1]

Napoleon regarded the left flank as the weakest part of the Russian position, and after a careful survey of the heights of Borodino he decided to concentrate all his efforts on this point, *i.e.* on an attack with his own right. Marshal Davout then requested the assistance of Poniatowski, whose forces were too weak for independent action, to help in outflanking the enemy. He proposed to move before daybreak with Poniatowski's troops and his own five divisions, numbering 35,000 men, under cover of the woods on which the Russians were resting, get behind them, along the old Smolensk road, and fall suddenly on the rear of the left flank. He pointed out that while the Emperor was leading the attack from the front, he would move rapidly from redoubt to redoubt and from reserve to

[1] It is stated that for a long time there was only one sapper attached to Miloradovitch's detachment.

reserve, disperse any force he found on the Mozjaisk road, annihilate the Russian army, and finish the war at a single blow.

This proposal furnished one more proof that Davout was the best tactician of all the marshals trained in the school of Napoleon. If his daring project had been carried out, it would most probably have thrown the Russian army into utter confusion. But Napoleon, after listening attentively to what the Marshal had to say, replied after a few minutes of silent deliberation—"No, it is too unheard-of a manœuvre; it will lead me away from my main object, and make me lose a great deal of time."

The Duke of Eckmühl, confident in the correctness of his views, still persisted. According to Ségur, he undertook to execute the whole manœuvre by six o'clock in the morning. He would answer, he said, for the utter rout of the Russians. But Napoleon, evidently displeased at the Marshal's persistence, interrupted him with—"Oh, you are always urging these flanking movements; it is too hazardous!" So Marshal Davout said no more, and, fortunately for the Russian army, left without gaining his point.

Kutuzof was not slow to divine the enemy's intentions. When the battle began, in the face of the enemy's fire he moved Boggavut's corps across from the right flank, against which Prince Eugène was making an ineffectual demonstration, to the support of the Second Army, and in his turn alarmed the French by a movement round their left flank with Uvarof's cavalry and the Cossacks.

Both sides appreciated the fact that the Semyonof heights were the real key to the position.

We must not omit to mention that throughout the night preceding the battle Napoleon was apprehensive lest the

Russian army should again retreat. The fear of this prevented him from sleeping; he kept calling to his attendants, asking what the time was, and whether any sound could be heard from the Russian camp, and sending to see whether the enemy was still in the same place. When he was reassured on this score, he began to express anxiety for his hungry and exhausted troops—how would they bear the shock of battle? He sent for Bessières, the Marshal in whom, apparently, he had the greatest confidence, and inquired whether the Guards had everything they needed. He more than once, in fact, made inquiries on this point.

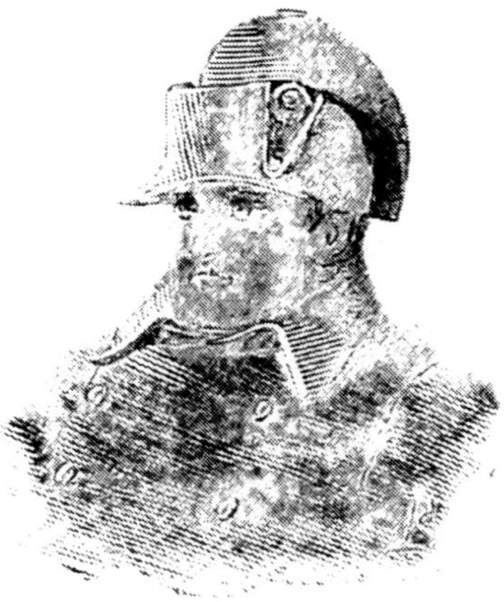

At last, still unsatisfied, he rose and asked the sentinels outside his tent whether they had had their rations served out to them. Receiving an affirmative answer, he lay down again and fell into a troubled sleep.

But he soon called out again. The aide-de-camp who entered found him with his head resting on his hand. He appeared to be musing on the vanity of human glory. Napoleon reviewed the critical situation in which he was placed, and added—"The eventful day draws near. It will be a terrible struggle!" Then he asked Rapp if he was confident of victory. "Certainly," the latter replied, "but we shall not get it without much bloodshed."

Once more Napoleon became restless and uneasy. Again he sent to inquire whether the Russians were in the same position, or whether they had slipped away. Receiving a reassuring report, he endeavoured to calm his agitation; but the exhausting journeys he had lately performed and his sleepless nights, together with his many cares and anxieties, had so told upon him that as the temperature fell during the night he grew feverish, and was seized with a dry cough and nervous irritation. During the latter part of the night he suffered from intense thirst. And to add to all this he was troubled by his old complaint, for on the previous day he had had an attack of dysuria, a disease from which he had long suffered.

Five o'clock struck at last. An officer came from Ney to report that the Russians were in front, and requesting leave to begin the attack. Napoleon brightened up, rose from his bed, summoned his attendants, and issued from his tent with the words—"They are in our hands at last! Forward! The gates of Moscow are before us!" Such is Ségur's account.

The battle of Borodino, famous in the annals of war, had begun. The roar of the guns, borne upon the wind, was heard eighty miles away from the battle-field. The Emperor was seen throughout the whole day sitting or slowly walking up and down near the landslip on the left front of the captured Shevardino redoubt; but he could scarcely view the battle from that place after it had been for some time in progress. He rose now and again, walked a few paces and seated himself once more. Those who attended him regarded him with astonishment. They were accustomed under such circumstances to see him managing affairs with a confident and tranquil air; but instead of this they now saw nothing but feebleness, lethargy, and inertia. Some ascribed his want of energy to fatigue; others thought that he was tired of everything, even of fighting, while some suspected internal sufferings.

The last supposition was probably the correct one. Napoleon's attendant, Constant, positively asserts that during the whole of the battle of Borodino he was suffering from an attack of his chronic malady. He had contracted, moreover, some time previously a severe cold which he had neglected, and it was rendered still worse by the anxieties of the day. So seriously, in fact, did it affect him that he almost lost his voice.

"Napoleon never once mounted his horse," says de la Fluse, "during the whole of the battle. He walked about with his officers, pacing up and down upon the same spot. It was said that his indisposition prevented him from riding.

"His aide-de-camp was kept busy in receiving and delivering his orders. Behind Napoleon were the Guards and a few corps in reserve. A regimental band was playing a succession of military airs, recalling the battle-fields of the first Revolution, such as '*Allons, enfants de la patrie!*' But at Borodino these strains had no effect on the soldiers, and some of the older officers laughed at the contrast of the two periods. The panorama of a bloody battle was spread before our eyes, but we could see nothing, owing to the smoke of a thousand guns thundering without a pause. I got as close as I could to the Emperor, who kept looking through his glass at the field of battle. He was dressed in his grey overcoat, and spoke but little. When a cannon-ball rolled towards his feet, as sometimes happened, he stepped on one side just like the rest of us."

By three o'clock in the afternoon the French had captured the redoubt on the Semyonof heights, but the Russian army, far from taking to flight, had no intention even of retiring. Napoleon, aghast at the unprecedented losses of men, officers, and generals, put a stop to any further attack, and, in spite of all representations, refused to allow the reserves to be used for a final decisive assault.

The marshals sent General Belliard for assistance. The

At Borodino

general declared that from the position they occupied they could see the whole of the Mozjaisk road, covered with men and wagons in full retreat, that nothing was needed but one vigorous onset to finally crush the Russian army. The Emperor wavered and hesitated ; then he bade the general return and report again.

Belliard rode off in some surprise, and soon returned with the news that the enemy was apparently rallying, that the opportunity for the decisive blow was passing, and that if they did not strike at once a second battle would be needed to decide the first. Bessières, however, returned at this moment from the hills to which he had been sent by Napoleon to inspect the Russian position. He insisted that the Russians, far from retreating in disorder, had only retired to their second position, and were actually preparing to attack. Then the Emperor informed Belliard that it was not yet clear what had happened ; that before making up his mind to allow his last reserves to be brought into action he wished to be more certain regarding the position of the pieces on his chess-board. He repeated this phrase several times.

Belliard returned completely dumfoundered to Murat and the other Marshals, who were impatiently awaiting reinforcements, and informed them that they were not forthcoming. "He had found the Emperor still at the same spot, evidently in pain, and in a state of despondency ; his features were downcast, his eyes dull and heavy, and he gave his orders in a listless way.

"Every one was surprised. Ney, in an access of ungovernable temper, said bluntly, 'What is the meaning of this? Have we come out here for the pleasure of taking the plain? What is the Emperor doing in the rear? There he can only see the reverses and not the successes. If he does not mean to lead the army himself, if he has ceased to be a general and is playing at Emperor, let him return to the Tuileries, and leave the command in our hands!'"

Daru, in his turn, was instigated by Dumas and Berthier to whisper to the Emperor that the universal cry was, "Now is the time for the Guards to attack!" But Napoleon answered, "And if I have to fight a second battle to-morrow, what troops shall I have to fight it with?"

Napoleon's sufferings were evidently increasing; it was as much as he could do to mount his horse and ride at a foot pace to the Semyonof hills. He saw that he was far from being master of the field of battle; that it was still disputed by the cannon-balls, and even the rifle-bullets, of the enemy.

Murat declared that he saw none of the genius of Napoleon displayed on this momentous day, and Prince Eugène, the Viceroy, admitted that he could not understand his adopted father's indecision. When Ney was appealed to for his opinion he was so angry that he recommended retreat.

The whole of the French army was disappointed with the result of the battle, and with the want of energy displayed by Napoleon. Bessières was especially blamed; for, at the critical moment, when the Emperor was on the point of making up his mind to let the reserves be brought into action, the Marshal approached him and whispered in his ear—"Sire, do not forget that you are eight hundred leagues from your capital."

There are, however, some who take the opposite view. Chambrey, for instance, assures us that "the whole of the French army was astonished at the stubbornness with which this terrible battle was fought," and Gourgot, in defending Napoleon, goes so far as to say, "If the ranks of the

Guards had been thinned at the battle of Borodino, the remains of the French army, of which it was the pillar and pride during the retreat, would hardly have managed to reach the Niemen."

Of the Russian authorities, some find fault with Napoleon, and others are of opinion that he adopted the only possible course. "Nothing," says Buturlin, "can justify Napoleon's course in stopping the fight at three o'clock when a little further effort might have ensured a victory. The last Russian reserves had already gone into action, while on the side of the French neither the Old Guard nor the Young, nor any of their cavalry, amounting to over 20,000 men, had taken any part in the battle. There is no doubt that if Napoleon had made use of the twenty-three battalions and twenty-seven squadrons of which this select force consisted, he would have utterly routed the Russians, and compelled them to spend the remaining four hours of the day in continual retreat instead of preparing for attack."

Danilevsky asserts that the French, after occupying the redoubt on the Semyonof hills, so far from pressing the Russians, who had fallen back on another position in the immediate neighbourhood, withdrew all along the line for the night; and reminds his readers of the fact, that until eleven o'clock on the following day the French made no attempt to renew the assault, but awaited an attack on the part of the Russians, and only advanced at last when their opponents began to retire.[1] He expresses an opinion that for Napoleon's refusal to use the Young Guard to support the cavalry in breaking through our left flank, our army was indebted to the movement made on the left by

[1] To be more accurate, it appears that the Russians had already begun to retire in the night.

Uvarof's cavalry,—that is to say, to a movement ordered by Kutuzof himself. We may add that neither Uvarof nor the Cossacks did all that might have been expected from them. Had the latter attacked the French more boldly in the rear, plundered their baggage, and generally caused confusion in that quarter, as they had every opportunity of doing, Napoleon would in all likelihood have had to send his reserves not to the front but to the rear; and the result would probably have been to demoralize, and perhaps to spread panic throughout the whole of the French army.

Many incline to Marshal Davout's opinion, which we have already mentioned, that Napoleon could have made much more certain of victory if, instead of attacking the Russian left, he had made a strong demonstration there, and sent a large force on to the old Smolensk road to support Poniatowski against Tutshkof. He would certainly have been enabled to fall on the rear of the Russian army, which, being thus cut off from Mozjaisk and cornered between the rivers Kolotsha and Moskva, would have been in a very critical position.

It was at first Prince Kutuzof's intention to accept battle on the following day in the position which the Russian army then occupied. But the reports sent in at night by the commanders of the various army corps as to the disordered condition of the different divisions, and above all as to the scantiness of ammunition, caused him to change his plans. Grabbe was sent that night to the First Army with orders to retire. Deep silence, he says, reigned at the village of Gorki. When he had found the cottage in which Barclay-de-Tolly was quartered, he obtained a candle with much difficulty and entered the parlour where the general was asleep on the floor, side by side with his aides-de-camps and orderlies. He gently awakened him, gave him the note which he had brought with him, and explained his mission. The general leaped to his feet, and, probably for the first time in his life, there burst from his lips, generally so mild and gentle, a torrent of bitter invective against Benigsen, whom, for some reason or other, he took to be the principal author of the decision to retreat.

The Russian army began once more to retreat, and the French to advance. The French had therefore nominally won the battle.

"Monsieur L'Evêque," writes Napoleon to the Bishop of Metz, "the passage of the Niemen, of the Dvina and the Dnieper, and the battles of Mohilef, Drissa, Polotsk, Smolensk, and lastly of Moskva [Borodino], call for thanksgiving to the God of Might. We desire that on receipt of this letter you will make the necessary arrangements. Summon my people to the churches and sing praises unto the Almighty according to the forms laid down by the Church for such occasions.

"In sending you this letter, I pray the Lord that, etc.

"*Given in our Imperial Quarters in Mozjaisk, 10th September*, 1812. NAPOLEON."

In accordance with these instructions, the Bishop of Metz issued the following proclamation :—

"Claudius Ignatius Laurent, by the Grace of God, Bishop of Metz, General Administrator of the District, and Baron of the Empire, to the clergy and to all true sons of the District of Metz, greeting.

"BELOVED BRETHREN,

"The whole universe now gazes in profound wonder upon new exploits and new triumphs yet more glorious than those that have hitherto filled us with astonishment. Napoleon has once more shown himself a veritable Titan, capable of the most gigantic achievements. His victorious phalanxes have swept like eagles from the mouth of the Guadalquivir to the sources of the Volga. No longer shall the Northern barbarians trample on the blessed valleys of the South; the glorious warrior of the West is driving the common foe before him to the ice-bound regions of the Pole.

"For more than a century have the presumptuous dwellers of the hyperborean shores, relying on a reputation they have ill deserved, menaced and intimidated the humble and confiding monarchs of civilized Europe. Long time, too long indeed, have they lent the hireling aid of their would-be invincible legions, to nations whom it was their aim thereafter to subdue, and whom they have set in arms one against another, only to break faith with their kings and lead them astray into difficulties from which there was no escape. He whom the Creator, the God of War, hath chosen to root out all manner of crafty cunning, to break the spells of witchcraft, to humble the proud, to cast down earthly idols, to triumph over the kings of the nations and subdue their chief cities, he has seen, beloved brethren, that the time has come to humble their intolerable pride and arrogance, and to show to all men that these savage warriors are no more invincible in their native steppes than in the valleys of Helvetia, or the plains of Poland and Moldavia.

"What the mind hath conceived, that the hand hath performed. Though few be the months that have passed, the rapidity of our successes and the splendour of our victories fill the whole world with astonishment.

"The immortal instrument by whom these wonders have been worked, he himself marvels, it would seem, at his own successes. He humbly acknowledges that it is the right hand of God, and not his own, that triumphs over the enemy who has summoned him to the fight.

"On the field of battle, in the midst of his victories, he is the first to raise the hymn of thanksgiving, and, from the ends of the earth, where he is now contending with the foe, he calls upon the pastors of his realm to summon the people to the churches, and join him in singing praises unto the Lord, in gratitude for His victories. Who is so proud that he will not bow down before the Most High when the victor, who casteth down the thrones of kings, himself falls at the throne of the Lord who giveth as He will, victory or defeat, life or death, peace or war?

"Never, my brethren, has Napoleon the Great missed any occasion of proclaiming these eternal truths whenever he has achieved one of his wondrous victories. The joyful epistle which his Imperial and Royal Majesty has graciously vouchsafed to us is a convincing testimony of the depth of his religious faith.

"Let us give thanks to the Fountain of these great mercies even as our most gracious Emperor lays his triumphs at the feet of the Almighty, the Lord of heaven and earth.

"And to this end that the praiseworthy intentions of our most august Emperor and King may be worthily fulfilled, we, having duly considered the matter, do hereby order and command . . . . "

It is admitted on all hands that the French losses at Borodino were quite as great as the Russian, namely, about 50,000. Ségur puts them at 40,000. Dumas says that "the losses were beyond calculation." At about nine o'clock in the evening Napoleon summoned Daru and Dumas. His camp was in the middle of a square formed by the Guards. "He had only just supped," says Dumas, "and was sitting all alone. He made one of us sit on his right, and the other on his left. After questioning us as to the arrangements made for giving assistance to the wounded, he began to talk of the result of the battle. Then, after dozing in his chair for about five minutes, he gave himself a shake, and began talking again. 'People are surprised, I dare say,' he said, 'that I did not let my reserves be used in order to secure a more decisive result;

but you see I was obliged to save them for the final blow which we must deal before we can enter Moscow. The success of the day was certain; I had to think of the issue of the campaign—that is why I kept the Guards out of action.'"

Napoleon attempted the same night to resume his routine work which had been interrupted for five days. But his voice failed him, and he could neither converse nor dictate. He was obliged to have recourse to the assistance of the pen, writing his orders on scraps of paper. His secretaries and all the members of his staff who could be of any assistance copied them out as fast as they could. Count Daru and the Prince of Neufchâtel set to work with the others; but the Emperor's handwriting was extremely difficult to decipher, for he was writing at the rate of an order a minute. He would frequently rap on the table as a sign to remove the papers which were accumulating in great piles.

Twelve long hours were spent in this work. Not a sound was to be heard but the scratching of Napoleon's pen and the rapping of his hammer.

* * * * * * *

The French army at last approached Moscow. Napoleon, who had been previously seated in a carriage, mounted his horse when half-way through the last march.

In the distance, through a cloud of dust, could be seen the long columns of Russian cavalry retiring in good order before the French troops. At last a number of towers came into view, with golden domes glittering in the sun—a vast city lay before the advancing host, and the van of the army, in a transport of enthusiasm, cried, "Moscow! Moscow at last!" The cry was taken up by the whole army; officers and men clambered on to the heights in order to gaze at the famous city, destined perhaps to be the new boundary of the French Empire.

Napoleon feasted his eyes upon the spectacle from the Pilgrim's Hill—Poklonnaya Gorà. Behind him was a group of delighted marshals.

To the left and right they could see Prince Eugène and Poniatowski approaching the city. In front, on the high-road, Murat and his scouts had almost reached the suburbs; but still no deputation of the inhabitants came out to meet them. It was afternoon, but Moscow gave no sign of life; it was like a city of the dead. Those officers who had already been in the city reported that Moscow was deserted! But for a long time no one dared to communicate these tidings to Napoleon; all feared an outburst of the Emperor's fury. When Napoleon was at last informed of the condition of the city he flatly refused to believe the report. Then he mounted his horse and rode up to the Dorogomilof gate. He gave orders that the strictest discipline should be observed, clinging to the hope that the rumour would prove to be untrue. Perhaps these people did not know the proper mode of surrendering. The whole situation was new to them; the French and their ways must be as strange to the Russians as they and their ways were to the French. But every fresh report confirmed the alarming news; doubt was no longer possible.

Napoleon summoned Daru—"Moscow is deserted! The thing is preposterous! Ride into the place and find the boyards."

Daru, however, was unsuccessful in his mission, for there was not a boyard in the city. There was no smoke from the chimneys—not a sign of habitation; unbroken silence brooded over the vast city.

But Napoleon insisted; he still waited and hoped. At

last one of the officers, evidently willing to oblige at any cost, rode in, seized a few vagrants in the streets and drove them out before him—as a deputation.

Rostopchin says that the deputation consisted of some twelve men clad in the worst of garments; the civic authorities, nobility, clergy, and principal merchants were represented on this solemn occasion by a simple type-setter. Napoleon saw the humorous side of the situation, and turned away. Convinced at last that Moscow was really deserted, he abandoned his hopes and projects, shrugged his shoulders, and said with a contemptuous air—"The Russians do not understand the impression that will be produced by the occupation of their capital."

One can well understand Napoleon's impatience to receive the keys of the city; for this would have meant the realization of a long-cherished ambition. An hour before reaching Moscow he summoned Count Durosnel, who was in charge of the Imperial head-quarters, and said—"Go into the city, get everything in order, and select a deputation to bring me the keys." There is no doubt that he had thought out all the details of his entry into Moscow; his speech to the nobility, in which he would have availed himself of the jealousy between the old capital and St. Petersburg, and the shortcomings of the constitution of the empire, to win these brave but barbarous people over to his side; his arrangements for a contribution to be paid in gold, and the issue of the false 100 rouble notes which he had had printed expressly in Paris, and with which he hoped to make good the expenses of the war. He had, of course, already decided whom he would punish, or reward, to whom he would extend his Imperial clemency; what changes he would make in the administration; and, last but not least, how he would conduct the negotiations for peace—whether slowly or quickly, haughtily and sternly, or graciously. He who had so long been accustomed to apply his genius to every detail of the subjugation, pacification, and organization of newly-conquered countries, must of course, now that he had reached the goal of his ambition, consider and decide everything beforehand. And, after all,—how aggravating to find that there was nothing, positively nothing, with which to satisfy the curiosity of the *Moniteur* and of Europe, which had been expecting this climax open-mouthed.

A Frenchman, who was an eye-witness of the scene, tells us that he came upon the Emperor in one of the suburbs, awaiting envoys from the Russians, and examining their cavalry, which was retiring on the left, through a field-glass. A few peasants and shopkeepers were marched up. They presented a pitiable spectacle, and were quaking with terror, under the impression, apparently, that their last hour had come.

Napoleon dismounted. He was evidently cold; he coughed as he gave his orders, and he seemed to be undecided as to what course to adopt. Apparently considering that it would be wisest not to run the risk of entering the city at that moment, he stationed himself in one of the neighbouring wooden houses.

This was in the suburb of Dorogomilof. Marshal Mortier was appointed Military Governor of the town. Napoleon said emphatically—"See to it that there is no plundering! You will be answerable with your own head—save me my Moscow from everybody and everything!"

At the Dorogomilof Bridge, Riess, the bookseller, was brought to Napoleon. Riess afterwards related that he had been compelled to remain at his shop, but hearing the drums and trumpets in the street he went out, was taken prisoner and brought before the Emperor.

"Who are you?" asked Napoleon.

"A French bookseller."

"Ah! then you are one of my subjects."

"Yes; but I have lived for a long time in Moscow."

"Where is Rostopchin?"

"He has gone."

"Where are the magistrates—municipal council——?"

"Gone also."

"Who is left in Moscow?"

"None of the Russians."

"*C'est impossible!*"

Riess apparently swore that what he said was true. Napoleon frowned and remained for some time buried in thought; then, as if he had made up his mind to some daring project, he gave the word, "Forward—march!"

One of the Russians says—"They went searching for the keys and for a deputation in the Government offices, the town-hall, the head-quarters of the police, the Governor-General's house, and, in fact, every place in which there was the least chance of finding an official. After a long but ineffectual search, the zealous Polish general who had undertaken the task returned to Napoleon and reported that there was not a single functionary left in Moscow, and that the town was deserted by all except a few foreigners who had stayed behind. The Emperor accordingly postponed his entry; he thought perhaps that by next day some of the inhabitants would have returned, and that a deputation would arrive after all, or that at any rate his French, Italian, and German subjects would come to the rescue and present themselves to pay him their respects."

He was again disappointed. He spent the night before the gates in an innkeeper's house, apparently unable to sleep. "There was such a horrible smell in the house," says his valet, "that his Majesty kept calling every minute, 'Are you awake, Constant?'

"'I am, your Majesty.'

"'Pray burn some vinegar, *mon cher;* I cannot stand this awful smell—it is simply torture to me!'

"The house was in such a filthy condition that they found next day specimens of those disgusting insects which are so plentiful in Russia, in the Emperor's bed, nay, in his clothes as well." The writer refers to our bugs, which, as is well known, attack new-comers with peculiar virulence.

It was said that Napoleon, "although he intended to establish himself in the Palace of the Kremlin, considered it best to wait a little before entering into possession, owing to a rumour that the ancient dwelling of the Tsars was mined with explosives."

The two armies moved simultaneously upon Moscow. The King of Naples and Marshal Ney crossed the bridge. The men and officers of the Russian rear-guard and of the French advance-guard met on the bridge, and the King found himself completely surrounded by Russians of General Miloradovitch's detachment. According to Ségur, Murat called out, "Is there any one here who can speak French?"

"There is, your Majesty," answered a young officer not far off.

"Who is in command of the rear-guard?" The young man pointed to a veteran in Cossack uniform who looked as if he had seen service.

"Please ask him if he knows me?"

"He says that he knows your Majesty well. He has always seen you in the thick of the fight."

The King hinted in the course of conversation that it was

time to make peace—that the war had already lasted too long. He also remarked incidentally that the fur coat which the worthy veteran was wearing must be most useful in camping out. The Cossack general at once pulled it off and offered it to Murat as a memento of the interview. Murat in return gave him a valuable watch which he took from one of the officers of his staff. This unfortunate officer was Napoleon's aide-de-camp, Gourgot, who afterwards bitterly lamented the loss of his watch, which he valued for its associations.

The narrative of Kerbeletzky, a Russian *chinovnik*, who was captured on the way to Moscow and brought before Napoleon, is interesting in its *naïveté* and simplicity—"The Duc d'Istry, Napoleon's State Secretary de Laurent, and his Polish aide-de-camp Lieutenant-Colonel Welsowicz, questioned me on the morning of September 1, in great detail, not only as to the number and disposition of all our armies, and the movements and performances of each of them, but also as to the intentions entertained by our Government with regard to peace. .

"All the officials whom I have named above, according to their own account, which they said was based on the most trustworthy information received by Napoleon, were thoroughly acquainted with the condition of Moscow. They knew that there were no Russian troops in the town, and supposed not only that the Russian army would not give battle before the gates of the city, but more than that, that the Russian Government would certainly sue for peace. Welsowicz further affirmed that on the morrow, namely on September 2, Napoleon, their Emperor, would dine in Moscow ; that whatever resistance might be offered by the Russian army which had taken part in the battle of Mozjaisk, he would take the city by force if need be;

would raise a good round sum by way of contribution; would restore Poland to her former dignity, and would join White Russia and Smolensk to her territories. He would further provide his troops with clothes and boots, and after spending a while in this capital of Russia would return to Paris. If the Russian Government remained obdurate and refused his terms, he would make over Moscow to Poland, while he himself marched to St. Petersburg and beyond, and subdued the whole of Russia.

"On the 1st, at ten o'clock in the morning, he proceeded towards Moscow with his huge army, which had passed the night camped round the country-house he had occupied. In the evening he halted at Viazum, a village some twenty-two miles from Moscow, belonging to Prince Galitzyn, and spent the night in the manor-house. That day Napoleon drove the first eight miles in his carriage, with the Prince of Neufchâtel (Berthier). Then, as he could no longer use the carriage, for the bridge on the high-road was burned, and the road that led round by the ravine was impassable, he mounted a horse and rode the rest of the way. On September 2 Napoleon left Viazum at daybreak, and at ten o'clock in the morning he reached a manor-house which lies on the right of the high-road to Smolensk, eight miles from Moscow. There he was met by the King of Naples. He did not enter the house with him, but turned to the left into a close near the church, and there they walked alone for more than an hour, discussing the steps that must be taken for the capture of Moscow.

"Murat then, without taking his dinner, proceeded towards Moscow, and the whole of the French army with its numerous artillery followed him without a halt. Napoleon made a hasty dinner in the house, and with his attendant generals—who took their dinner outside—and a special body-guard, consisting of a squadron of Chasseurs and another of Polish Uhlans, under the guidance of the Russian prisoners, set off post-haste after Murat.

"Napoleon arrived at two o'clock in the afternoon at the Pilgrim's Hill—Poklonnaya Gorà—distant some two miles from Moscow. He found the vanguard already drawn up in battle array at the foot of the hill by order of the King of Naples. The Emperor, holding in his hand a plan which was given to him, dismounted, and some of the generals who accompanied him did the same. The army was preparing for battle.

"After waiting half-an-hour without any challenge from Moscow, Napoleon gave orders to fire a gun as a signal; then, when five more minutes had elapsed, he and his staff mounted their horses and galloped at full speed towards the city. At the same moment the vanguard and the division which was posted in the rear of the centre advanced with indescribable impetuosity; the cavalry and artillery galloped at full speed, keeping step together, and the infantry charged along as fast as they could double. The thud of horses' hoofs, the creaking of wheels, and the rattling of guns, added to the noise of running men, made a remarkable uproar. The daylight was dimmed by the dense cloud of dust which they raised! Within twelve minutes they had reached the Dorogomilof gate.

"The unexpected news that Moscow was deserted both by the Russian army and by the inhabitants seemed to astound Napoleon. He was seized with the profoundest amazement, which for the moment wrought in him a kind of ecstasy or self-forgetfulness. His tranquil and measured step at once became quick and feverish. He looked all round and about him, recovered himself, stopped in his walk, shivered, fell into a stupor, scratched

Looking Towards Moscow.

his nose, pulled off his glove, and pulled it on again; drew out his handkerchief from his pocket, crumpled it between his hands and put it in another pocket as though by mistake, then took it out again and put it back; then he pulled off his glove once more and pulled it on again, repeating this action many times. He continued thus for a whole hour, and during that time the generals surrounding him stood motionless, like lifeless images of men, not one of them daring to stir. Then Napoleon recovered himself a little, mounted his horse and rode into Moscow, followed by the cavalry, which had hitherto stood without the gates. When he had passed through Dorogomilof Post-boy Ward and come to the edge of the river Moskva, he stopped on the right side of the street on the slope of the bank, dismounted, and began once more to pace up and down; but this time he was more tranquil.

"Napoleon and his escort lay that night in the Dorogomilof suburb in private dwellings. Of the inhabitants of Moscow none were to be seen except four stable-boys."

The night which Napoleon passed in the suburb was a sad and dreary one. To say nothing of the bugs—and perhaps also other parasites by no means rare in Russia—he was kept awake by the gloomy reports that were continually brought in, warning him, among other things, that the city was about to be burnt. "The Emperor was uneasy and could not lie still; he kept calling his attendants and making them repeat the rumours. Apparently he could not quite bring himself to believe them, but about two o'clock in the morning he received word that the fires had begun.

"He entered Moscow on Tuesday, September 3, at half-past ten in the morning. The Arbat Ward was absolutely empty. He mounted his little Arab, dressed in his grey overcoat and an ordinary cocked hat, without any sign of distinction. He was surrounded by a very large suite of marshals and other officials. The various colours and the richness of their uniforms, and the many-tinted ribbons of the orders which they wore, made a most brilliant picture, and gave a certain distinction to the simplicity of Napoleon's attire. The conqueror of Moscow rode as far as the Borovitzky gate without seeing a single inhabitant. His wrath was visible in every line of his face. He was not, indeed, at any pains to conceal what was passing in his mind."

It was at this time that new fires broke out in many parts of the Arbat Ward, and after Napoleon had entered the Palace of the Kremlin, the Bazaar and the so-called Carriage Mart, together with a number of dwelling-houses round the Kremlin, burst into flames. Napoleon hurried to the scene, issuing orders interspersed with curses and threats against the troops and Marshal Mortier.

"The sight of the Kremlin, however," says Ségur, "the majestic dwelling of the line of Rurik and the Romanofs, the throne still standing in its accustomed place, the Cross of Ivan the Great, and the beautiful part of the city commanded by the Palace, restored, in some degree, his peace of mind. His hopes revived; the conquest was at least flattering to his pride, and he said with some complacency, "*Me voilà, enfin!* Here am I at last in Moscow, in the ancient palace of the Tsars! in the Kremlin itself!" He examined everything with mingled pride, curiosity, and pleasure; made inquiries as to the resources of the town, and began to consider the possibility of making peace."

The enthusiasm in Paris on receipt of the news that Napoleon had entered Moscow was indescribable. The only anxiety was lest he should rest satisfied with his laurels and not march triumphantly into India! Innumerable sonnets, epistles, odes, and eulogistic rhymes of all kinds were published in honour of the occasion.

Here are a few specimens in the original, for they would suffer by translation; we have merely left out a few descriptive passages of a purely imaginary character—

ODE À SA MAJESTÉ L'EMPEREUR ET ROI, SUR LA PRISE DE MOSCOU, PAR M. QUAYNAT.

"Elevons nos chants d'allégresse!
Vantons nos triomphes heureux!
Jadis l'Italie et la Grèce
Eurent des soutiens valeureux;
Jusqu'à nos jours, Athène et Rome
Doutaient de voir paraître un homme
Qui pût égaler leurs succès.
Maintenant, elles sont moins fières,
En trouvant les preuves contraires
Dans le monarque des Français.
* * * * * *
Ton vainqueur, témoin de ces crimes,
Moscou, déplore tes malheurs,
Et par des secours magnanimes
S'efforce d'essuyer tes pleurs;
Mais tes maux sont trop innombrables,
Sur ces pertes irréparables,
Moscou, tu gémiras longtemps.
Pleure, vingt siècles sans orages
N'effaceraient pas les ravages
Des brandons de monstres sanglans."

Another lyric poet, Paul Chanin, anathematizes Russia in a 'Poem on the Campaign of Russia by the United Armies of France and Germany.'

"Une nation factieuse
S'oppose au bien que nous voulons;
Son influence désastreuse
Corrompt l'air que nous respirons.

Une île de nous se sépare !
C'est du Scythe, c'est du Tartare
Qu'elle ose appeler le secours !
Le crime de ce pacte impie,
Aux yeux de l'Europe trahie,
La déshonore pour toujours."

And now M. A. J. B. Barjaud rises to the epic strain, in a poem entitled 'Conquest of Moscow.'

"Le Russe espère, en vain, par un excès d'audace,
Se soustraire au péril dont ton bras le menace ;
Sa bouche ose indiquer le prix du déshonneur
A ce perfide appel, la voix de la Patrie
Répond : qu'il soit marqué du sceau de l'infamie,
Le font du suborneur !
* * * * * * *
Tremblant à ton aspect, contre l'airain qui gronde
Il se fait un rempart de la flamme et de l'onde,
De ses propres foyers il est le destructeur :
Mais loin de retarder ta marche triomphale,
C'est la sombre clarté de sa torche fatale
Qui guide son vainqueur."

Next comes an 'Ode to His Majesty the Emperor on his Entry into Moscow,' by A. de la Garancière.

"En vain tes ennemis se flattent dans leur rage
Que leurs climats glacés dompteront ton courage ;
Tu dis en contemplant tes valeureux soldats :
'Si jamais la victoire, en caprices féconde,
Fuyait, pour m'échapper, dans un troisième monde
J'y guiderais leurs pas !'"

And M. Mazarie, in his turn, celebrates 'The Taking of Moscow' in "fiery stanzas."

"Le fils aînés de la Victoire
Suivent ce héros que la gloire
A ceint du laurier des Césars ;
Par lui les destins s'accomplissent,
Et dans la tombe, au loin gémissent
Les mânes effrayés des Tzars."

I bring these citations to a close with a verse from an anonymous ode on 'The Campaign of His Imperial and Royal Majesty in Russia and his Entry into Moscow.'

> " Lâches, où courez-vous ? Quels seront vos asiles ?
> Ne lancez-vous les feux que sur vos propres villes ?
> Ah ! tournez contre nous ce salpêtre éclatant.
> Des coups de vos ayeux, élancés du Bosphore,
> L'Europe fume encore ;
> Et les Parthes, du moins, fuyaient en combattant ! "

"Let us see what the Russians mean to do now," said the Emperor. "If they still refuse to enter into negotiations, we shall have to take our own course. We are provided with winter quarters now. We will show the world that our army can winter comfortably in the midst of a hostile nation—like an ice-bound ship in Arctic seas. In the spring we can continue the war—though Alexander will not compel me to do that—we shall come to terms and peace will be signed."

Apparently Napoleon had provided for almost every contingency. One thing, however, he had not foreseen—the terrible fires that spread so rapidly in the gusty wind that prevailed on the night of his entry into the Kremlin. There was nothing to be seen on any side of the fortress but flames rising high into the air, almost, as it seemed, into the clouds.

Numbers of the inhabitants who had remained in Moscow, and who now fled from house to house in terror of the fire and of marauding soldiers, were arrested and shot, under suspicion of incendiarism.

Napoleon spent his first night in the Kremlin in a state of great excitement; abusing his soldiers, his officers, and Marshal Mortier, stamping his feet, and demanding that the fires should be stopped.

When he was told that the Kremlin was surrounded with flames, he sent Berthier on to an elevated terrace of the Palace to see if this was really the case, but the force of the wind and the draught created by the fires was so great that the Prince and his officers had considerable difficulty in preventing themselves from being carried away.

The Emperor was stupefied at times by the strength of his emotions; his face was red and streaming with perspiration. The King of Naples, Prince Eugène, and the Prince of Neufchâtel begged him to leave the Palace, but he could not make up his mind to retreat. "These ruffians," he said to his servant Constant, in his indignation against the incendiaries, "will not leave one stone upon another in Moscow."

Fire broke out at last within the very walls of the Kremlin; the arsenal was found to be in flames. They found a Russian in the fortress. He was brought before Napoleon, who questioned him narrowly and ordered the soldiers to despatch him with their bayonets. He was the custodian of the arsenal!

"There is no such word as *cannot* in my dictionary," was one of Napoleon's favourite sayings. But the time had apparently arrived for incorporating the unwelcome expression, especially when Berthier represented that if he did not leave the Kremlin and Kutuzof delivered an attack, he would find himself cut off from his troops.

Napoleon resolved to abandon the Kremlin and remove to Peter's Palace—Petrofsky Dvoretz—but the change of quarters was by no means an easy undertaking. Around the fortress swirled an eddying sea of fire closing every exit. At last the fugitives discovered a path to the river Moskva; and the Emperor with his suite and his guards sallied forth across the stream, only to find themselves in a veritable inferno. The officers of Napoleon's suite wished to wrap him in a cloak and carry him through the flames in their arms; but he refused, and solved the question of the means of escape by dashing boldly forward. They had to fight their way through an avenue of fire, scorching their faces and burning their hands, which they put up to ward off the sparks and cinders that fell in a shower around them. It was fortunate for the Emperor that some soldiers, who were marauding in the vicinity, recognized him and showed him a way of escape. His hair was singed, his clothes were burnt into holes, his hands blistered, and his boots scorched.

The Prince of Eckmühl, it is said, though still suffering from the wound he had received at Borodino, as soon as he heard of the danger to which Napoleon was exposed, hurried to meet him, intending to rescue him or perish in the attempt. It is said that when Napoleon and the Marshal met they fell into each other's arms.

The principal officers accompanied Napoleon to the Petrofsky Palace. Dumas, the Intendant-General, gives the following account of his escape—" It was night when I left the house I was proceeding to occupy. We issued from Moscow under a perfect hail of fire; the wind was so strong that it tore the red-hot iron from the roofs and hurled it down into the streets. All our horses had their legs burnt. It is impossible to describe the confusion of our headlong flight. The roar of the flames can be likened to nothing but the noise of the waves of the ocean—it was indeed a storm raging over a sea of fire. The whole length of the road to the Petrofsky Palace was littered with odds and ends of all kinds, especially with broken bottles thrown away by the soldiers. We bivouacked at the edge of the forest in full view of this image of the infernal regions. The whole of the huge city was a vast sheet of flame, and the heavens themselves seemed to be on fire. At a distance of two miles from the conflagration I was able to read the orders which were brought to me from the major-general."

After a five days' stay in the Petrofsky Palace, a period of the most intense anxiety, Napoleon returned to Moscow. It should be mentioned that from the time he entered the Kremlin, and throughout his stay at the Petrofsky Palace, he made no military arrangements of any kind. It is evident that he was so overwhelmed by the fire that he was unable to determine upon any course of action.

When Napoleon re-entered Moscow a fearful sight met his eyes. Of all the huge city there remained nothing but heaps of ruins surmounted at intervals with stacks of chimneys. A heavy stifling atmosphere hung over the fallen Colossus. Heaps of cinders and ashes, with here and there the fragments of half-ruined walls or pillars, alone marked the course of the streets.

The Emperor saw his troops scattered over all parts of the town. His own progress was hindered by the multitude of plunderers, searching for booty or dragging it away in noisy crowds. Soldiers were grouped at the entrance of every cellar, before every large house, and before the shops and churches towards which the fire was making its way. Before the flames reached these buildings the doors were broken open by impatient pillagers. The Emperor's path was impeded at every turn by remnants of broken furniture flung from windows, and various articles thrown away by the plunderers to make room for more delicate or costly booty. Napoleon rode on in silence.

But disorder soon reached a climax. Even the Old Guard joined in the pillage, and Napoleon resolved upon stern measures, which had a certain good effect. After returning to Moscow, the Emperor's mood became somewhat more cheerful, and the change was reflected in his *entourage*. When, however, he looked out of the window upon the scene of desolation that met his view on every side, he was once more oppressed with gloomy thoughts, and his bitterness was vented on those who had the ill-fortune to present themselves at such moments. But he no longer displayed such constant signs of impatience, nor did he give rein to such furious outbursts of anger, as had marked his previous demeanour. It need scarcely be said that Rostopchin—who was, fortunately for himself, at a safe distance—and the incendiaries were the principal objects of his wrath.

Napoleon was very satirical in chronicling the fact that the Russians had celebrated Borodino as the first victorious encounter of their forces with the invader. He says in one of his despatches—"The Russians have offered up a *Te Deum* in thanksgiving for the battles of Ostrovnaya and Smolensk—and of course the army entered Moscow to the strains of hymns of thanksgiving."

"At the ruffian Rostopchin's house," he continues, "they found rifles, papers, and a letter which he had begun—he ran away without having time to finish it. Moscow, one of the wealthiest cities in the world, is no more. This is an incalculable misfortune for the Russians, both for their merchants and for their nobility; the loss must amount to milliards. Some hundred incendiaries have been taken and shot. Thirty thousand Russian sick and wounded were burnt alive. The richest commercial houses of Russia are ruined. They were unable to take anything away with them; and when they saw that everything had fallen into the hands of the French, they set fire to their own ancient capital, their holy city, the centre of the empire. Rostopchin is the author of this crime. We did what we could to subdue the fire, but the ruffianly Governor had taken his precautions only too well—he had carried off or destroyed all the fire-engines and apparatus."

As an answer to this bulletin he learned that the surprise, terror, and indignation produced in Paris by the news of the burning of Moscow defied description. It was easy to see that a despatch announcing that the soldiers were provided with shelter, food, and clothing would have re-assured the Parisians far more than any news of victories.

Napoleon, however, after bewailing the treacherous welcome he had received from the city, declared—"The army is doing well; there is plenty of corn, potatoes, cabbages, and other vegetables, beef, salt meat, wine, brandy, sugar, coffee, etc., etc. The men have secured a quantity of furs and coats for the winter. One advance-guard is posted on the road to Kazan, the other on the road to St. Petersburg."

He referred in carefully-chosen terms to the Emperor Alexander, who, in his opinion, would not have hesitated to make peace if he had but received any one of the letters sent to him—letters, by the way, of a most gloomy, melancholy character.

Napoleon expounded his magnanimous intentions to Yakovlef, a Russian nobleman who was captured when about to leave Moscow, robbed by the soldiers, and brought to the Emperor dressed in the coat of his valet. After various complaints and reproaches, Napoleon, adopting a much gentler tone, asked—"If I write a letter, will you consent to deliver it? Will you promise that it shall come into Alexander's own hands? If you can promise me this, I will let you go—but are you certain that you have access to your Emperor, and can you assure me that he will get my letter?"

Yakovlef of course promised.

Napoleon got up at night on purpose to write the letter—"I have fought your Majesty without ill-feeling. A word from you before or after the last battle, and I would have stopped, and abandoned my right to enter Moscow. If your Majesty yet cherishes any kind feeling towards me, you will consider my appeal to you. Common humanity, your Majesty's own interest and the interests of this great city, should have induced you to trust to my hands the capital which your troops had left."

At three o'clock in the morning he despatched the letter to his prisoner, who passed with it through the French lines, delighted that his carelessness in allowing himself to be taken prisoner had had no graver consequences.

Tutolmin, the Governor of the Foundling Hospital, also had the honour of a conversation with Napoleon, of hearing from his own Imperial lips of the respect and brotherly tenderness with which he regarded the Emperor Alexander, and of his readiness to make peace. "I have never adopted this method of warfare," said Napoleon to Tutolmin; "my troops can fight, but not burn. All the way from Smolensk I have seen nothing but ashes. Some limit must be put to this bloodshed; it is time for peace. I have no business here in Russia."

As Tutolmin's official duties prevented him from leaving Moscow, Napoleon begged him in his next report to the Empress—to be sent through the outposts—not to omit to mention Napoleon's peaceful inclinations and his readiness to enter into negotiations.

Napoleon was very uneasy during the first few days after his entry into Moscow regarding the movements of the Russian army, which had been completely lost sight of in the confusion of the fire, the looting, and all his other troubles. He spoke very sharply to General Sebastiani, losing his temper and abusing him roundly, for not keeping an eye on Kutuzof. Imagining that frequent communication with the Russian outposts was the cause of the disorders that had occurred, he ordered Marshal Berthier to instruct Murat to forbid all communication with the enemy on pain of death. "It is his Majesty's wish," said Berthier, "that the only communication with the enemy should be through the medium of powder and ball." Napoleon, however, was not the only person who was uneasy at the disappearance of the Russians. The marshals were apprehensive at one time lest Kutuzof should cut their communications.

"On the 11th September," according to Kerbeletzky, "Napoleon, preceded by two pages and accompanied by his generals, Court officials, three Russian prisoners and a body-guard consisting of a squadron of Chasseurs and some Polish Uhlans, left the Kremlin for the first time to gaze upon the ruins of Moscow, and, also for the first time, doffed his light-grey overcoat and appeared in uniform. It might have been expected that, as his marshals and all his generals were in uniforms, richly embroidered back and front with gold, the Emperor would be distinguished by the peculiar brilliance of his attire. On the contrary, he was dressed in a plain military uniform of dark-green cloth, with a red collar, without embroidery, but with epaulettes, the star of the Legion of Honour on the left breast, and a crimson ribbon round the tunic. He wore a low cocked hat and a small cockade. His charger was an ordinary Polish horse, while his generals and Court officials had English horses, in a very famished condition. When Napoleon came out, many of the inhabitants of Moscow, who had drunk deep of the cup of suffering, ran away as soon as they caught sight of his numerous suite. Others, of a more daring disposition, ventured to peep stealthily from behind ruined walls. And lastly, in a street near the poultry market, a group of small burgesses, numbering about forty, whose clothes were in tatters, and whose faces, through the combined effects of fear, hunger, and cold, retained scarcely any semblance of humanity, waited till the suite approached the end of the street, then fell on their knees, stretching out their arms to the Emperor, bewailing what they had suffered, lamenting their utter ruin, and begging for mercy and bread!

"But this inhuman creature turned his horse away to the right, and merely bade his secretary learn what they wanted.

"From end to end Moscow was a scene of indescribable horror and utter desolation. The houses which had survived the fire were plundered, and the churches looted. All the pavements and side-walks were littered with fragments of chandeliers, mirrors, furniture, pictures, books, church-plate, and even the sacred *ikons* of the saints."

As we have already said, when the plundering began, even the severest prohibitions scarcely availed to check the reign of lawlessness. Sebastiani, for instance, when complaints were made, was obliged to declare that he was unable to restrain his men. In the orders of September 22, Napoleon says—"In spite of all orders, the patrols neglect their duty; at night the sentinels fail to challenge those who pass." On September 24 he says—"To-day the officers omitted to salute the Emperor with their swords on parade."

"At the Kremlin," says Constant, "the days were long and tedious." Napoleon was waiting for the answer from Alexander that never came. Among other things his spirits were depressed by the flocks of crows and jackdaws that appeared in the city. "*Mon Dieu!*" he cried, "do they mean to follow us everywhere?"

Napoleon rode daily through the city, mounted on a little white Arab, and accompanied by a few generals and aides-de-camp and fifty Uhlans. He spoke to nobody while in the street. A theatre was opened for the men and officers of the army in one of the houses which were still left, but Napoleon did not visit it himself. Sometimes in the evening he would play a game of cards with Duroc. A few concerts were given at the Palace; the Italian Tarquinio, who had lately come from Milan, sang, and Martini played the piano; but the Emperor listened with a heavy heart. "Music," observes Constant, "had lost its power over his disordered spirit." Evidently these distractions and the rides through the streets were insufficient to counteract his gloomy meditations on the solution of the insoluble problem, how to present the utter failure of the campaign to Europe as a gigantic success, and by what stratagem to evade the inevitable.

Napoleon paraded and reviewed the Guards and the garrison in all weathers, distributing rewards and crosses of the Legion of Honour. The latter ceremony is described as follows by an eye-witness—"A fat little man marched down the steps of the Palace, surrounded by a numerous suite of marshals and generals. The band struck up, and he advanced to within some fifty paces of the front of the line. He wore a green uniform, and his hat was pulled right down over his evil, penetrating eyes. The ribbon of the Legion of Honour which he wore was so hidden under his uniform that it was not always visible. He sometimes made speeches on these occasions. At the announcement of the names of the newly-appointed chevaliers the band gave a flourish. To judge by Napoleon's haughty look, he was quite conscious of his own power."

It had meanwhile become plain that Alexander would not condescend to reply. This was a terrible insult, and Napoleon was correspondingly enraged.

"On October 3," says Constant, "after passing a sleepless night, he summoned his marshals. As soon as they appeared, he said—'Come in! Come in! Listen to the new plan I have thought of. Prince Eugène, read it! Burn the remains of Moscow; and march through Tver to St. Petersburg, where Macdonald is to join us, Murat and Davout to command the rear-guard.' He gazed at his generals in a state of great excitement; but they remained impassive and silent, apparently only surprised. He tried to kindle some enthusiasm in them, and cried out—'What! Are you not delighted at the notion? Was there ever a more glorious feat of arms? What glory we shall reap! What will the world say when it hears that we have subdued the two great capitals of the North in three months?'"

Davout and Daru tried to damp his enthusiasm by pointing out the lateness of the season, the scarcity of provisions, the bare and exposed nature of the road from Tver to St. Petersburg, a track through marshes which three hundred peasants could render impassable within a few hours! Why, they urged, go north to meet the winter so eagerly, when it was even then at their very doors? And what of the 6000 wounded in Moscow? Must they be given up to

Kutuzof? The latter would certainly pursue, and the army would then have to act simultaneously on the offensive and defensive. The time, they added, had come to end the campaign, not to prolong it. The question was not that of securing a superfluous victory, but of getting as quickly as possible into winter quarters. They must abandon all thoughts of Kutuzof and of fighting, and retire.

Napoleon had not only to listen to this advice, he had to follow it. The time had passed when he could say of his marshals—"These people think that they are indispensable; they do not understand that I have a hundred brigade-commanders who could amply fill their places."

The marshals clearly saw not merely the dangers of the approach of winter, but also the precarious condition of the army. From the moment of Napoleon's arrival at Moscow, his pride kept him in a state of absolute ignorance upon this subject. He always took the army to be in the condition in which he wished to see it, and he boldly adapted his orders to this view, refusing to listen to his generals when they endeavoured to disabuse him of his error. He was resolved, indeed, to make no serious arrangements until their absolute necessity became apparent; until, in fact, it was too late.

Seeing the stubbornness of his marshals, and Russia's unwillingness to take the hand which he had proffered too late, Napoleon showed remarkable consideration for the happiness of the two contending nations, and resolved to secure peace at any price. In vain did Caulaincourt, whom he wished at first to send as an envoy to St. Petersburg, represent that at this season of the year Russia must feel her own strength and superiority, and that any such attempt would do more harm than good, inasmuch as it would betray the difficulty of his position. Napoleon, whose chief fear was lest he should have to utter the word "Retreat," resolved once more to try the charm of his own personality. He could not admit, with Tilsit and Erfurt in his mind, that this charm would be less effective in Moscow than in Paris, and resolved to send General Lauriston to Kutuzof's head-quarters. Lauriston also ventured to submit that at this season of the year it was time, not to be negotiating from Moscow, but to be retiring to Kaluga, and that as quickly as might be. Napoleon answered bitterly that he himself was in favour of the simplest plan, and the straightest road—the high-road—and in the present case the road by which they had come; but he would not travel along it until peace had been concluded. He then showed to Lauriston, as he had showed to Caulaincourt, his letter to Alexander, bade him approach Kutuzof and request a pass to St. Petersburg. The hopelessness of Napoleon's position was expressed at this interview in his last words to Lauriston—"I desire peace; you hear my words. Get me peace, *coûte que coûte!* But save my honour by any means you can!"

The "old fox," Kutuzof, fully appreciated the necessity of keeping Napoleon in Moscow, and humoured Lauriston so cleverly that the poor envoy flattered himself with the most extravagant hopes of a speedy peace, and, what is more, inspired his Emperor with the same delusion.

The position of the French army, however, began in the meanwhile to assume a critical aspect. A desultory guerilla warfare broke out, and in order to procure forage it was necessary to send large detachments with a powerful escort of cavalry and artillery. Every measure of oats and every truss of hay was obtained by hard fighting. Then the peasants began to take part in the war. These men whom Napoleon had taught his troops to look upon as hereditary helots and barbarians, exhibited an unlooked-for independence, and refused to accept the favours which the foreigner endeavoured to foist upon them.

Recognizing the danger of his position, and feeling that he was being hoodwinked, yet not daring to break off his overtures to the Russian Government, Napoleon cast around for some means of making peace necessary to his adversary. He began to collect information regarding Pugachof's rebellion, and endeavoured to procure a copy of one of the Pretender's latest manifestoes, expecting to find in it a guide to the families that could lay claim to the Russian throne. In the course of his inquiry he was ready to turn for advice to any one whom he chanced to meet. He soon saw, however, that it would be difficult to effect anything by this means, and abandoned the idea of using Pugachof.

The Tartars were invited to go to Kazan and summon their brethren to declare their independence. They were promised support as soon as they should rise; but nothing came of this proposal. False reports of all kinds were then circulated. It was pretended that Riga had been taken by assault, that the whole length of the road from Vilna to Smolensk was covered with a train of wagons bearing winter clothing to the army, that Marshal Victor was bringing up large reinforcements, that next spring the army would be as strong and well-equipped as when it crossed the frontier; in short, that if the Russians did not make peace that winter the Emperor would adopt stern measures.

None of these reports and projects, however, came to anything. No reply was received from St. Petersburg, and the war assumed a more and more serious aspect. An armed band, with a priest at its head, captured the town of Vereya, near Moscow, under the very nose of the Grande Armée. Others seized two immense convoys on the high-road to Smolensk, the only route by which Napoleon was able to communicate with Europe, and with France. It was becoming clear that the great invasion was a fiasco, and Napoleon was obliged to reconsider his opinion as to the system by which the Russians should defend their country. When they were attacked in the centre they directed all their forces on the flanks, and seemed almost as if they would overpower them.

Worst of all, winter was now approaching. Napoleon at last realized the fact. He grew uneasy, and began to make unobtrusive preparations for departure.

Poor Moscow bore the brunt of his resentment. He gave orders to strip the covers from the *ikons* and fling them, with the censers, crosses, and plates, into the melting-pot. Two and a quarter hundred-weight of gold and six tons of silver were converted into bullion for transmission to France. In addition to this Napoleon took a number of so-called "trophies"—the arms of Moscow from the Senate House, the eagle from the gates of St. Nicholas, the cross from the belfry of John the Great. The removal of this gigantic cross cost no little time and labour. The Emperor wished to use it as an adornment for the Church of the Hôtel des Invalides. While personally superintending its removal he lost all patience with the clouds of "accursed jackdaws which hovered over the belfry as if they had a mind to defend the cross!" It is said that Berthier, the Duke of Wagram, who was standing with General Dumas on a balcony outside the Empress' apartments while the work of removing the cross was in progress, unable to restrain his anger, exclaimed—"To think of a man doing a thing like this when he as good as has peace in his pocket!"[1]

Shortly before the departure from Moscow a very curious order was issued. The Commanders of Army Corps were directed to present tables showing the number of sick who could recover, (1) within a week; (2) within a fortnight; (3) within a month; and secondly, the number who would probably die, (1) within a fortnight; (2) within three weeks. Provision was to be made only for the departure of Class 1—all the rest were to be left behind. Not less extraordinary, considering the depopulated and devastated state of the country, was the order to purchase exactly 20,000 horses, neither more nor less; and to procure fodder for two months—and that in a position where even the most distant and dangerous expeditions were insufficient to procure enough forage for daily needs.

During the latter half of his stay in Moscow Napoleon's anxieties once more gave rise to constant outbursts of temper. At his morning *levées*, for instance, when he was surrounded by his chief officers, he would challenge their inquiring looks, which seemed to him to be full of reproach, with his stern impassive glance; but his hard abrupt way of speaking and the pallor of his countenance showed that he knew the truth, and that it gave him no peace. He would vent his wrath at times in harsh, even cruel, reproaches, which afforded him no relief, but rather added to the tension of his feelings by the consciousness of his injustice.

It was only, according to Ségur, in his conversations with

[1] The state of Napoleon's temper and the keenness with which he felt his position were reflected in his treatment of his servants. "His trusty henchman, Roustan," says Soltyk, "who happened one day to put Napoleon's left boot on his right foot, found himself stretched on the broad of his back by a vigorous kick."

Disillusion.

Count Daru during his sleepless nights, that he entirely unburdened his mind. "He wished," he said, "to attack Kutuzof and either annihilate or drive him from before him, and then to fall rapidly back upon Smolensk." But Daru answered that though this might have been done before, it was now no longer feasible. The Russian army, he pointed out, was stronger than ever, and his own weaker; the victory of Mozjaisk was already forgotten; and as soon as his army turned back towards France it would slip like water through his fingers, for every soldier was loaded with booty, and would hurry forward into France to dispose of it.

"Then what am I to do?"

"Stay here," said Daru; "turn Moscow into a great fortified camp, and so pass the winter. There is plenty of 'bread and salt'—I can answer for that. For all else, great foraging expeditions can provide. I will salt down all the horses for which there is no forage. As for quarters, if there are not houses enough, there are plenty of cellars. This will help us to last out till the spring, when our reinforcements, backed by all Lithuania in arms, will come to the rescue and help us to complete our conquest."

At this suggestion, the Emperor was silent a while, evidently buried in thought; then he answered, "*Conseil de lion!* but what will Paris say? What will they do? What have they been doing these past three weeks? No one can foresee the impression which six months of uncertainty may have upon the Parisians. No; France is not accustomed to my absence. Prussia and Austria will take advantage of it."

Napoleon was already engaged in imparting an artificial warmth to the zeal of his allies. In confirming the instructions he had before given to Schwarzenberg, and adding new ones, he did not forget to allow him "12,000 francs per month for secret expenses; and ordered 500,000 to be paid to the account of the future;" nor did he refuse any of the rewards solicited by Schwarzenberg for his nominees. He even begged the Emperor of Austria to confer upon him the dignity of Field-Marshal, and suggested various distinctions for his army.

Schwarzenberg, requiting one good turn with another, secretly informed Berthier that the Emperor could count on him personally, but that he must not rely upon Austria.

Napoleon, however, was still reluctant to announce his intention of retreating. Already half defeated, he deferred from day to day a public avowal of the disaster that had overtaken his arms. Amid the gathering clouds of military and political disaster, Napoleon, who had always shown a morbid activity, was absolutely inert. He spent his days in discussing the merits of various odes and sonnets that had lately arrived from France, specimens of which we have given above, or in revising the regulations for the Comédie Française — a task on which he spent three evenings.

It was generally remarked that his dinners and suppers, usually simple and short, were now prolonged, and that he began to sustain his flagging energies with spirits. He grew heavy and sluggish, and would pass whole hours half-sitting, half-lying, with a novel in his hand, his eyes fixed upon vacancy, awaiting the *dénouement* of this terrible drama. The letter to Alexander at St. Petersburg, which he sent by Lauriston under the escort of Volkonsky, should have arrived on September 24. A reply could not be expected until October 20, and Napoleon was evidently awaiting that date. According to Constant, "the last days spent at Moscow, preceding October 18, were terribly gloomy; his Majesty seemed deliberately cold and uncommunicative; for whole hours together no one who was with him would dare to begin a conversation."

Throughout this period the official sources of information, the despatches and the *Moniteur*, carefully concealed the truth. Thus we read—"On October 3 winter began to make itself felt in Moscow. Our troops are in quarters, and preserve the most excellent discipline. We found in Moscow all the Turkish standards taken during the last hundred years and more."

Murat at this time sent a despairing report from the advance-guard regarding the scarcity from which they were suffering and the rapid disappearance of the remains of the cavalry. Berthier was alarmed at this information. Napoleon summoned the officer who brought the report, and so questioned and cross-questioned him that in the end he began to doubt his own information. Napoleon at once availed himself of this hesitation to support Berthier's flagging hopes, and assure him that they were still in a position to wait, and finally sent the officer back to Murat with the full conviction that he would spread the notion in the advance-guard that the Emperor had his plans fully thought out and decided upon.

It is impossible to believe that Napoleon had entire confidence in his own optimism, for his every action was stamped with the mark of indecision. All who came into contact with him were astounded by the entire absence of his former promptitude and audacity, which had always been equal to the necessities of the moment. They recognized that his genius was no longer able to adapt itself to circumstances, as in the days when his star was in the ascendant. He was now obstinate and rebellious, and could not reconcile himself to the shipwreck of his plans. Not only his military projects, but all his other schemes—

which the world regards as strokes of genius if they are sanctified by success, and dishonourable cunning if they fail—missed their aim and vanished in smoke. To the list of these abortive plans—besides the endeavours of which we have spoken to raise the peasants and the Tartars —we must add the miserable fiasco of the bank-notes, which he had forged to the extent of 100,000,000 roubles. It is impossible to refuse to credit the existence of these hundred-rouble notes of Parisian manufacture. Berthier, in one of his letters, laments the loss of his last carriage which contained "the most secret papers." In this carriage was found a *pièce de conviction* of the most damning character—a plate for printing Russian hundred-rouble notes.

Every precaution was taken before the war to prevent the Parisian artists, who were engaged to engrave the plates, from learning the true character of the nefarious task upon which they were employed. The forgery was carried on very slowly, to Napoleon's great annoyance; he more than once insisted upon the work being advanced more quickly. The campaign had already begun when they brought him twenty-eight cases of forged notes, and if he did not succeed in uttering them, it was only because there were no inhabitants on his road—there was no one to pay and no one to reward.

In the spring of 1812 the Duke of Bassano handed over to Frenckel, a banker of Warsaw, forged notes to the amount of 20,000,000 roubles, with instructions to circulate them beyond the Russian frontier as the French advanced. In order to facilitate this operation, a rumour was spread that when the French occupied Vilna they seized notes to the amount of many millions, but the report proved ineffectual. The merchant Nakhodkin, who was acting as Mayor of Moscow, received 100,000 roubles for his services.

Pozdnykof, Kolchúgin, and others were rewarded in the same way, but they could not bring themselves to put the notes into circulation. Tutolmin, the honourable director of the Foundling, refused outright to accept any bribe. "It was mere maliciousness on their part," he wrote in his report to the Emperor, "that led them to offer me forged notes, of which they had brought a great quantity, and with which they even paid the troops at Napoleon's own order." It was with great reluctance that the Guards accepted these notes in payment, though the forgeries were cleverly executed, and afterwards accepted in error even by the Russian banks.

Napoleon's inactivity was infectious. It was not until October 7 that leather was distributed, by the orders of Berthier, the head of the staff, to repair the soldiers' boots, and then it was too late. It was also too late when the slightly wounded and the convalescent, together with the trophies that had been captured, were despatched to Mozjaisk. The rest of the sick and wounded were moved into the Foundling, and French doctors were told off to attend them, in the hope that the Russian wounded who were among them would serve as a kind of protection.

Napoleon concentrated the various army corps that were stationed outside the city on the Moskva, and reviewed them even more frequently than before. The obvious weakness of the battalions was a constant source of annoyance to him, and he ordered the troops to be drawn up two instead of three deep. It is difficult to find a reason for this change, unless we assume that Napoleon was endeavouring to deceive himself and others by lengthening the lines.

During one of these reviews in the courtyard of the Kremlin, a rumour was circulated among his suite that artillery fire was to be heard in the direction of the advance-guard. At first no one dared to call Napoleon's attention to the fact; but Duroc summoned up courage to inform him of the news, and all observed that the Emperor was seriously disturbed. He soon recovered himself and was about to continue the review, when an aide-de-camp from Murat came galloping up with the information that the King's first line had been taken by surprise and routed; that his left flank had been surrounded under cover of the woods, his right attacked, and his communications cut. Twelve guns, twenty caissons, and a number of baggage-wagons had been captured, two generals killed, and three to four thousand men lost. He added that the King himself had been wounded, but he had saved the remnants of his command by means of repeated attacks on the overwhelming forces of the enemy, who had just begun to occupy the only road by which he could retreat. Murat's report was that "the advance-guard no longer exists, for the exhausted remnant of it could certainly not survive more than one more battle with the enemy, who have become bolder than ever."

This was on October 18. The war was being renewed, said the French—it was just beginning, said Kutuzof.

At the news of this attack, Napoleon recovered all his former energy. He issued a thousand orders, embracing the most important movements and the most trivial details, and before nightfall the whole army was in motion. At dawn on the 19th, the Emperor himself left Moscow, with a bold declaration that he was moving on Kaluga—"And woe to him who tries to bar my way."

He left Moscow by the old Kaluga road, meaning to reach the frontier of Poland by way of Kaluga, Medyn, Yelnya, and Smolensk. Rapp, who accompanied him, observed that it was getting late in the year and winter would overtake them on the way; but the Emperor replied that the soldiers must be given time to rest and recover, and the sick must be moved from Mozjaisk, Moscow, and the Kolotzky monastery to Smolensk. Then he pointed to the clear blue sky, and asked if they did not see the star of his fortune in the sun above them and in the continued fine weather. "The sinister expression of his countenance," says an eye-witness, "gave the lie direct to these words of hope and simulated confidence."

In this instance, as in every other, it was hard even for those who were brought most closely into contact with him to decide whether he spoke from conviction or not. Considering the explicit nature of the reports that were sent in to him, it is impossible to suppose, for instance, that it was through ignorance that he so entirely misrepresented the truth as to the engagement of the advance-guard under Murat. This was the celebrated battle of Tarutina, the real beginning of the *débâcle* of the French army. About 50,000 were engaged and utterly routed, losing some 4000 killed and wounded, thirty-eight guns, one flag, and the whole of the baggage.[1]

Napoleon in his despatches gives the following account of the engagement—"A number of Cossacks have begun

[1] The battle would certainly have ended in the capture of the whole of Murat's force, had not Kutuzof, who disapproved of the engagement, refused to support Benigsen. Kutuzof was of opinion that Napoleon and his troops should be left as long as possible undisturbed in and around Moscow, in order that they might be tempted to stay until the frosts began, and in this he was right; but when once he allowed an attack on his recklessly incautious adversary, it was unpardonable not to send the help which was demanded when the battle was at its height. For the opportunity of escaping, though not without serious losses, the French were entirely indebted to Kutuzof and his chief advisers Tol and Kaissarof. Some say that General O. D. could hardly keep in his saddle that day, and some say . . . all kinds of things.

to make their appearance, and given our cavalry some trouble. The cavalry advance-guard, which was stationed by Vinkovo, was surprised by a mob of these Cossacks, who made their way into the camp before our men had time to mount, captured General Sebastiani's baggage, consisting of 100 wagons, and made about 100 prisoners. The King of Naples placed himself at the head of his Cuirassiers and Carabineers and attacked a column of the enemy's light infantry, consisting of four battalions, which had been sent to support the Cossacks, with such success that he routed and annihilated it. General Desi, the King's adjutant, and a brave officer, was killed in this skirmish. The Carabineers distinguished themselves."

When Napoleon learned from a new envoy to the Russian camp that Kutuzof had made no forward movement, he started for Kaluga, making a circuit round the Russian troops with the object of avoiding an engagement. We are forced to the conclusion that he only spoke of dashing Kutuzof to pieces, and opening the road before his troops, with a view to rousing the drooping spirits of his men, and distracting the attention of Europe. He must have seen that though his troops could fight in defence of the enormous booty they had taken, they could no longer win victories.[1]

[1] It is impossible to read without a smile Thiers' eulogy of Napoleon's plan—if indeed such an absurd plan could ever have existed—of wintering with the army in *the more temperate climate* of Kaluga; and of keeping up communication with Smolensk, and with Moscow in the rear. According to this project, Napoleon was to have maintained possession of the Kremlin (?) and entrusted its defence to Marshal Mortier and 4000 dismounted cavalry (?), who would have formed infantry battalions. He was to have left there the more cumbrous part of his *matériel*, together with the wounded, sick, etc., and have provided that experienced soldier, the Marshal, with a garrison 10,000 strong, and with provisions for six months.

The retreating French army covered a vast extent of ground. Of the column—which consisted of nearly 150,000 men, with 50,000 horses—the 100,000 who formed the vanguard, with haversacks and rifles, 550 guns, and 2000 artillery-wagons, still recalled the warriors who had conquered Europe. The rest resembled a Tartar horde returning from a successful raid. Along three or four endless lines of march there was a hopeless tangle of carriages and caissons, of smart barouches mixed up with wagons of every description. In one place were trophies of Russian, Turkish, and Persian flags, and the huge cross of Ivan the Great; in another were bearded Russian peasants dragging along French booty of which they themselves formed part. Others were drawing wagons laden with everything on which they had been able to lay hands. They had no chance of reaching even the first *étape*, but their greed made nothing of 2000 miles or more. Elegant carriages passed along drawn by undersized horses harnessed with ropes. These carriages were filled with plunder and with French women, former inhabitants of Moscow, flying before the anticipated vengeance of the Muscovites. Many Russian women were also to be seen, some following the army of necessity, and some of their own free will. One might have fancied, say those who witnessed the scene, that this was some caravan of nomads, or some army of early days returning from a foray with women, slaves, and all kinds of spoil.

In spite of the breadth of the road and the cries of his body-guard, Napoleon could scarcely manage to make his way through this endless host—they no longer paid much attention to him. He pushed forward in silence, and proceeded along the old Kaluga road. For some hours he pursued this direction, but at mid-day, on the heights of Krasnaya Pakhra, he turned the line of march suddenly to the right and reached the new road to Kaluga in three marches across country, the movement being covered by Ney's corps and the remains of Murat's cavalry. Berthier's letter to Kutuzof, received on the day of the evacuation of Moscow, descanting upon the theme of humanity and love of one's fellows, was a military stratagem intended to throw dust in the eyes of the Russians and gain a day of undisturbed retreat.

This ruse very nearly achieved its end; but it so happened that the Russian free-lance, Figner, detected the retreat of the army and carried the news to Kutuzof, who was lying without precaution at Letashefka. The Russian general immediately moved parallel to Napoleon upon Kaluga.

There can be no doubt that if Napoleon had cared less for the preservation of his plunder and more for speed he would have arrived before the Russians; but moving as he did without haste, no faster than circumstances conveniently permitted, he made the irretrievable mistake of arriving too late.

"Never," says Fezensac, "did the French army carry such a quantity of baggage. Every squadron was provided with a wagon for its provisions, and burnt what it could not carry without the formality of asking permission from the battalion commander."

"The troops," says René Bourgeois, "and especially the Guards, were laden with gold, silver, and precious things, stuffed into every possible place, regardless of the provisions. The result was that they had not got far from Moscow before the army began to want for the first necessaries of life. There were few of the officers who were not provided with furs, but the majority of the soldiers had no clothing beyond their uniforms and great-coats, while their boots were in a most lamentable plight."

The French army slowly made its way to Malo Jaroslavetz. The advance-guard had already occupied the town, and the principal obstacle to their progress seemed to be successfully surmounted. Napoleon was taking his *déjeuner* in the open with Murat, Berthier, and General Lariboisière, when he suddenly heard artillery fire from the direction of the advance-guard. Fighting had begun at Malo Jaroslavetz. The Emperor mounted and galloped in the direction of the cannonade. The Viceroy's aide-de-camp, who brought news that all the available forces had gone into action, received the answer—"Ride back to the Viceroy and tell him that now he has begun he must drink the cup to the dregs. I have ordered Davout to support him!"

The battle was a sharp one. Malo Jaroslavetz was captured and re-captured eleven times. The town was utterly destroyed, and the course of the streets was indicated only by the piles of corpses with which they were strewn. The houses were mere heaps of ruins, among which might be seen the limbs of charred corpses. When the Emperor reached the scene of action, he was shown redoubts which the Russians, when repulsed, had hastily constructed. The general opinion of the French was that Kutuzof would not retire, and that the action would end in a general engagement, to which the vigour of the French troops and the ammunition of their artillery were alike unequal.

"At Malo Jaroslavetz," says Fezensac, "the advantage of the day rested with the French, but Kutuzof fell back upon a new position and strengthened it with redoubts. One of his divisions actually began to make its way round our right along the Medyn road. We were obliged either to retreat or engage in a serious battle."

The position was extremely grave. In the village of Gorodnya, on the road to Malo Jaroslavetz, a Council of War was summoned to consider the question. Marshal Bessières and the other generals were of opinion that they must retreat—not that they were doubtful of victory, but they dreaded the losses that must ensue, and the probable demoralization and disorganization of the army.

The cavalry and the artillery horses were worn out with work and want of food, and it was impossible to replace those that were lost. How were they to transport their artillery, their ammunition, and the wounded, of whom there would certainly be a large number? Under these circumstances the march to Kaluga seemed a very risky enterprise, and prudence counselled retreat through Mozjaisk to Smolensk. Bessières was the first to suggest retreat, and the others followed suit. Napoleon hesitated for a long time, but at last, after passing the whole day in inspecting and studying the locality and in hearing the opinion and advice of his generals, he resolved to retire to Mozjaisk, and thence to retreat along the devastated route of his advance.

In Bulletin XXII. Napoleon gave the following account of the important battle of Malo Jaroslavetz and the subsequent decision to retire—

"At Malo Jaroslavetz the Russians brought two or three armies into action, but without effect. The enemy retired in such disorder that they were obliged to throw twenty guns into the river. The Emperor rode into Malo Jaroslavetz and inspected the enemy's position. He ordered an attack, but the enemy escaped in the night. The Emperor then returned by way of Vereya to Smolensk, *i.e.* to the road on which he had previously travelled. . . . The weather is brilliant and the roads are excellent. The Italian Guards have distinguished themselves. General Baron Delsome, a first-rate officer, received three bullet wounds and was killed. The old Russian infantry was annihilated. It is stated upon good authority that only the front ranks of the Russians consist of soldiers. The rest are made up of recruits and militiamen, with whom the Government has broken faith in keeping them under arms." And so forth.

Napoleon now increased the rate of march, and reprimanded Davout continually for the slowness of the rear-guard. What this slowness really amounted to may be gathered from the report given by Platof, Hetman of the Cossacks, who followed Davout from Mozjaisk. He stated that the enemy was in flight—"no army can be said to retire under such circumstances—they abandon their wounded, their sick, and their heavy baggage by the way."

After leaving Mozjaisk the French army passed by the plain of Borodino, on which more than 30,000 corpses had been left. At the approach of the troops, flocks of carrion-crows rose with hideous cries from the torn and mangled bodies of the dead. In spite of the cold, the latter emitted a most nauseating odour. Napoleon neither turned his head nor uttered a word; he merely quickened his step—for he was on foot.

It is said that when the Emperor's column approached Gzhatsk they found the road strewn with freshly-slain Russians, all with their heads blown open in the same manner, by a point-blank shot, and their blood and brains scattered around. They knew that 2000 Russian prisoners had gone on in front under escort, and they understood that these were the bodies of those who could not keep up with the rest, and who had been shot to save further trouble. Some of the suite were filled with indignation, others held their peace, while yet others justified this cold-blooded butchery. None of those who were with the Emperor dared to express their feelings, except Caulaincourt, who exclaimed—"This is the foulest brutality! And this is the civilization which we have imported into Russia! The enemy will requite our barbarity; there are numbers of wounded and captive Frenchmen in their hands, and there is nothing to prevent them revenging themselves on us." Napoleon was stern and silent, but next day the butchery ceased—no doubt he had taken measures to stop it.

With regard to these prisoners, the testimony of eyewitnesses at head-quarters is all to the same effect. "There was a column of Russian prisoners marching in front of us," says Fain, "guarded by soldiers of the Rhine Federation. They flung them fragments of horse-flesh for their food, and their guards had orders to kill those who fainted by the way and could not proceed. The road was scattered with their dead bodies, their brains blown out."

"The Baden Grenadiers," says Rooss, "who escorted Napoleon's baggage, had orders, if any of the Russian prisoners succumbed and were unable to proceed, to shoot them on the spot. Two of these Grenadiers informed me that it was Napoleon himself who gave the order."

"My pen positively refuses," says M. de B., "to describe our treatment of the Russian prisoners during the retreat, the cruelty and savagery of which it has in vain been sought to excuse by the law of necessity, and by the exceptional circumstances in which the French troops were placed."

Labaume describes what he himself saw. "On the road

they had no means of feeding the 3000 Russian prisoners taken in Moscow. They drove them along like so many cattle, and would not allow them to leave the narrow space allotted to them under any pretext. Fireless and frozen, they lay upon snow and ice, and in their unwillingness to die, longing to stay the pangs of hunger with any nourishment, they ate the bodies of such of their comrades as succumbed. It must be added that these were not captives taken with arms in their hands, but a rabble composed of men of every class who were found in the streets of Moscow."

Perofsky, an officer of noble birth, who was kept prisoner in spite of all the rules of war, gives the following account of this butchery. "Suddenly, a few paces in our rear we heard a rifle-shot, to which I at first paid no attention. A non-commissioned officer came and reported to the officer in command that he had shot one of the prisoners. I could not believe my ears, and I asked the officer to explain the statement. 'I have written instructions,' he replied politely, 'to shoot all prisoners who, from fatigue or any other cause, fall more than fifty paces behind the rear of the column. The escort has received decisive orders to that effect.' In the course of the day some six or seven men were shot, and among them was one of the civil officials. Sometimes we heard as many as fifteen shots in a day. I once saw a veteran sink upon the road from fatigue; three times the Frenchman who stopped to shoot him put the muzzle of his gun to the Russian's head, three times did he pull the trigger—the rifle missed fire! At last he left him, and sent a comrade whose musket proved more effective. Some of the prisoners, when they saw that their end was approaching, espied a church ahead in the distance. They strove to drag themselves to the porch, and were there shot dead with prayers upon their lips."

The author of this last statement, who afterwards became a count, would doubtless have shared their fate but for his deliverance by a band of free-lances under the command of Cheznyshof.

On October 31, Napoleon reached Vyazma. For the first time since leaving Moscow he wore a sable cap, a green pelisse edged with sable, and slashed with gold frogs, and fur-lined boots. He continued to wear this costume during the rest of the retreat, and when the severe frosts began, and it was impossible to sit in the saddle, he either drove in a carriage or went on foot. The infantry of the Old Guard camped round his head-quarters as before in a square, finding shelter, as far as possible, in such houses as were still standing.

The troops, who had orders to burn everything, smashed in the doors and windows of the houses and set fire to them with torches, cartridges, and even ammunition-boxes. The towns and villages were filled with the smoke of burning houses and the stench of decomposing corpses. Davout, who despaired of preserving his men under such circumstances, wrote to Napoleon saying—"It should be left for the rear-guard to fire such villages as remain." The daily losses of the army in men and horses were greatly increased by this destruction of every dwelling on the road.

The battle of Vyazma was most disastrous to the French. Miloradovitch took a number of prisoners, artillery, and baggage. Napoleon, however, only informed France of the loss of a few individuals who had been captured by the Cossacks,—some engineers and topographers who were taking plans, and a few wounded officers who were march-

On the way Home.

ing without sufficient caution, running into danger instead of marching in their place with the baggage.

"On November 6," says Ségur, "there was a complete change in the weather, and the blue sky entirely disappeared. The French army had for some time past been moving through a frosty mist which grew constantly thicker and thicker; but on that day the mist turned into flakes of snow—it seemed as if the icy sky had united with the frozen earth. Everything took on a new and unknown form. The troops marched without knowing where they were or where they were going to, meeting obstacles at every step. While the soldiers were struggling forward against the icy hurricane, the snow, whirled up by the wind, drifted over the hollows and concealed their depth; the soldiers fell into them and were buried in the drifts, and many who were already enfeebled lay where they fell. Those who came behind them tried in vain to turn aside; the wind blinded their eyes with falling and drifting snow, buffeted and confused them, and prevented them from advancing. Their wet clothing froze upon them, and a garment of ice clung to their bodies and numbed their limbs. The strong bitterly cold wind caught their breath as it issued from their mouths and turned it into icicles on their beards and coats. Trembling in every limb they would plod on until the snow, forming balls under their feet, absolutely prevented all progress; then, stumbling over a piece of wood or the dead body of a comrade, they would fall and lie groaning and lamenting while the snow covered them up, leaving on the surface nothing but an almost invisible hillock—a soldier's grave. The whole road was scattered with these tiny eminences, like a churchyard. There was snow, snow everywhere, as far as the eye could see nothing but a melancholy vista of snow. The effect on the imagination was profound; it seemed to be a winding-sheet which Nature was wrapping around the unfortunate French army! The only objects that stood out were the fir-trees with their funereal green, standing motionless and huge, their black boughs outspread, filling the heart with sadness and foreboding.

"Everything, even their weapons which had been serviceable at Malo Jaroslavetz, but were now only contemptible, hindered the wretched soldiers in their progress. They seemed insufferably heavy; when the miserable men stumbled, their muskets would fall and break or become buried in the snow. They would rise to their feet without them—not that they lost them intentionally—hunger and cold had snatched them from their grasp. Many had their hands frost-bitten, while their fingers clung stiff and numbed to their muskets.

"Then came the sixteen-hour nights. With the snow everywhere, covering everything, there was no place to lean against, to stop at, to sit or rest upon, there was no spot in which they could dig for roots to stay the pangs of hunger or obtain fuel for fires. The troops did their best to form a camp, but the wind cared for nobody, and rudely scattered all their preparations. The fir-wood was covered with hoar-frost and would not take fire, fresh snow fell from the sky, the old snow melted beneath, and even when, at infinite pains, the fire was kindled, it could not be kept alight. At last something like a fire might be obtained, and officers and soldiers began to prepare their wretched supper of scraps of lean meat from horses slaughtered or dead of fatigue, with perhaps a few spoonfuls of oatmeal soaked in melting snow. Next day a heap of frozen soldiers marked the position of the camp-fires, and all around lay thousands of dead horses!"

On the day on which winter broke in all its horror on the unfortunate French army, Count Daru stopped the head-quarters staff on the march and made a secret communication to the Emperor. It appeared that an *estafette*, the first that had arrived for a whole week, had reached the army with news of Malet's conspiracy. On the march, under the public gaze, Napoleon received the news with the utmost *sang-froid*, but afterwards in camp he expressed the greatest wrath.

He was still more angry at Smolensk, where the army, after all its expectations of rest, found an insufficiency both of quarters and provisions. The Emperor was simply furious. "I never saw him," says his servant Constant, "forget himself to such an extent. He sent for the Intendant; I could hear his cries from the adjoining room. Napoleon gave orders that this officer should be shot, and it was only by grovelling at the Emperor's feet that the wretched man managed to get off."

The calamities of this stage of the retreat were accentuated by the fact that no notice had been received of the return of the army, and officials at Smolensk and elsewhere, taken by surprise, completely lost their heads when they saw these crowds of ravenous fugitives storming and plundering their stores without much advantage to themselves, but to the ruin of all who came after them.

The army not only obtained no respite in Smolensk, it proceeded on its march in a worse condition than ever. There is no doubt that the Emperor hoped to give his disordered flight the air of a dignified and regular retreat, for, among other things, he directed that the walls of Smolensk should be razed to the ground, in order, to use his own expression, "that they might not stand in his way another time;" as if, at this moment of disaster, he could have dreamt of a new invasion.

As we have already said, Napoleon rode the first part of the way in a carriage. In this vehicle, which was closed and contained an abundant supply of furs, the Emperor, who was warmly clad, did not of course feel the cold himself. Moreover, shut up with Murat in his carriage, he ran less risk of being subjected to insults from his angry soldiery, nor was he haunted by the spectacle of their famine and despair, or the sound of their clamour for bread, bread, bread!

After Smolensk he covered a great part of the distance on foot, and in the course of the march he of course had ample opportunity of assuring himself of the terrible plight of his troops, who were suffering unspeakable hardships.

The Emperor gave orders that the greater part of the ill-starred trophies, as well as a quantity of cannon and weapons of every description, should be sunk in the Dnieper and in the Semlefsky Lake. But, come what might, he wished to convey the cross of Ivan the Great to Paris, and he seems to have brought it as far as Vilna.

We have already given some description of the sufferings which the army underwent on its retreat, but the details furnished by eye-witnesses are so full of character, interest, and instruction, that I may add a few more extracts.

At every step were to be seen gallant officers, dressed in tatters, and leaning on sticks of pinewood, with their hair and beards covered with icicles. Again and again one might hear them imploring assistance. "Comrades," cried one in piteous tones, "help me to rise, give me a hand; I cannot be left behind!" Every one passed on without even glancing at him. Misery levelled all ranks and abolished all distinctions. In vain did many of the officers insist upon their right to command—no one paid any attention to their orders; the starving colonel had to beg for a scrap of biscuit from the common soldier; he who had a store of provisions, were he merely a simple officer's orderly, was surrounded by a little court of sycophants, who laid aside rank and distinction, and flattered and fawned upon their more fortunate comrade. Officers accustomed to command, and unacquainted with want, were in the most grievous plight of all—every one shunned them to avoid rendering them any service.

"*À moi, mes amis!* help me to rise, I am a Captain of Engineers," cried an officer piteously. A passing grenadier stopped, "What, you are a Captain of Engineers?"—"Yes, dear friend, I am!"—"Work away at your plans then!" The road was covered with soldiers who no longer bore the semblance of humanity, and whom the enemy would not even trouble to take prisoners. Many were reduced by cold and hunger to idiocy; they cooked and ate the dead bodies of their fellow-soldiers or gnawed their own arms. Others were so weak that they could not fetch a log of wood nor carry a stone to sit upon; they seated themselves on the bodies of their comrades and turned a dull fixed stare upon the burning embers. Soon the fire would die out, and these living skeletons, having no strength to rise, would fall dead beside the bodies on which they sat. Many tried to warm themselves by thrusting their naked feet into the midst of the fire.

All the corps were mixed up: the remnants formed a number of little detachments, or rather groups, of eight or ten men, who kept together and had everything in common. Each group had a Russian horse—a *conya* as they called it, under the impression they were speaking Russian—for their baggage, their cooking apparatus, and provisions; and every member of the group had also a sack for provisions. Each of these little communities lived apart from all the rest, repulsing every one who did not belong to them. The members kept close together and did their utmost not to get separated in the crowd, and woe betide him who lost sight of his mates—he would certainly find no one else to take the least interest in him or give him any assistance.

"We were a gang of ruffians," says Labaume, "respecting neither person nor property. Necessity made thieves and rogues of us. Without the slightest feeling of shame we stole from one another whatever we wanted. Arson, murder, and destruction of every kind were incidents of everyday life, and crime became second nature. With the same indifference with which the soldiers set houses on fire for the sake of a moment's warmth, they would deprive a weaker comrade of all his little store for their own maintenance."

In spite of the fearful condition of the troops, Napoleon ordered occasional manœuvres—with what result may be imagined. Such divisions as could still be made to perform any evolutions, after wandering about over snow-blocked roads, would end the day by retiring without their artillery and baggage, which had been abandoned in the ditches.

The staff encampment, according to the testimony of an eye-witness, presented a sad and pitiable spectacle. "In a wretched outhouse, with a crazy roof, some twenty officers, sandwiched with as many servants, were gathered round a little fire. Behind them stood their horses, ranged in a circle to keep off the wind. The smoke was so thick that one could hardly discern the forms even of those who were sitting close to the fire blowing up a flame under the cauldron in which their food was simmering. The rest, wrapped in cloaks and fur-coats, were lying side by side almost on the top of one another for the sake of warmth. They did not stir a limb, but every now and then one might hear the voice of a man abusing his comrades for moving about and treading on him, or cursing the neighing of the horses, or the sparks from the fire that burnt his coat."

Napoleon, who now travelled for the most part on foot, clearly recognized the condition of the army, but he saw no need for giving Europe any inkling of the truth in his bulletins. "The roads are very slippery," he says in Bulletin XXVIII., "and are difficult travelling for the draught-horses — we have lost a considerable number through cold and fatigue." From Vyazma he wrote— "Twelve thousand Russian infantry, under cover of swarms of Cossacks, cut the road between the Duke of Eckmühl and the Viceroy. The Duke and the Viceroy attacked them, drove them from the line of march, pursued them into the forest, and took a number of prisoners, including a general and six guns. Since then we have heard no more of the Russian infantry; only the Cossacks are to be seen moving about in the distance."

Not a word about the number of prisoners, guns, and baggage taken by Miloradovitch in this battle, which proved so disastrous to the French army, or of the fact that the French had by this time lost some 40,000 prisoners, about 25 generals, 500 guns, 30 flags, and, in addition to a stupendous quantity of other baggage, all the trophies from Moscow which they had not yet burnt or destroyed! If to this total we add some 50,000 who had died of their sufferings, or been killed in different engagements since they left Moscow, we may calculate that the army contained not more than 70,000 men, and of these, inclusive of the Imperial Guard, there were only about 10,000 able to carry arms.

Kutuzof strictly enjoined his generals not to drive the enemy to despair, and for Napoleon and the Old Guard in particular, from which he expected a most desperate resistance, he ordered them to *faire des ponts d'or*, reckoning that even if they survived cold and hunger they would be unable to pass the Beresina, where they would have to deal with three armies at once. This is the only supposition upon which it is possible to explain the unnecessary caution displayed by the Russian Commander-in-Chief whenever his generals showed any intention of attacking their enfeebled adversary, and making an end of him and the war at a blow. The French army—or rather the remains of it—was indebted for its escape, not so much to its prestige, as to Kutuzof and Chichagof, and especially to the latter.

In consequence of Kutuzof's plan, the Emperor and his picked troops were not harassed on the road to Krasnoye, while Marshals Davout and Ney, who brought up the rear, were exposed to the most determined attacks.

At Krasnoye, Napoleon, after a series of vacillating and contradictory movements, once more displayed his characteristic skill and audacity. By a bold manœuvre he held the Russians in check, and gave the remains of his two divisions an opportunity of escaping.

While he was manœvring with the Guards, an indescribable mass of broken-down fugitives absolutely incapable of defence filed past him. In spite of his self-command it was evident that the sight of these destitute remnants of his once invincible troops affected him deeply. Throughout the night that followed he was unable to sleep, and complained that he could not bear to think of the condition of his troops. "The very sight of them," he said, "fills my soul with horror."

"Imagine, if possible," says René Bourgeois, "60,000 destitutes with sacks over their shoulders and long sticks in their hands, covered with rags of the filthiest description stuck together anyhow, swarming with vermin, and absolutely starving! Add to this picture pale, cadaverous faces covered with the dirt of camps and blackened by the smoke of fires, glazed and sunken eyes, dishevelled hair, long filthy beards—and you will still have but a faint notion of the appearance presented by the army! No men had brothers, friends, countrymen, or officers. *Sauve qui peut* was the order of the day. We were waging a desperate warfare, each man against his neighbour; and it may truthfully be said, both in the literal and the figurative sense, that the strong devoured the weak. Wherever one turned one's eyes they fell upon scenes of horror and barbarity. If a man was suspected of concealing provisions his comrades attacked him furiously, and snatched them from him in spite of all his struggles and curses. All day and every day one might hear the sound of dead men's bones crunching beneath the feet of horses and the wheels of the wagons, as they were crushed into the ruts."

In the face of these horrors one cannot but be surprised that any fraction, however small, of the Grande Armée ever managed to reach the frontier and the long-wished-for winter quarters, and it will therefore not be without interest to see how the fugitives lived their daily life.

"Whenever we halted," says Bourgogne, "to take a mouthful of food, the soldiers laid eager hands on the horses that had been abandoned, or on those which were not guarded, cut them up, collected their blood in saucepans, boiled and ate it. . . . If it happened that the order to advance was given before they had time to finish, or the Russians were seen approaching and they had to make off, they carried their saucepans with them, and ate the contents on the march. Their hands of course became smeared with blood.

"They fought on the slightest provocation, and the air was filled with evil words. The foulest abuse and the vilest epithets were bandied about on the most frivolous occasion. Every quarrel ended, as a rule, in the disputants falling upon one another with fists and sticks; the troops had in fact arrived at such a condition of savagery that they were ready to tear one another in pieces.

"At the halting-places they rushed like madmen into the houses, sheds, outhouses, and buildings of whatever kind that were to be found, and in a few moments packed them so full that it was impossible either to leave or enter. Those who could not get in settled down outside, as near as possible to the walls. The first task was to get firewood and straw for the bivouac, and for this purpose they would climb on to the neighbouring houses and carry off roofs, rafters, partitions, and everything combustible, reducing the whole building to ruins, despite the cries, threats, and resistance of those who were within. The inmates had to stand a regular siege and drive away their assailants by a sortie, or rather by a series of sorties, for the place of those who were repulsed would be taken by other besiegers stronger and more resolute. They had to yield at last to superior force and escape in order to avoid being buried in the ruins. When it was impossible to effect a forcible entry the assailants would fire the building from outside in order to expel those who were warming themselves within. This happened as a rule when a building was tenanted by

Napoleon. Berthier. Murat Rapp

BIVOUAC.

generals who had expelled its first occupants. The latter would then threaten to set the house on fire, and actually put their threat into execution. The unfortunate officers would rush for the door with execrations on their lips, falling and crushing one another in their eagerness to escape."

Even those highest in command now admitted that Napoleon in leading his army to Moscow had made the same error as Charles XII. when he invaded the Ukraine; that from a military point of view the campaign was lost by irresolution during the critical battle, and from a political point of view by the burning of Moscow; and that if the army had returned in time it might have retired in good order. After its entry into Moscow the Russian Commander-in-Chief and the Russian winter both gave the French ample grace; the former forty days, the latter fifty, to rest and retreat. And while they lamented the time wasted in Moscow and the indecision shown at Malo Jaroslavetz they reviewed the long catalogue of their own misfortunes. Since leaving Moscow they had lost all their baggage, half their artillery, thirty flags, some thirty generals, 40,000 prisoners, 60,000 dead. There remained some 50,000 helpless vagrants, and perhaps 10,000 who were still in a condition to defend themselves! It was, moreover, a grave mistake to entrust the task of covering the retreat of the army and all its stores to the Austrians without leaving some one in authority at Vilna or Minsk to correct their errors and omissions. The French were unanimous in charging Schwarzenberg with treachery, though Napoleon himself held his peace—perhaps out of policy, perhaps because he had not looked for any greater degree of zeal from his Austrian ally.

Napoleon endeavoured to check the general demoralization and despondency. In private, as we have already said, he bitterly bewailed the sufferings of his troops, but in public he assumed a tranquil air, and gave orders that every one should keep his proper place in the ranks. Failing obedience, he ordered that "officers be reduced to the ranks, and soldiers shot." But this threat proved entirely ineffectual, for the soldiers were naturally less afraid of death than of the prolongation of such a state of misery.

At Orcha Napoleon burned his baggage with his own hands in order to prevent it from falling into the clutches of the enemy. Thus perished the documents which he had collected for the history of his own life, with the composition of which he had intended to occupy himself when he started on this campaign. He then counted upon establishing himself in a threatening position on the banks of the Dvina or Beresina, and during the six tedious months of winter devoting his leisure hours to writing his reminiscences. All these plans and hopes were now scattered to the winds.

A rumour gained currency that Chichagof had occupied Minsk, and that the line of retreat was therefore endangered. The Emperor, however, attached little importance to the report, for he was convinced that he commanded the passage of the Beresina at Borisof. The bridge at Borisof was protected by a strong fortress occupied by a Polish regiment. Napoleon was so confident upon this point that in order to relieve the burdens of the army, he gave orders at Orcha to burn all his pontoons. It must indeed have been a blow to learn after this that Chichagof had taken the town of Borisof, which commanded the passage of the river.

There is an interesting description of the arrival of an officer of the Young Guard who brought this unwelcome news—"On November 26 we were marching along the high-road in the direction of Borisof. The town was not far off. Bonaparte was walking, like the rest of us, with a stick in his hand. He was dressed in a fur-coat and hat, and was walking along the middle of the road a few paces from me, behind the Prince of Neûfchatel (Berthier). On every side reigned a melancholy silence. Suddenly we saw an officer riding to meet us. It was Colonel de F., attached to the staff. He halted in front of the Prince and made a report of something to him—I only heard the words 'Beresina' and 'Russians.' We all stopped. Bonaparte also halted; he was about six paces from the Chief of the Staff and the colonel. I moved a little closer in order to learn what it was all about. I could hear Bonaparte asking angrily, 'What is he talking about? eh? What is he talking about? What is he talking about?'

"The Prince ordered the colonel to repeat his message to Bonaparte. I seem to hear them even now.

"*De F.*—'Monsieur le Maréchal has sent me to inform you that the Russian army of Moldavia has reached the Beresina and occupied all the crossings.'

"*Bonaparte.*—'It's not true, it's not true, it's not true!'

"*De F.*—'That two divisions of the enemy have captured the bridge and occupied the left bank; also that the river is not frozen sufficiently to cross on the ice.'

"*Bonaparte* (angrily).—'You lie, you lie! It's not true.'

"*De F.* (coldly, in a louder tone).—'I was not sent to ascertain the position of the enemy. Monsieur le Maréchal sent me to bring this report, and I am performing my duty.'

"Seeing Napoleon beginning to brandish his stick, I thought he meant to strike the colonel with it; but at that moment he stepped back with his legs spread wide apart. Leaning his left hand on his stick and grinding his teeth together, he cast a furious glance at the heavens and shook his fist! A cry of passionate anger broke from his lips; he repeated his menacing gesture, and added one short expressive word—a word blasphemous enough by itself. I assure you that in all my life I never saw a more fearful expression of face and figure! He was evidently quite forgetful of the care with which he had striven till then to hide his feelings from us, and his endeavours to appear cheerful—though, of course, no one was deceived. We were so attentively engaged in watching his movements, and were so much surprised at the scene, that we only recollected ourselves at last when he gave orders to continue the advance."

"That night," says Ségur, "Napoleon had no sleep. Duroc and Daru, thinking he was asleep, began to talk of the desperate position in which the French were placed, unaware that he could hear all they said. When they uttered the words 'royal prisoner' he could keep silence no longer, but broke in, 'Do you think that they would dare?' Daru, after the first moment of surprise, replied that if the Emperor was obliged to yield at last he must be prepared for the worst; that he must not count on the magnanimity of his adversary, for politics, in the widest sense of the word, knew nothing of the ethics of everyday life, they have their own code."

"'And France?' asked Napoleon. 'What will France say?'

"'Oh! as for Francc—one may fit one's conjectures to one's fancy, for it would be hard to say what the result will really be in France. The best thing,' added Daru, 'both for us and for your Majesty, would be if you could somehow get back into France, through the air, if it may not be along the road; for you would be more likely to save us by being there, than by staying here.'

"'In fact, I am in the way?' asked Napoleon.

"'Yes, your Majesty.'

"'And would not you like to be a royal prisoner?'

"Daru answered in the same jesting strain that 'he would be satisfied to be an ordinary prisoner of war.'

"To this the Emperor made no reply; but after a long pause he asked if all the despatches had been burnt.

"'Your Majesty did not wish that to be done?'

"'Go at once and burn everything—our position, to be frank, is not one to boast of.'"

Marshal St. Cyr received strict orders to drive the Russians over the river. He performed this task; but the problem how the French army was to cross under the enemy's fire without any pontoons still remained unsolved, and troubled the minds of every soldier from the highest to the lowest.

There was no longer any hope that the fugitives would be able to slip through between the Russian armies. Driven on by Kutuzof and Vittgenstein to the Beresina, they must cross the river without delay in spite of the threatening position occupied by Chichagof on the further bank.

On November 23 Napoleon began his preparations for this desperate step. The remains of the cavalry, under the command of Latour-Maubourg, were rapidly dwindling in number, and there were now only 150 left. The Emperor collected all the officers who could still sit in the saddle and formed them into a body of some 500, which he called his "Holy Squadron." Divisional commanders acted in this squadron as captains; Grouchy and Sebastiani were appointed commanders. Napoleon further ordered that all superfluous vehicles should be burnt, and that no officer should have more than one; so that half the vans and wagons in the various corps were destroyed, and the horses distributed among the Horse Guards.

The retreating host soon came up with Marshal Victor's army, which was awaiting Napoleon's arrival.

"Still in good condition, having suffered but little, it welcomed the Emperor with the usual enthusiastic cries, which had long been unheard among the fugitives from Moscow," says Ségur. "These troops knew nothing of the sufferings of the main army, so that they were perfectly astounded when, in the place of the well-appointed columns of the victors of Moscow, they saw Napoleon followed by this rabble of skeletons, clad in tatters, in women's jackets, in fragments of old carpets or filthy remnants of rusty cloaks, burnt into holes, with their legs wrapped in all manner of scraps and rags. The real soldiers gazed in horror on these unfortunate warriors, their sunken cheeks, the earthy colour of their countenances, their straggling beards; defenceless, weaponless, jostling one another like a herd of cattle, their heads hanging down and their eyes cast upon the ground. What astonished them more than anything was the number of generals and colonels, marching by themselves, in solitary dejection, with no soldiers to command. Busied only with themselves, their persons, or their goods, they marched unnoticed and uncared for among the common soldiers—soldiers from whom they no longer looked for obedience, for every tie was broken and every rank levelled by misfortune. Victor's and Oudinot's troops could not believe their eyes. The impression produced by this fearful *débâcle* had an immediate effect upon the discipline of the 2nd and 9th corps—disorder soon showed itself in their ranks; the soldiers threw away their muskets and laid hands on valuable walking-sticks."

The Grande Armée reached the river, and it was decided to make the crossing at Studyanka. The only chance of success lay in deceiving the Russians as to the place in which the passage was to be attempted, for it was evidently impossible to effect a crossing by force. On the 24th, therefore, three hundred soldiers and a few hundred fugitives were sent down the river to Ukholda with orders to prepare materials for the construction of a bridge, and to make as much noise as possible over it. The remains of the Cuirassiers were sent to the same place by a road that was well within sight of the Russians. In addition—and this was the most cunning stroke of all—the Chief of the Staff summoned some Jews of the neighbourhood and questioned them with the greatest show of secrecy as to the fords and roads leading to Minsk. Then, as if delighted with the result of his examination, and allowing them to imagine that in his opinion this was the only way out of his difficulties, he retained some of the rogues as guides and dismissed the rest beyond his outposts. In order to make certain that they would repeat all they knew, the general forced them to take an oath that they would meet the French lower down the Beresina and inform them of the enemy's movements.

While endeavouring in this way to hoodwink Chichagof, they made all necessary preparations for the passage of the river at Studyanka. The presence, however, of a division of the enemy on the far side of the river caused them to doubt seriously whether the Russians would fall into the trap. They expected every minute that the Russian guns would open fire on the workmen engaged in building the bridge. Even if the enemy had delayed until dawn the work would not have been sufficiently far advanced, and the opposite bank, which was low and marshy, was only too well adapted for opposing the passage.

Napoleon was aware of this, and when he left Borisof at ten o'clock in the evening he prepared for the last desperate stroke. He halted with the 6000 Guards which remained to him at Staro-Borisof in a house belonging to Radziwill. He did not go to bed that night, but was continuously on the alert, listening and making inquiries as to the movements of the enemy. In his anxiety he was haunted by the idea that the night was drawing to a close and dawn about to break. His attendants had great difficulty in assuring him that this was not the case. He went out to wait in a little hut on the banks of the river.

"Well, Berthier, how shall we get out of this?" he said to the Chief of the Staff, who was continually with him. In a quiet moment, when Napoleon was sitting in a room of the hut, they saw the tears rise to his eyes and course down his pale cheeks, paler now than ever.

The King of Naples openly expressed his doubts as to the possibility of effecting a crossing, and in the name of the army begged the Emperor to think of his own safety.

"There are brave Poles ready to escort the Emperor; they will take him up along the banks of the Beresina and will get him to Vilna within five days." Napoleon hung his head in sign of refusal, but said nothing.

Hardly had the first piles of the bridge been driven when Marshal Ney and the King of Naples came running out of breath to the Emperor, crying that the enemy had abandoned their position on the other bank. Napoleon, beside himself with delight, and unable to believe his ears, ran to the river—it was indeed true! In an ecstasy of joy, he

cried breathlessly, "Then I have deceived the Admiral!" And the Russians were indeed in the fullest sense of the word deceived. Their officers did not consider the work that had been going on at Studyanka for forty-eight hours as worthy of any attention. The carelessness and incautiousness of the French served to convince Admiral Chichagof that they meant to cross lower down the river, and he accordingly moved the whole of Chapletz's corps, which was stationed opposite the bridge then in course of construction at Studyanka, and which could of course see and hear the work that was proceeding.

Admiral Chichagof was an excellent type of the crafty courtier. He had gained his promotion by the accident of interest and favour; he was proud, bold, and overbearing. Most aptly did Krylof characterize him in the fable of the pike that went mouse-hunting. The Jews sent out by the French, and the demonstration at Ukholda, firmly convinced him that the crossing was to be effected below Studyanka, and in spite of all reports of the progress of the works at that point, he drew off the whole division to the very last man.

Napoleon, however firmly he might believe in his lucky star, could scarcely have counted on such simplicity, and the French are right in saying that the historian will have to solve an interesting problem; how was it that a demoralized and exhausted army, hemmed in on every side by an enemy incomparably superior in numbers, who literally had only to put out their hand to seize their prey, found the way left open before them? The Russians retired—there were no obstacles, and the French army was allowed to retreat in peace along a route that was neither burnt nor devastated. Whatever the cause may have been —whether carelessness, misunderstanding, or indolence—

the retreating army owed thanks to Heaven that among its enemies there was at least one stupendous fool.

Ségur graphically describes his own impressions and Napoleon's feelings at this time. "Every stroke of our sappers' axes which had been ringing in the adjacent woods for a whole day must have been heard by the enemy. We expected that at the first rays of dawn we should see the Russian battalions and guns drawn up before the frail construction which General Ebler had erected, while eight hours' work were still wanting to complete the bridge. No doubt, we thought, the enemy is waiting for daylight in order to train his guns with more effect. Day broke, and our eyes beheld the camp-fires abandoned, the river-bank deserted, and in the distance, on the heights, thirty guns—moving away.

"A single cannon-ball would have sufficed to demolish our only hope of safety. But their artillery was retiring before our very eyes, moving further and further into the distance, while ours was at the same time being brought into position.

"Far away we could see the end of the long Russian column retiring to Borisof—they had but to look round. An infantry regiment of twelve guns remained, but scattered about, and evidently with no intention of interfering with us; while at the edge of the forest we could see a detachment of Cossacks—the rear-guard of Chapletz's division, 6000 strong—withdrawing so as to leave the road open to us.

"The French simply could not believe their eyes. At last, delirious with joy, they began cheering and clapping their hands. Rapp and Oudinot ran in to the Emperor—'Your Majesty, the enemy have struck their tents and abandoned the position!'—'Impossible!' answered the

Emperor; but Ney and Murat in their turn came running up to confirm the news. Napoleon rushed out of his hut, looked, and saw the extreme end of Chapletz's column in full retreat just disappearing into the woods."

By one o'clock the Cossacks had completely abandoned the bank, and the bridge for the passage of the infantry was finished. Legrand's division immediately crossed with its artillery before Napoleon's eyes, to loud cries of "*Vive l'Empereur!*" Napoleon had been hurrying on the work, and he now assisted the passage of the artillery by his encouraging words and example of cheerfulness. When the foremost troops at last reached the further bank, he could not forbear from crying out—"My lucky star, again my star!"

Chichagof to his first mistake added yet another, into which no intelligent sergeant-major would have fallen, and which is really beyond forgiveness. Zemlin lies on the far side of the river in the middle of an extensive marsh, over which passes the Vilna road. The latter is constructed on a causeway of twenty-two wooden bridges, which the Russian general could and ought to have burnt before he retired. Combustible materials had indeed been put under them for this very purpose, but no one took the trouble to set fire to them. If Chichagof had been less self-confident he would at least, in withdrawing to Ukholda, have ensured the impossibility of the passage of the river at Studyanka by ordering the Vilna road to be destroyed. The French army would have been irretrievably lost, and all their labours and sacrifices at the passage of the Beresina would have availed them nothing, for the deep marshes which surround Zemlin would inevitably have stopped them.

The crowding, jostling, confusion, fighting, and killing which took place at the passage of the Beresina, according to the testimony of those who witnessed the scene, defy description. All rushed like madmen for the bridges; no one was master of himself, a universal frenzy possessed the whole army. They hewed a passage with their swords or whatever weapon they possessed, and hurled down every obstacle in their way. The word "Emperor," which a month before had been one to conjure with, had lost its magic. Caulaincourt, the great Master of the Horse, was hustled and jostled, almost knocked from the saddle, before he managed with infinite difficulty to get the Emperor's horses and carriages over.

By the evening the Russian guns (of Witgenstein's army) were in position, and opened fire on the masses of soldiers who covered the banks and the bridges. It is difficult, nay impossible, to paint the scenes of horror, of butchery, which were enacted under the fire of the Russian batteries. The terrified troops were so closely huddled and packed together that every shot told with fearful effect. With the cries of despair which rang out on every side, with the groans of men and the neighing of horses as they fell and were trampled under-foot, mingled the ceaseless shrieking of the cannon-balls, the booming of the guns, the rain of lead upon wagons, carriages and caissons, broken, shattered and dispersed, their flying splinters still further adding to the slaughter. It was a scene of horror beyond the power of words to paint.

At last night put an end to the massacre. Some portion of the 9th Army Corps managed to cross the river, but the greater part was destroyed. The whole of General Portuneau's division laid down its arms; it had lost its way, blundered among the Russians, and been surrounded. Marbot declares, but it seems improbable, that the general was accompanied by a guide from Borisof, who endeavoured to explain with all the expressiveness at his command that the camp in front of them was a Russian camp; but, having no interpreter, they did not understand him. The result was that the French lost from 7000 to 8000 men. There is no proof of Napoleon's grave accusation that, to judge by report, "the commander lost his division because he took an independent line."

By eight o'clock the next morning the bridge destined for the horses and wagons was broken, and the baggage and artillery proceeded to occupy the other bridge. This was the signal for a regular battle, in the truest sense of the word, between the infantry and cavalry. Many fell in this struggle, and still more at the beginning of the bridge, where the path was so blocked with the bodies of men and horses that the troops had literally to pass over heaps of dead.

"The last to cross was Gérard's division, who made their way at the point of the sword, after clambering over the pile of corpses which cumbered the road. They had hardly reached the further shore when the Russians charged down after them; and the French immediately set the bridge on fire, thus sacrificing all that remained on the left bank, in order to prevent the Russians from crossing."

Those who had not succeeded in getting across were mad with terror. Many endeavoured to dash over the burning bridge, and to avoid being roasted alive were forced to leap into the river, where they were drowned.

Thousands of fires lined the heights occupied by the Russians, while in the valley beneath, by the bank of the river, tens of thousands of wretched men were dying or preparing to die, without food or shelter. There was nothing but the sound of their moaning to tell that these hosts of men lay there, still breathing, in the darkness.

"Much has been said," writes Marbot, "of the disasters of the Beresina; but no one has yet said that most of them might have been avoided if the staff had better understood its duties and availed itself of the night of the 27th and 28th for the transport of the baggage and of all those thousands of men who next day blocked the way across the river. That night the bridges were empty; not a soul crossed them, though within a hundred paces one might have seen by the light of the moon a rabble of more than 50,000 men of all sorts, stragglers from their own regiments, who went by the name of 'broilers.' These men sat calmly by their enormous fires cooking their supper of horse-flesh, unconscious that the passage of the river must cost many of them their lives on the following day, while at that very moment they might be crossing at their leisure and could cook their supper in safety on the other side. Their conduct is not to be wondered at, for no officer came from the Emperor, no aide-de-camp from the staff, nor from any one of the marshals, to warn these poor wretches, or, if necessary, to drive them by force to the bridges.

"Had the authorities borrowed a few battalions from Oudinot's corps, or from the Guards, who still maintained discipline, they might easily have forced all these masses to cross the bridge. In vain did I urge, as I passed the Head-quarters Staff and that of Marshal Oudinot, that the bridges were lying idle, and that all these unarmed troops should be made to cross while the enemy remained quiet. I received only evasive replies, and found myself referred from one to another."

The battle of the Beresina may be regarded as having decided the fate of the Grande Armée—the magnificent force that had once caused Europe to tremble.

It has often been said that the destruction of the French

army was due to the cold; but, as we have seen, many other causes were at work. The 2nd and 9th Army Corps kept perfect order, though they had to endure much the same cold as the main army. The chief cause of the *débâcle* was hunger, followed by rapid and ceaseless marches and bivouacs without sleep or rest; and lastly, the cold when it became very intense. We must not, however, forget the steadiness and endurance of the Russian troops. Napoleon and the whole of the French army were astonished by the fact that at "the great battle," though there were hosts of Russians slain there were no prisoners. As for the horses, they sustained the cold very well so long as they were fed; and they too perished chiefly of hunger and fatigue.

Kutuzof, as has been said, was not alone responsible for Napoleon's escape from Russia. The Russian Commander-in-Chief took a thoroughly sound view of the position of the French Emperor; and in this connection his conversations with one of his prisoners, a man occupying a high rank in the administrative branch of the French army, are full of interest. Kutuzof told him that he had thoroughly studied Napoleon's character, and was sure that when once he had crossed the Niemen he would be tempted to extend his conquests indefinitely. "We have given him plenty of space to exhaust and dissipate his army, to give strategy, famine, and frost free play. What blindness is it that has prevented Napoleon alone from recognizing the trap that was so evident to everybody else?"

The Field-Marshal expressed astonishment at the ease with which Napoleon had been induced to stay in Moscow and encouraged in his absurd hopes of concluding an honourable peace, when he was helplessly caught in the toils.

"Napoleon's intelligence," he remarked, "has deteriorated—the whole campaign shows that. It is a pity he did not think of going further than Moscow, we would have given him another 5000 versts to conquer."

He admitted that it would have been hard to imagine anything more dangerous for Russia than Napoleon's original plan of remaining in Smolensk, covering Poland, and renewing the war in the spring. But he was convinced that the plan did not originate with Napoleon himself, for he was too much accustomed to short campaigns to devote two whole years to the conquest of a single empire. "One must know but little of Napoleon," said Kutuzof, "to imagine him capable of the patient execution of an enterprise demanding time, caution, and tedious elaboration of detail."

"When I left the Field-Marshal," says this French officer, "he expressed the conviction that Bonaparte would inevitably be crushed at the passage of the Beresina."

* * * * * * *

Beyond the Beresina, the retreat became more disastrous than ever. It was a headlong flight in which there was no longer any pretence of order. The fugitives behaved, in the most literal sense, like wild beasts. Muravyof, Fenschaw, Chichagof, and many others affirm that they saw the French devouring their dead comrades. They often found them in outhouses seated round a fire on the bodies of the dead, cutting out the best portions to roast and eat. When, on one occasion, a Russian officer expressed his horror and disgust, one of these cannibals replied with perfect equanimity, "Of course this stuff isn't very nice, but at any rate it's better than beastly horse-flesh."

In the hospital at Minsk the French convalescents, for want of tables, played cards on the dead and stiffened bodies of their comrades, and the walls of the room were ornamented with the bodies of the dead dressed in fantastic costumes and with their faces daubed, by way of jest, with coal and brick-dust.

Fuel was so scarce that even the Viceroy Eugène, for instance, had to make shift without a fire. It is said that on one occasion, in order to scrape together a few billets of wood, his attendants had to remind the Bavarians that Prince Eugène was married to their king's daughter, and consequently had a right to command them!

To make matters worse, on the far side of the Beresina, and during the first stages of the retreat, the arrival of the fugitives came as a complete surprise to the towns and halting-places along the road. At Vilna, for instance, there was a supply of flour for 100,000 men for forty days, exclusive of the corn in the granaries; there was meat for 100,000 men for thirty-six days, unkilled; beer and brandy in still larger proportions; 30,000 pairs of boots; 27,000 rifles, and an immense quantity of clothing, ammunition, saddlery, harness, and equipments of every kind. The officials, however, having received no instructions, did not dare to make an immediate distribution of these stores. They waited so long that the greater part of the supplies fell into the hands of the Russians, who followed close upon the heels of the French.

Vilna was, like Smolensk, a sort of Promised Land in the eyes of the soldiers. Here, they thought, they would be able to eat their fill at last and enjoy at least some rest from their flight. But they were disappointed in their hopes, and forced to continue their flight without a pause. The town was nothing but a plague-stricken cesspool. Thousands of corpses lay unburied, simply flung out of the houses into the yards, where the invalids also lay, forming a confused mass of sick and dead.

Most of the houses in the town were turned into hospitals, crammed full of sick and wounded. As soon as the French left Vilna the house-owners, who were Jews, stripped the sick of all their money and clothes and turned them, stark naked, into the streets. The Russian authorities, including the Emperor Alexander himself, were obliged to take stern and vigorous measures for housing the wounded and relieving their sufferings.

A few miles beyond Vilna is a steep hill, which was at that time covered with ice. It gave the French baggage as much trouble as the Beresina. In vain did the horses put forth every effort to surmount it—the French saved hardly a gun or private carriage. At the foot of the hill they were forced to abandon the whole of the artillery of the Guard, the Emperor's baggage, and the army treasure-chest.

As the troops went by they smashed open the carriages and took the most valuable of their contents—clothes, furs, and money. Many poor wretches dying of hunger were to be seen covered with gold; articles of luxury of all kinds were strewn upon the snow. The plundering was only stopped by the appearance of the Cossacks, who swooped down and seized all the booty that remained. One of the officers gives us an account of the retreat from Vilna and of this last disaster—which, if we may trust eye-witnesses of the scene, might have been avoided, inasmuch as there was an easy road round the hill. "We passed out in silence, leaving the streets covered from end to end with soldiers, some asleep, some dead. The court-yards, the galleries, and the steps of the buildings were covered with them, but none were willing to rise and follow us, nor even to stir at the summons of their officers.

"We arrived at the foot of a hill, the ascent of which was rendered quite impracticable by reason of its steepness and the ice with which it was covered. All around lay Napoleon's carriages and baggage, which were abandoned at Vilna, together with the army treasure-chest.

"It was decided to entrust the salvage of the Imperial treasure to the escort. As there was about five million francs, principally in silver écus, they had to distribute them at random among the soldiers. Many, seeing that they could not possibly keep up with us, made free with what had been entrusted to them. The flags which had been taken from the enemy, and which had no further interest for the troops, were shamefully thrown away at the bottom of the hill, as well as the famous cross of Ivan the Great—a trophy which we had set our hearts upon carrying away! The Russians, who are generally regarded as barbarians, subsequently afforded a most noble example of moderation such as is rarely displayed after victory.

"New-comers kept increasing the number of the plunderers, and it was indeed an edifying spectacle to see these men dying of hunger, and at the same time loaded with such quantities of treasure that they could move only with difficulty. On every side lay open trunks and broken chests. Gorgeous gold-embroidered court dresses and rich furs were donned by persons of the most repulsive exterior. Sixty francs were offered for a Napoleon d'or, and ten crowns was the price of a glass of brandy. One of the Grenadiers in my presence offered a cask of silver coin for sale; it was finally bought by one of the principal officers, who took it away in his sledge.

"All the soldiers, turned second-hand dealers, were selling their plunder to those who had looted the treasure-chests. Their conversation turned exclusively on bullion and jewellery; every one had plenty of silver, and no one a rifle. Is it surprising that the mere appearance of the Cossacks was enough to inspire the fugitives with terror? Nor were they long in coming upon the scene." An eye-witness tells us that on this occasion the lust for gold abolished all distinction between the bold and the timorous, between friend and foe, and that the Cossacks set to plundering side by side with the French!

At this point the most terrible frosts overtook the fugitives. Even the discipline of the Guards was destroyed; and when the drum summoned them to march, this brave army of tried veterans, the last hope of the army, refused to leave the camp-fires and fall in. Reproaches, entreaties, and menaces sufficed to persuade some; others did not stir—they were frost-bitten, for even the fires were not enough to save them from the cold.

Even for so high an officer as Murat the Grenadiers refused to fetch firewood or snow for water, lest, as they expressed it, they should be "nipped on the way."

On one occasion the whole of the 4th Army Corps refused to move, and it was only by the most vigorous persuasion that the Duke of Neufchâtel induced them to stir out of the room,—for one roomful constituted the whole of this corps of the Grande Armée!

As for the rear-guard, it was no longer in existence. The result of the campaign was the complete annihilation of an army of nearly half a million men. The whole of the artillery, consisting of 1200 guns and caissons, fell into the hands of the enemy, together with many thousands of wagons and officers' carriages, and an enormous quantity of warlike stores and provisions. According to official accounts, 253,000 bodies were burnt in the provinces of Moscow, Vitebsk, and Mohilef, and 53,000 in Vilna and its immediate neighbourhood. More than 100,000 men were taken prisoners. Within historical memory, from the time of Cambyses to the present day, there is no parallel to such a disaster affecting so great a host.

To return once more to Napoleon—it should be said that after the passage of the Beresina he had but one thought—how best to return to France, collect a fresh army, and if he could not induce his allies to keep faith with him, at any rate prevent them from immediately joining forces against him. His intention of leaving the army and proceeding direct to Paris was kept a profound secret, although some of those nearest to him knew, and for the most part approved, the plan. They saw, in fact, no hope of rescue except in the organization of a new army of half a million men.

For some time previous to the Emperor's departure from the army he, too, suffered extreme discomfort and even privation. The soldiers occupied filthy, foul-smelling huts close to his head-quarters, and it was necessary to use force to repel them. The bread baked for Napoleon at this time consisted of black rye loaves; the meal was badly ground, the dough had hardly risen, in addition to which it had a disagreeable musty smell.

In the little town of Zanifka the head-quarters were established in a small, two-roomed hut. The back room was occupied by Napoleon, the front apartment by his suite, who disposed themselves for sleep packed side by side so closely that the Emperor's valet could not avoid treading on their legs and arms. At Smorgoni the Emperor was stationed at head-quarters for the last time.

He there made his final arrangements, and wrote his last bulletin, No. XXIX., filled, as usual, with half-truths and glaring falsehoods. In this bulletin he attributed his disasters to fortuitous circumstances, explaining that they might soon be repaired by vigorous action.

"More than 30,000 horses," he says, "fell within a few days. Our cavalry had no mounts, our artillery and transport had no beasts of draught. We had to abandon or destroy a large number of our guns with their appurtenances. The enemy, coming upon these traces of the French army, were encouraged to surround our columns with Cossacks, who cut off all straggling baggage and wagons like Arabs in the desert. This wretched (*méprisable*) cavalry, whose strength lies in noise alone, and which could not seriously attack a company of riflemen, was rendered formidable by circumstances. However, we caused the enemy to regret every serious attempt they made against us." . . . "Horses and necessaries of every sort," he continues, "are beginning to pour in. General Boursier has more than 20,000 horses in various depôts. The artillery has already repaired all its losses."

Every precaution was taken to prevent any knowledge of Napoleon's intention of leaving the army from leaking out until the last moment. But the presentiment of the coming disaster was in the minds of every member of his suite—every one wished to accompany him and escape from this living hell as quickly as possible.

"In the evening the chief officers of the army were summoned together," says Ségur. "The marshals appeared. As they entered Napoleon took each of them aside and revealed his project, sparing neither arguments nor expressions of confidence and affection.

"When he caught sight of Davout he went to meet

At a Council of War

him, and asked whether he was vexed with him. Why did he not see more of him? To the Marshal's reply that he seemed to have fallen under his displeasure, Napoleon, accepting all his explanations, expounded in detail his intention of departing, and indicated the direction of his route. He was genial and affectionate to all. At table he praised all for their admirable conduct in the course of the campaign. 'As for himself,' he said, 'it would have been easier, no doubt, to avoid mistakes, had I been a Bourbon.'

"When dinner was over Napoleon told Prince Eugène to read out Despatch XXIX., and explained publicly what he had before spoken of in confidence. That night he would leave with Duroc, Caulaincourt, and Lobau for Paris, where his presence was essential both for France and for the remains of the army. Only from Paris could he keep his thumb on the Austrians and Prussians, who would no doubt hesitate to declare war against him if they saw that he was once more at the head of the French nation, and an army of a million soldiers!

"He stated that he was handing over the chief command to the King of Naples. 'I hope,' he added, 'that you will obey him as myself, and that there will be no differences among you.'"

Nobody, of course, raised any opposition. Marshal Berthier, without endeavouring to dissuade Napoleon, merely announced that he must be included in the number of those who were going. This request drew upon him a very severe rebuke. Napoleon loaded him with reproaches for preferring such a claim; reminded him of all the kindnesses and benefits he had received at his hands, and finally called upon him to change his mind and submit, or return at once to his estate in France and await the announcement of his punishment for rebelling against the will of the Emperor.

At ten o'clock that evening he shook hands with them, kissed them all in turn, and issued at the front door between two lines formed by the officers of his suite, smiling pitiful forced smiles to the right and left.

Napoleon and Caulaincourt got into a covered sledge, on the box of which sat Roustan, the Mameluke, and a Polish officer, who was to be his driver. Duroc and Lobau followed in open sledges.

As soon as the news of the Emperor's departure spread through the army, the last traces of discipline disappeared. Groups of armed soldiers had till now been gathered round the colours; but even they dispersed at last, hiding the eagles in their valises. Napoleon alone was able to maintain any semblance of order; with his disappearance, Murat and the other officers lost all authority.

"An hour after the Emperor's departure," says an eye-witness, "one of the senior officers turned to another with the words, 'Well, has the ruffian gone?'

"'Yes,' replied the other; 'he has played us the same trick as in Egypt.'"

Napoleon, after barely escaping capture at the hands of the free-lance Seslavin's Cossacks, and that only by the most remarkable good fortune, arrived at Warsaw. When he had somewhat recovered from the fatigues of his journey, he gave the following explanation of the disastrous issue of the campaign—"When I left Paris it was my intention," he said, "to carry the war no further than the former confines of Poland. Circumstances drew me on. Perhaps I was guilty of an error in going so far as Moscow, perhaps I was wrong in staying there so long as I did; but from the sublime to the ridiculous is but a step, and posterity shall be my judge! My French soldiers," he added, "are worthless in the frost, the cold turns them into mere dummies.

"During the retreat I had no cavalry, and I must admit that when the Cossacks attacked my column I found myself in a dilemma. It was impossible to mass the army together, for that would have retarded the retreat; it was equally impossible to deploy it, for the Cossacks would have broken through our line. We were obliged to continue our retreat, to fill up the gaps, and deceive the enemy. I confess that I needed all my skill and experience to escape."

He did indeed escape, but with this campaign began the decline of his power.

II

THE BURNING OF MOSCOW

Vassily Blajenni Cathedral.

THE restoration of the kingdom of Poland and the abolition of serfdom were among the pretexts put forward by Napoleon for his invasion of Russia. The proposed liberation of the serfs was presumably intended merely to embarrass his adversary, for Napoleon can scarcely be credited with any sentimental weakness in favour of liberty for its own sake. He expected to find in Russia a people ready to throw off its fetters, and to some extent at least his estimate of the social and political situation was correct. The masses were ardently longing for freedom, and the idea of enfranchisement was in the air; but Napoleon failed to recognize that the means which he employed, instead of encouraging the people to revolt against their masters, were calculated merely to turn them into irreconcilable enemies of the invader. There were, it is true, some disturbances and seditious plots at the beginning of the campaign, but they were comparatively insignificant; the excesses of the French, and especially of their allies—Germans, Poles, Italians, and others—soon provoked a wide-spread revulsion of public opinion. The announcement that the provinces occupied by the Grande Armée would be retained by France, and that the nobility and officials would, under no circumstances, be allowed to return, encouraged the peasantry in some districts to assist in provisioning the invading army. In many instances, however, they broke out into open revolt against their masters, and refused to assist their escape by supplying them with horses. "Why," they asked, "should we lend horses to remove our masters' goods, when Bonaparte is coming to set us free?"

Of the gentry, some, like Engelgard, behaved as true patriots, remaining on their estates, harassing the French to the utmost of their power, and frequently meeting death in the service of their country. On the other hand, we find Prince Bagration tearing the Cross of Honour from the neck of a certain dignitary, and branding him as a traitor unworthy to serve his sovereign. Again, in the captured barouche of the French General Montbrun a note was found, among other papers, giving information as to the plan of a proposed Russian attack. This note was, in all probability, delivered to the general by an officer attached to the Russian head-quarters.

The behaviour of the clergy was, in some cases, extraordinary. The Bishop of Mogileff and the ecclesiastical dignitaries of Vitebsk in so far admitted that the conquered provinces no longer belonged to Russia as to swear allegiance to Napoleon, and issue an order to the priests directing them to take the same oath, and, in the public prayers in their churches, to substitute the name of Napoleon for that of Alexander.[1] Following the example of the Bishop,

[1] "I, the undersigned, swear by Almighty God to be faithful to the Government appointed by his Imperial Majesty the French Emperor

the priest Dobrovolsky, and many others, in Holy Mass or the *Te Deums*, omitted to mention any member of the Russian Imperial Family, while praying for the health of Napoleon, Emperor of the French and King of Italy.

After the departure of the French many proceedings were instituted in respect of seditious acts among the ecclesiastical and civil authorities. Archbishop Theofilakt, who was sent to restore ecclesiastical order in the provinces, wrote to the Minister:—"In the civil departments it is necessary to shut one's eyes, for the civil governor, Count Tolstoi, knowing full well who the traitors are, is nevertheless obliged to retain them in the service."

It is interesting to learn that Marshal Davout entered into a doctrinal discussion with the Archbishop of Mogileff. He urged upon the Archbishop that, having accepted the *fait accompli*, he was bound to mention the name of Napoleon in public prayer, quoting the words of the Gospel—"Render unto Cæsar the things that are Cæsar's."—"That is exactly what I am doing," answered the Archbishop, "mentioning the name of my own sovereign."—"By no means," replied Davout. "By Cæsar we must understand the stronger, and, at the present moment, the stronger is certainly not your Emperor Alexander."

"There is no denying the fact that there was discontent among the people," says A. F. de B., an officer in the Russian service, "and the further the enemy advanced, the more this discontent spread. The attitude of the people was extremely doubtful, but it was Napoleon himself, or rather his troops, who contributed most to destroy the confidence of the peasantry in the sincerity of his promises.

---

and the King of Italy, Napoleon, to fulfil all his orders, and to ensure that these orders be fulfilled by others."

Rumours soon began to spread that the enemy were plundering all along the line of march; that they were turning the churches into stables, trampling the holy images under-foot or chopping them up for firewood; that they were ill-treating the inhabitants, women, girls, and even young children, suffering at their hands. Small wonder that the peasants betook themselves to the woods, taking with them everything they could carry, and burning whatever they were unable to remove."

The atrocities committed by the French in other countries are sufficiently notorious, but they were surpassed in this campaign. Many Frenchmen, eye-witnesses of what they relate, give harrowing details of the wanton destruction and rapine that marked the advance of the invading army. Labaume gives some instances of barbarous violation of private property. "We entered," he says, "into a large domain, called Vedenskoye, a charming estate with a mansion beautifully appointed within and without. In a few minutes everything was broken or torn in pieces." "On another occasion," he says, "we stopped at a large house with a beautiful garden. Apparently the place had been but recently furnished, but it was now dismantled in a most painful manner. Broken furniture was scattered about the passages; fragments of china and expensive pictures, torn out of their frames, were scattered to the winds."

Bourgeois tells us that "the inhabitants, driven by fire out of their homes, took shelter wherever they could. Sometimes they sought refuge among the inhuman soldiery, who plundered them to the last extremity. . . . The women were seized and exposed to every kind of insult. . . . Even the dead were disinterred, in the search for hidden treasure. It is not surprising, therefore, that the Russians themselves set fire to their homes, and that the French met with nothing but villages in ashes, and wells filled with carrion."

We know how nobly the populace of Moscow responded to the appeal of their Emperor. The gentry provided numerous volunteers, and the merchants large sums of money. Some of the volunteers, it is true, arrived too late, and the money was not all collected until 1819, and, even then, under considerable pressure. But the spirit that animated the people was none the less heroic. The inhabitants of Moscow resolutely refused to entertain the idea of making any concessions to the invader, and, with a few insignificant exceptions, were true to their duty as patriots.

How was it, then, that the French army found Moscow filled with provisions, wealth, and merchandise of all descriptions? The explanation is simple. When Napoleon won the battle of Borodino, Kutuzof saw clearly that he could do nothing more at the moment, and that he could not venture to fight another battle under the walls of Moscow. Nevertheless, he led the Governor-General of the city, Count Rostopchin, to believe that he was preparing to assist him with his army, and the latter, trusting in this, and unwilling to alarm the inhabitants, made few preparations for retreat, sending away only the most precious objects and the treasures of the Tsars. He did not even touch the arsenal. At the last moment, when the entry of the enemy was inevitable, and Rostopchin recognized that the Russian general was concealing his real plans, he tried to hide what was left; but horses were scarce, and the whole city, abandoned by its inhabitants, remained with the greater part of its wealth at the discretion of the enemy.

The dissensions between the two commanders, at first restrained, soon developed into an open rupture. While Rostopchin made an exhibition of his patriotism, Kutuzof was compelled to remain silent; but he suffered keenly nevertheless, for, although he decided to sacrifice the sacred city, it was only because he saw the impossibility of defending it.

In spite of the field-day opinions of such generals as Beningsen, Ermolov, and others, the "old fox" Kutuzof thought, with Barclay, that Moscow should be sacrificed like any other city if the safety of the Empire demanded such a step. He authorized Miloradovitch to make some show of resistance merely with the object of satisfying the inhabitants, but he resolutely kept Rostopchin, the old courtier of Paul I., at arm's length from his councils. The latter did not hesitate to call Kutuzof "an old one-eyed Baba" (peasant woman), and wrote to him—"It rests with you to decide whether I shall act with you before Moscow, or without you in Moscow."

The "Baba," who had no great opinion of the armed mob which Rostopchin offered to place at his disposal, replied only with a demand for provisions, and did not even invite the commandant of Moscow to attend the Council of War at which the retreat of the Russian armies was decided upon.

"When the masters are fighting," says a proverb of Southern Russia, "the peasant's head is aching." The truth of this adage was now bitterly felt by the inhabitants of Moscow. It was owing to the quarrels of their leaders that they were surprised by the French.

Rostopchin had just sufficient time, putting a good face on the trick played upon him by Kutuzof, to open the gates of the arsenal to the public, empty the numerous barrels of vodka into the street, and, most difficult of all, to escape with his wife and family.

The populace which he had armed, and who were excited by his "placards," which have become legendary, opposed his departure. They gathered in front of the governor's palace, and demanded to be led against Napoleon. To save himself, Rostopchin hit upon the idea of throwing a victim to the mob, as to a pack of famished wolves. He promptly found a scapegoat in the person of Verestchagin, the son of a merchant. The victim was accused of having translated an article relating to Napoleon, and Rostopchin handed him over to the mob as "the wretch through whom Moscow and Russia would perish." As no hand was raised to execute justice on this so-called traitor—a pale, delicate young man—the Governor-General ordered a dragoon to cut him down. At the sight of blood the passions of the mob broke loose. Verestchagin was fastened to the tail of a horse and dragged through the streets, while the Governor-General escaped by the back door and fled the city. The body of the victim, after being dragged through the market-place, was dropped in front of a small church, and was buried at the very spot on which it fell. Some time later, when the Sophiyaka Street was opened, the body was found intact, and was believed by many to be that of a holy martyr.

Although the Emperor Alexander had, since the battle of Austerlitz, been prejudiced against Kutuzof (a feeling, by the way, by no means justified, inasmuch as that general had only carried out the plan drawn up by the head of the Austrian chief staff, Weinrotter, and approved by both Emperors) he placed him at the moment of danger in command of his armies. This appointment was demanded by public opinion.

Armed Peasant.

On taking over the command, Kutuzof did his best to reanimate the courage of his troops, upon whom the constant retreat before the invader had necessarily had a depressing effect.

In some quarters, however, he was by no means trusted. The gallant but irascible Bagration asserted that he regarded Kutuzof as "a scoundrel ready to sell his country." As a matter of fact, Kutuzof had but one idea—to deceive Napoleon, and, by avoiding a pitched battle, cause him to stay as long as possible in Moscow. If he could be tempted to remain in the city until the winter time, Kutuzof hoped to be able to block up the road to the southern provinces, throwing Napoleon back on to the route which he had already traversed—a devastated line of march.

The plan succeeded, and if Kutuzof subsequently failed to pursue Napoleon, it was because, as a Russian and a patriot, he thought it sufficient to drive the invader from the country, and did not care to be mixed up in the affairs of Europe. This is evident from the reports of the English military *attaché*, Wilson, which are nothing more than a long and violent diatribe against the "traitor" Kutuzof.

After the retreat had been decided upon by the Council at Filli, the Russian troops began to move through the town towards the Kiazan road. Glinka saw Kutuzof sitting in a *droshky* near the town-gate lost in deep thought. Colonel Toll approached him and reported that the French had already entered Moscow. "Thanks be to God," answered Kutuzof, "this is their last triumph." The regiments moved slowly past the general, who was sitting motionless, his right elbow resting on his knee, apparently seeing and hearing nothing. The troops were in great disorder; luggage-carts were colliding; various detachments were seeking their respective regiments; private soldiers were seizing the opportunity to plunder. The people surrounded the transport train containing the wounded, and kind-hearted women threw money into the carts, forgetful that the copper coins might seriously hurt the sufferers.

If at this time Napoleon had sent a few regiments of cavalry against the retreating Russians he could easily have destroyed the rear-guard. But at this time he had other matters to think about. He was standing behind the Dorogomilovsky gate waiting for a deputation from Moscow. He had summoned this *canaille* of a Rostopchin to appear before him, together with the commandant, the chief of police, and the mayor, but no one came.

Kutuzof, having enticed him into Moscow, turned aside, and, without leaving any trace behind, succeeded in completely hoodwinking his enemy. While Napoleon was announcing to Europe that the Russians were fleeing in disorder along the Kazan road, Kutuzof suddenly turned off this road on to the Kaluga road, and placed himself in position to protect the fertile provinces that had not yet been touched by the invaders. Whose idea this was is not known, but it was a very happy one, full of results advantageous to the Russians and ruinous to the French.

Meantime complete confusion reigned in Moscow. Of the well-to-do only those remained in the city who, relying upon Rostopchin's proclamations, had not removed their wealth. In addition to these and others who remained perhaps to fish in troubled waters, there was the vast army of beggars and criminals. The Postmaster-General, Kluchareff, suspected of being a freethinker, was banished; young Verestchagin, as we have seen, was murdered, and an ex-student, Uroosoff, who tried to show that Napoleon's invasion was a good thing, was first imprisoned and then banished.

When the order directing the broaching of wine and spirit casks was issued, the people fell to work at once, and soon became intoxicated. Wine and spirits literally flowed in the streets, and the mob, lying on the pavement yelling and fighting, lapped up the liquor from the gutters.

"My father was an obstinate man," says the wife of a citizen.

"'I will not leave the city,' he said, 'no, on no account; there is no reason to be afraid of the French.'

"Arms were distributed in the Kremlin, and he received a gun, but it was without a hammer.

"'Never mind,' he said, 'although it is out of order, it may prove handy to frighten a Frenchman with. . .'

"When we reached the stone bridge there was a crowd of about a hundred men, and a regiment of the enemy was marching across. Father took it into his head to threaten them with his gun, but one of the soldiers snatched it out of his hands, and with the butt-end hit my father a blow on the back of his head that caused blood to flow."

"I was sitting at a window knitting a stocking," says the wife of a priest, "when suddenly the deacon's wife came running up. 'Mother,' said she, 'they say that "Bonaparte has passed through the gates of Dorogomilovsk and Kaluga."' I dropped the stocking and called aloud — 'Dmitry Vlasich, do you hear?' My husband was sitting in another room writing. 'What is the matter?' he asked. 'The matter is that the deacon's wife tells me that Bonaparte has come,' I answered. He laughed. 'What a foolish woman you are to believe the deacon's wife rather than the Governor-General. There is the Count's proclamation, have I not read it to you? You had better go and order the tea.'

"Later," says the same authority, "we sent the cook to the bazaar to do her marketing, and she took with her my cousin, Sidor Karpowitch. The latter was carrying a pot and a good wooden spoon. 'I have a great mind,' he said, 'to lay in my stock of honey, as I know there are several casks of it.' They found the bazaar empty, but from time to time a Russian, or one of the enemy, passed by. The cook went for her sugar and tea, and he for his honey. 'When you are ready,' he said, 'wait for me, I shall soon find what I want.' She put tea and sugar into her napkin and waited for her companion, but for some time no one appeared. So she took refuge in a shop and said her prayers. Suddenly she heard Sidor call, 'Anicioushka, my pigeon, where are you?' She stept outside and stood spell-bound with fear; all the shops were empty, but coming towards her was a man—no, not a man—a monster. She could not make out what it was. When, however, it came closer, and she discovered what it was, she thought she must have died with laughter. There stood Sidor dripping with honey from head to foot. On his head one might have thought he wore a hood; of the face there was not a trace.

"The victim explained that when he began to fill his pot with honey, three men came up and said, 'Give up your pot!' He refused. 'Why,' he said, 'did you come empty-handed?' 'Give up the pot!' they repeated. Sidor Karpowitch clutched his pot tightly, and made off, but he was soon overtaken. His pursuers snatched the pot out of his hands, and threw him into the cask, head downwards. 'I saw nothing; I was stifled; I began to wriggle and managed to raise my head. But then my feet sank in; my nose, eyes, mouth, were all covered with honey. I do not know how long my martyrdom lasted, but at last I felt that I was growing giddy. Then I summoned up all my courage, caught hold of the edge of the cask, and pulled myself out!' Later, many years later," adds the Matouschka, "we could never think of this incident without laughing. The wife of the sexton, who is fond of her joke, says, whenever she sees my cousin, 'Will you not take some honey, Sidor Karpowitch, you are so very fond of it, are you not?'"

Long processions of the citizens of Moscow, carrying the sacred *ikons* and the vessels of the Mass, left by all the gates of the city, lamenting and singing plaintive songs.

A legend states that on that terrible day a sword of fire was seen in the heavens at Moscow—a miracle that helped to complete the terror of the few thousands who remained behind, out of a population of nearly a third of a million.

Meantime the French were occupying Moscow, spreading, as Kutuzof said, like a sponge in water. Some of them only passed through the streets and bivouacked in the suburbs and adjoining villages; others, belonging to the Guard, took up their quarters in the Kremlin itself.

Labaume writes—"We were greatly impressed by our first view of Moscow, and our vanguard saluted the town with transports of enthusiasm, crying, 'Moscow! Moscow!' All ran to the hills and vied with each other in discovering and pointing out the beauties of the sight. Houses painted in various colours, domes covered with iron, silver, and gold; the balconies and terraces of the palaces, the monuments, and especially the belfries, combined to realize one of those beautiful cities of Asia which we had hitherto supposed to exist only in the imagination of the Arabian poets."

Miloradovitch, who commanded the Russian rear-guard, warned Murat against pressing forward too hastily, threatening that if the Russian troops were not allowed to retire in peace, he would set fire to the city. The King of Naples, with the consent of Napoleon, agreed not to harass the Russian retreat, and the French troops marching in mingled with the rear-guard of the Russians marching out. This gave Murat an opportunity of making a display of the splendour of his attire before the "barbarians."

The longer the French troops remained in the vast city the more they were amazed at the death-like quiet and desolation that reigned on all sides. The strange stillness caused them involuntarily to keep silence, nervously listening to the rumbling clatter of the horses' hoofs on the pavements. Even the bravest were depressed, owing to the length of the streets. It was sometimes impossible to distinguish the uniforms of troops marching at some distance from one another along the same thoroughfare, and in some instances detachments fled in panic from their own comrades.

The soldier Bourgogne naïvely expresses his astonishment at the aspect of the deserted city. "We were greatly surprised at seeing no one in the streets, not a single young woman listening to our regimental band playing 'Ours is the Victory!' We could not account for this complete desolation; such a glorious city, but now so mute, so gloomy, and so empty! Nothing was to be heard but the sound of our own footsteps, drums, and music. Nor, of course, were we ourselves in very talkative humour. We kept looking at one another, wondering whether the inhabitants, not daring to show themselves in the streets, were spying at us through the chinks of the shutters. It was impossible to imagine that such magnificent palaces and such beautiful buildings were abandoned by their owners. . . . An hour after our entry into the city the fires began. We, of course, thought that some of our own people, in plundering, had set fire to the buildings through carelessness. . . . We could not believe that the inhabitants were so barbarous as to burn their own property, and destroy one of the finest cities of the world."

Labaume writes—"In all these richly-furnished houses and palaces we found only children, old men, and Russian officers who had been wounded in previous battles. In the churches all the altars were decorated as on holy-days; and, judging from the number of candles and burning lamps before the holy images, it was evident that just before leaving the city the pious Muscovites had been at prayer. These striking testimonies of the citizens' piety and love of religion raised this conquered people in our estimation, and made us feel ashamed of the injustice we had done them. Sometimes, in an involuntary feeling of fear, we found ourselves listening eagerly, and our imagination, nervously strained in this huge conquered city, caused us to fear ambuscades on every side, and to imagine that we heard the clash and sound of arms or the cries of combatants.

"A humble officer found himself sole occupant of a beautifully-furnished suite of apartments, for no one was present but the porter who, with trembling hands, presented him with the keys of the place."

Madame Fusil, an actress at the French theatre at Moscow, tells us—"I left my lodgings on August 25 (September 6). Passing through the city, I was strongly impressed by the melancholy of the scene. The streets were empty, but now and then I met a passer-by, one of the common people. Suddenly I heard in the distance the sounds of mournful singing, and, coming nearer, I saw a large crowd of men, women, and children carrying holy images and following the priests, who were singing sacred hymns. It was impossible to witness such a sight without tears—the people leaving the city and carrying away with them the treasures of their faith. Suddenly I was called away. 'Come and look on this wonderful phenomenon in the sky, it is like a fiery sword. Surely some great calamity must be about to happen!' And I really saw something quite out of the common, a sign indeed. . . ."

The strength of the French army that entered Moscow may be estimated at about 110,000 men. With the exception of the Guard, the French left the city the next day and encamped in the suburbs; the Spaniards, Portuguese, Swiss, Bavarians, Wurtembergers, and Saxons remaining in the city. The presence in Moscow of the "alien element" probably accounts for the extraordinary cruelties perpetrated in the city. Numerous Russian stragglers roamed about the streets. Fezensac says that he alone stopped about fifty, and sent them to head-quarters. "The general to whom I reported this, expressed his regret that I had not shot them all, and instructed me to dispose of them in this way in future."

Meantime the fires, far from subsiding, began to spread with ever-increasing fury.

"It was horrible," relates the daughter of a merchant. "The Russians themselves were burning Moscow."—"We were struck with terror at seeing fires all round us," says another witness.—"Moscow," says yet another, "was burned to drive out Bonaparte. I do not know how it happened, but one thing is certain, that our house was set on fire."

A drunken man, dressed in a peasant's smock, was seen leaving the house of Prince Kourakin, the steward and four footmen driving him out with blows. He uttered a shout of triumph, exclaiming, "How well it burns!" Kourakin's servants declared that he was an incendiary, and that they were about to give him up to the French. He was at once shot.

It is impossible to attribute the burning of Moscow to a concerted plan. It was due in great measure to the fact that a large proportion of the houses were built of wood, and to the determination of the Russians not to allow their property to fall into the hands of the enemy. At first the responsibility was thrown on Rostopchin, who assured Bagration that if the worst came to the worst he was resolved to reduce the city to ashes. The fact that the Governor caused all fire-extinguishing appliances to be removed may suggest the theory that the destruction of the city was due to the action of the Governor-General. But subsequent inquiries demonstrated that the conflagration was, in the main, accidental, and Rostopchin himself confirms this idea. "It is a trait in the Russian character," he says in his *Explanation*, "to destroy rather than to suffer anything to fall into the hands of the enemy. Let everything perish!" After Napoleon and his army occupied the city, several generals and officers visited the principal carriage-manufactories. Each selected a carriage and wrote his name upon it. The merchants, of one accord, set fire to their shops that they might not become "purveyors" to the enemy.

On the other hand, the French officers seem to have suspected their own men, and this suspicion was a source of no little vexation. Ségur states that a number of officers took refuge in the halls of the Palace. Other generals, among them Mortier, who had been fighting the flames for thirty-six hours, arrived in a state of exhaustion. Some were taciturn. Others charged their companions with responsibility for the outbreak. All believed that drunkenness and want of discipline among the soldiers had helped to spread the conflagration. They looked at each other with dismay. What would Europe say? They spoke with downcast eyes, as if awestruck by so terrible a catastrophe, which tarnished their glory, destroyed the fruits of their victory, and endangered their lives. Would not Providence—the whole civilized world—punish such criminals?

These sad thoughts were at last mitigated by the news that the Russians themselves were setting fire to the city. It was impossible to doubt it. Officers who came in from all sides agreed on this point. A hurricane had sprung up, and the fire was raging with unheard-of fury. In less than an hour it had engulfed ten different parts of the city, and an enormous district on the far side of the river was transformed into a sea of flame, spreading terror and destruction far and wide. A cupola of fire hung over the whole city, the air was alive with sparks and burning embers.

"At night-time," says Labaume, "the city was set on fire in various places, and the conflagration soon reached the finest portions. In a moment, the palaces which we had admired for their architecture and the taste of their fittings were wrapped in a sheet of flame. Their superb pediments, adorned with statues and bas-reliefs, fell with a crash on the ruins of the columns. The churches, although covered with sheet-iron and lead, also fell in, and with them the gorgeous domes of gold and silver, which we had seen the day before glittering in the sun. The hospitals, containing over 20,000 wounded, were not long in catching fire, and the scene which then presented itself was revolting and horrible to the last degree. Nearly all the inmates perished. A few of the survivors might be seen dragging

In a Russian Church.

themselves half burnt through the smoking ruins; others lay groaning under piles of corpses, convulsively endeavouring to lift the ghastly weight above them in their efforts to escape."

What must have been at this time the thoughts of Napoleon, who was in Peter's Palace? Probably, like other witnesses of this awful night, he did not close his eyes, for about six in the morning one of his aides-de-camp was despatched to the next camp to command the attendance of Madame O——, who had taken refuge there. The two were met at the Palace gate by Marshal Mortier, who showed the visitor into the large hall. Napoleon was waiting for her in the recess of a window.

"I was told that you were very unhappy, Madame; is it so?" asked Napoleon, and for a full hour he plied her with questions on various matters.

Great must have been the difficulties of the conqueror if he had to seek counsel from this lady in matters of politics and administration. Among other things, Napoleon asked what she thought about the liberation of the serfs. "I think, your Imperial Majesty," she answered, "that they would scarcely understand what you mean by it."

This lady was not alone in having the honour of advising the Emperor. Several others ventured to give their advice. Napoleon, indeed, invited their opinions, for advice costs nothing.

"How shall I describe the scenes that took place in the city?" says an eye-witness. "Soldiers, sutlers, convicts let loose from prison, and prostitutes, were roaming the streets, breaking into deserted houses and seizing all that attracted their cupidity. Some clothed themselves in silken dresses embroidered with gold, others piled upon their shoulders as many furs as they could carry. Soldiers, and the rabble in general, attired themselves in court dresses. Crowds broke open the doors of the cellars, drank to intoxication, and reeled about the streets laden with plunder. It was not only deserted buildings that were pillaged in this way. The soldiers forcibly entered inhabited houses, and abused every woman they met. When the generals received orders to abandon Moscow, licentiousness reached its culminating point. Unrestrained by the presence of their leaders, the troops gave themselves up to the most monstrous excesses. Nothing was sacred to their unbridled licence."

One eye-witness tells us—"Nothing so inflamed the greed of the plunderers as the Archangel Cathedral in the Kremlin, in the royal tombs of which they hoped to find enormous treasures. In this expectation the Grenadiers descended with torches into the vaults, and without compunction disturbed even the bones of the dead. . . .

"We hoped that night would put a stop to these horrors, but the darkness merely served to render the conflagration more terrible. The flames, spreading from north to south, shot up into the heavens, illuminating the pall of smoke that hung like a thick fog over the city. Our blood chilled as we listened to the babel of cries, growing louder and ever louder in the darkness; the moans of the unfortunate wretches who were being tortured and slain; the screams of maidens vainly seeking refuge in the arms of their mothers; the howling of the dogs which, in the Moscow custom, were chained to the gates of the houses, and were thus slowly burned alive.

"Through the thick smoke long files of wagons were to be seen loaded with booty. These were continually stopping, and above the din rose the shouts of the drivers, who, fearful of being burned to death, spurred on their horses and forced a way to an accompaniment of recrimination and abuse."

"We met a Jew," says Bourgogne, "who was tearing his hair and beard at the sight of a burning synagogue of which he had been the Rabbi. As he was able to speak a little German we learned that, together with other Jews, he had brought to his place of worship all his valuables.

"We went with him into the Jewish quarter. There we found that everything was burned to the ground. Our friend, on seeing the ruins of his house, uttered a cry and fainted.

"Whenever the troops discovered a house still intact, they broke in the door as if fearful of missing any chance of plunder. If they found anything more valuable than what they already possessed, they threw away the treasures previously collected to make room for the new booty, and when their carts could hold no more they brought away loads of plunder upon their shoulders.

"Sometimes when their road was barred by fire, they were forced to turn back and roam about the strange city, seeking an outlet from the labyrinth of flame. Notwithstanding their danger, the greed of the plunderers conquered their dread of the flames. Covered with blood, they made their way over dead bodies to any spot where they expected to find treasure, heedless of the burning ruins which were falling about them. Nothing but the unbearable heat eventually drove them away, and compelled them to seek shelter in the camp."

The earth was so hot that it was impossible to touch it. Boots were no protection; the ground scorched the feet even through leather soles. Eye-witnesses assert that molten lead and copper were flowing in streams along the streets. Strangers were astonished to observe that the inhabitants looked upon their burning houses without a trace of emotion. Their religious faith must undoubtedly have sustained them, for they placed *ikons* before the houses they abandoned, after quietly making the sign of the cross, without lamentation, or weeping, or wringing of hands.

A lady who determined to leave Moscow with her friends, called upon one of her acquaintances, an old woman named Poliakoff, to urge her to accompany them.

"I found her," she said, "near the *ikons*, lighting her lamp. She was dressed as if for a holiday, all in white, with a white kerchief about her head. 'What is the matter, Babouchka (granny)?' I asked. 'Do you not know that your house is on fire? Let us pack up your traps and clothes as quickly as possible, and with God's help we may escape; we came to take you with us.' But she only replied—'Thank you, my pigeons, for remembering me. For my part, I have spent all my life in this house, and I will not leave it alive. When it was set on fire I put on my wedding chemise and my burial garment. I shall begin to pray. And it is thus that death will find me.' We tried to reason with her; why should she become a martyr when the good God pointed out a way of escape? 'I shall not burn,' she rejoined, 'I shall be suffocated before the flames can reach me. Go; there is still time. The smoke is already filling the room, and I have my prayers to make. Let us say good-bye, and then go. God bless you.'

"Weeping, we embraced her. With tears in her eyes, she blessed us all. 'Forgive me,' she said, 'a wretched sinner, if ever I have done you any injury, and when you see any of my family, give them my last greeting.' We bowed before her as before one who was dead. The room was already full of smoke."

The small property of the Convent of St. Alexis, hidden in the store-room, was plundered. The soldiers dressed themselves in the long habits of the nuns; several took up their quarters in the cell of the Lady Superior, and caroused there for two whole days, inviting the young nuns to join them. One of them—her name is known—willingly submitted to this disgrace.

"The young ones among us," relates one of the nuns, "were dying of curiosity to find out what was taking place in the cell. We had gathered together in a room, and gently opened the door to steal out one by one. An old nun ran up to us. 'Where are you going?' she exclaimed. 'Go back at once. You wish to look at the soldiers, shameless women that you are. See how you blush. If you had been modest girls you had been pale with fear.' One of the elder nuns insulted the French whenever she met them, but they made no reply. She went to the well to draw water. A Frenchman ran up and offered to help her draw up the bucket. Then she gave reins to her indignation. 'What, drink water drawn by your impious hand? Be off, accursed one, or I will throw it over you.' A man of another nation would have been angry; he merely laughed and withdrew.

"At the Convent of the Nativity the older nuns hit upon the device of rubbing soot over the faces of the novices. In passing through the courtyard they encountered a number of soldiers, who surrounded them. The old women spat on the ground, pretending, by their gestures, that the novices were black and ugly. Near at hand was a bucket of water. One of the soldiers picked it up, advising the nuns to wash their faces. Then they became frightened and tried to escape, but the Frenchmen caught them and commenced to scrub them. All the nuns, young and old, then began to shriek, while the soldiers laughed heartily, saying—'*Jolies filles.*'"

If the testimony of numerous eye-witnesses is to be credited, the French soldiers were less cruel than their allies, and, according to private reports, much more polite, and even obliging. Although their name is associated with all the monstrosities and cruelties committed during the invasion, this is merely because the Russians made no distinction between them and the Germans, Wurtembergers, Saxons, Bavarians, Poles, Italians, and others, and only spoke of the "Frenchman," on whom they placed all responsibility.

An old neighbour of mine, of whom I made inquiries on this point, knowing that his village had been occupied by Frenchmen only, informed me that—"They did us no harm. They only fed at our expense."

In one case the troops stole all the sacramental vessels of a village church. The priest sought out Murat, who encamped within a short distance of the village, and, with tears in his eyes, besought the King to restore the vessels necessary for divine service. They were found and given back, and this act of grace is attested by an inscription on one of the silver vessels. The priest of the church of Kolominskoë told me that his father-in-law, who was a child at the time of the invasion, was so much afraid of the French that he hid himself in the stove, until, being hungry and impatient, he began to cry. The soldiers pulled him out, petted him, and solaced him with sugar.

From the beginning, according to Ségur, the conflagration might have had terrible consequences for the invaders, whose want of foresight and carelessness were incredible. "Not only did the Kremlin contain, unknown to us, a powder-magazine, but at night the worn-out and badly-placed sentries allowed a battery of artillery to enter and take up position under the windows of Napoleon. . . . The pick of the army, and the Emperor himself, would have been blown to pieces if but one of the burning cinders which flew over our heads had alighted on a powder-chest. For several hours, therefore, the fate of the whole army hung upon that of every spark scattered abroad by the conflagration."

The courage of the people of Moscow excited the admiration of their foes. "Although," says Labaume, "we suffered so terribly by the fire, we could not but admire the generous self-sacrifice of the inhabitants of the city, who, by their courage and steadfastness, have attained to that high degree of true glory that marks the greatness of a nation. . . ."

The same writer admires the firmness of the Russians who were condemned to be shot. "At the moment of death, each stepped forward to be, if possible, the first to receive the fatal bullet. With a demeanour that bore eloquent witness to their calmness and courage, they made the sign of the cross, and fell riddled with bullets. . . ."

The Abbé Surrugues, a Catholic priest, and an eye-witness, says—"The soldiers did not respect the modesty of women, the innocence of children, nor the grey hairs of age. . . . The wretched inhabitants of Sloboda, pursued from place to place by the flames, were obliged to take refuge in the cemeteries. . . . The unfortunate beings, with terror stamped on their faces, seen fitfully by the light of the burning dwellings flitting among the tombs, might have been taken for so many ghosts that had left their graves. . . . The sacramental vases, the images, all the monuments consecrated by the piety of the faithful, were pillaged or dragged ignominiously about the streets.

The churches were turned into guard-houses, slaughter-houses, or stables."

No town taken by assault ever witnessed such excesses. An officer asserted that since the Revolution in France he had never seen such insubordination in an army. All the streets were strewn with bodies of the dead, lying side by side with the carcases of horses and other animals that had perished by fire or famine.

The author of the *Journal de la Guerre* confirms these details—"In one quarter," he relates, "cries of 'Murder!' were heard, dying away into sighs and groans; in another, the inhabitants were besieged in their houses, defending their already pillaged and devastated hearths against a soldiery infuriated by drunkenness and exasperated by resistance. In yet another quarter one saw men and women, scarcely clothed, dragged through the streets and threatened with death if they did not reveal the spot in which their supposed wealth was concealed. . . . The shops were wide open, the shopmen had left, and the goods were scattered about in every direction."

The Russian author, A. F. de B——, gives the following details—"So soon as one troop of marauders left the house, another took its place, so that not even a shirt or a shoe was left. . . . People no longer dared to go out into the streets. Even the soldiers placed on guard began to loot, imposing silence on the wretched inhabitants by threats and blows. . . . Some, having lost all their wardrobe, were obliged to wear female apparel. Men were to be seen wearing elegant bonnets trimmed with feathers or flowers . . . on their shoulders were fur tippets, and their feet were squeezed into ladies' boots. . . ."

Even the French officers took part in this absurd masquerade. The weather was becoming cold, and satin pelisses trimmed with fur were for this reason worn over military uniforms and accoutrements.

What concealment could be effectual against men who had made war and plundered in every corner of Europe? Hearths and ovens were broken to pieces in the search for treasure. The earth was turned up with sword and bayonet; even the cemeteries were visited, the resting-places of the dead violated, new graves opened, and coffins ransacked. . . . The sick were thrown out of their beds in order that the plunderers might search the mattresses. . . . The tubs in which orange-trees were planted, the flower-pots in hot-houses, were emptied of their contents in the same frenzied hunt for loot.

An Englishman living in Moscow succeeded in outwitting the pillagers. He dug a deep hole, put into it all his coffers, and, without quite filling up the cavity, interred the body of a French soldier, which he then covered over with a slight layer of earth. The French, feeling certain that there must be something hidden, began to dig, but immediately desisted when they recognized their dead comrade.

"It is impossible," remarks Perovski, "to imagine the state of Moscow. The streets are encumbered with furniture and other wares; on all sides one hears the songs of drunken soldiers and the shouts of the pillagers fighting among themselves. Here a bearded grenadier is to be seen clothed in priestly vestments, with the three-cornered hat on his head. Another is wearing a woman's tippet, with a stole round his neck. A third appears in a mantilla, wide trousers, and a helmet; while a fourth is decked out in a white cloak and wears red *kakochniks* as a head-dress. An elderly warrior, again, is strutting about in the surplice of a deacon; a cavalryman is masquerading as a monk, with his shako adorned with a red plume; a soldier of the line is promenading in a woman's skirt. When the soldiers returned into camp in their various disguises, they could only be identified by their side-arms. To make matters worse, many of the officers, following the example of their men, went looting from house to house. The less bold among them contented themselves with pillaging houses in which they were quartered. Even the generals, under pretence of investigation, made house to house visits, and ordered any objects that pleased them to be laid aside."

Madame Fusil has left an interesting account of these lugubrious days. "In my house," she relates, "were two officers of the Gendarmerie of the Guard. Everything was upside down; my papers were scattered over the floor. I returned by the light of the burning houses; the glare was horrible, and the fire was spreading with inconceivable rapidity. A violent wind was blowing, and everything seemed to have conspired to assist the destruction of the doomed city. . . . Grandly horrible was the sight. For four nights we did not require a lamp, the light was more brilliant than at mid-day. . . . On one occasion we wished to take the usual road to the boulevards, but we found it impossible to pass, the way being blocked by a sheet of flame. We stood in the middle of the street, and the flames, fanned by the wind, formed an arch of fire over the thoroughfare. This may seem to be an exaggeration, but it is literally true. We could neither advance nor make a *détour*. Putting our horses to the gallop, we managed to regain the boulevard. . . . The house to which we intended to return was burning. We went from street to street, from house to house. All bore the marks of devastation. . . . We had scarcely eaten anything since the previous day. A table and some chairs were still intact. These were carried down into the street, and a sort of dinner was prepared and dished up in the middle of the road. Imagine a table in the middle of the street, houses in flames or smoking ruins on all sides, the wind driving dust and smoke into our faces, incendiaries shot down near us, drunken soldiers carrying away the booty which they had just pillaged."

In the midst of these horrors they had the heart to open a theatre. Those actors who were left in the city were called together, some being ordered to sing in the Kremlin, others to assist in a play. A theatre was hurriedly run up in the house of Pozniakoff, and pieces were chosen. The curtain and the costumes were of rich materials willingly supplied by the soldiers, and a huge lustre, stolen from one of the churches, gave the necessary light. The orchestra was selected from the bands of the various regiments, and two Russians are said to have given their services. Neither the Emperor nor the marshals attended, but many generals and officers were among the soldiers who filled the hall.

The wax candles taken from the cathedrals were used to illuminate some houses spared by the conflagration, in which balls were arranged. The French, obliged to dance with one another, were unceasing in their questions as to the whereabouts of the Russian women. "Where," they asked, "are the *barinas*, your daughters?"—naïvely expressing deep regret at their absence.

Thus the invaders led at times a jovial life in Moscow. Bourgogne, referring to this period, says—"As we thought we should remain some time in the city, we stored up for the winter seven large cases of champagne, and several of sherry and port. We were the happy possessors of five hundred bottles of Jamaica rum, and over a hundred large loaves of sugar to be divided among six sergeants, a cook, and two women. Meat was scarce, but we had a cow. . . . We had also several hams, which had been found in large quantities, a good supply of salt fish, some sacks of flour, two large barrels of tallow, which we had taken for butter, and some beer. . . . We slept in a billiard-room on sables, lions' skins, fox and bear hides, each with his head wrapped in a rich shawl, forming an immense turban."

Those who did not attend the roll-call would come back laden with the richest and most valuable booty. The loot included silver plates with designs in relief; a bar of the same metal, as large as a brick; ornaments, Indian shawls, and silk stuffs woven in gold or silver. . . . "We, the non-commissioned officers, levied a tax of at least twenty per cent. on all the loot brought in by the soldiers."

Bourgogne then gives an account of an improvised ball. "We began," he says, "by dressing our Russian women as French marchionesses, and as they knew nothing about the dress, Flamand and I were told off to superintend their toilette. Our two Russian tailors were disguised as Chinese; I as a boyard (Russian nobleman), Flamand as a marquis; in short, we all assumed a different dress. Our *cantinière*, Mother Dubois, who turned up at that moment, donned the rich national dress of a Russian lady. As we had no wigs for our *marquises*, the company haircutter dressed their hair, using tallow in place of pomatum, and flour instead of powder,—their toilette was indeed a marvel.

"When everybody was ready, dancing began. I must admit that during the preparations for the ball we drank somewhat freely of punch, with which Mellet, an old dragoon, took care to supply us, and which got into the heads of our *marquises*, and also affected the old *cantinière*.

"Our band consisted of a flute, played by the sergeant-major, while the company drummer tapped the time.

"They began with the tune '*On va leur percer le flanc . . . ran, ran, tan plan, tire lire, ran plan.*' But when the band struck up and Mother Dubois was advancing towards her *vis-à-vis*, the quartermaster-sergeant, our *marquises*, evidently delighted by our stirring music, began to jump about in Tartar fashion, bounding from side to side, and cutting all sorts of capers, so that one might have thought them possessed. This would not have been remarkable had they been dressed in their national costume, but the sight of French *marquises*, usually so decorous, jumping about as if possessed, was so irresistibly comic that we were convulsed with laughter, and the flute-player was unable to continue. The drummer, however, stuck to his post, beating the advance, at the sound of which our *marquises* began anew until they could hold out no longer, and fell down on the floor through sheer fatigue. We picked them up and applauded, and then continued dancing and drinking till four in the morning."

At the Kremlin, too, they were not without amusement. "At each gate of this fortress-palace," says the author of the *Journal de la Guerre*, "were posted sentries of the Grenadiers of the Guard. They had wrapped themselves in Russian furs, fastened round the waist with cashmere shawls, and close to them were vases of opal crystal, two or three feet high, filled with preserved fruits of the most expensive kind, in which were stuck large wooden soup-ladles. Around these vases were piled enormous quantities of flagons and bottles, the necks of which were broken—to save time. Some of these men had donned Russian head-dresses in place of their shakos. They were all more or less drunk, had dropped their muskets, and literally did sentry with their wooden spoons."

Although officially forbidden, pillaging continued. Very strict orders, threatening the execution of all mutineers, were necessary to produce any effect. But the harm done was immense and irreparable. Thirteen thousand eight hundred houses, to say nothing of palaces, had been reduced to ashes. The shops of six thousand tradesmen, forming in themselves a small town, had disappeared. Huge warehouses had also been burned. When the inhabitants ventured to leave their cellars, they failed to recognize the city. They only found isolated houses standing in the midst of ruins. Piles of burned rubbish marked where the streets had stood, and the ruins were encumbered with the bodies of men and animals. Several men were to be seen still hanging; these were the incendiaries, real or suspected, who had first been shot and then strung up. The soldiers passed by these ghastly trophies with complete indifference.

The army had wine and sugar in abundance, but neither bread nor meat. In vain were detachments sent into the forests where the peasantry were concealed with their cattle:—the men returned empty-handed.

"If, from the beginning," says the Abbé Surrugues, whom I have already quoted, "the authorities had seized the store-houses containing flour, wine, and brandy, and established a certain order in the distribution of the provisions, there is no doubt that Moscow might have been preserved from want during the whole winter. . . . The result of the pillaging was that at the approach of the frost, the prime necessaries of life were wanting."

The peasants of the village of Ostankino came indeed to Moscow with thirty cart-loads of oats and flour which were duly bought and paid for. Having received their money they left, with the injunction to come again as soon as possible. But scarcely had they left Moscow than they were assaulted, beaten, and compelled to return to the city, where they were put to forced labour. Two other peasants who had sold their wares to the French were robbed, and one of them was killed. From that time forth no one had any desire to deal with the soldiers or the army, and, in spite of all their efforts, de Lesseps, the former Consul-General, who had been appointed Civil Governor of Moscow, and his Russian assistants, could not succeed in establishing an open and well-supplied market.

But in Moscow itself the inhabitants, less timid and more greedy for gain, did not hesitate to enter into relations with their invaders. A large quantity of copper money, found at the Mint in bags, containing twenty-five roubles each, was used to pay all arrears due to the soldiers. When the populace heard that the Imperial Guard wished to sell these sacks, large numbers hastened, like a flock of birds of prey, to the Nikolskäia, the principal centre of trade. For fifty copecks, or a silver rouble each, they could buy as many sacks as they wished. It is said that several of the great business houses of Moscow date the beginning of their prosperity from that time. The most difficult part was to force a way, when laden with sacks, through the crowd. Even the women hoisted them on their shoulders, but some strong hand would snatch them away, and the thief would manage to escape in spite of cries and blows. Great was the competition to obtain a sack. There were cries of "Monsieur! monsieur! make me a present of it."—"What will you give for it?"—"Be off, be off!"—"Give it to me, monsieur." Then would follow blows from the flat end of the sword, rained down on the outstretched hand, but this treatment was borne with patience, when fortune was so close at hand.

The next morning some soldiers took their stand at the windows of the Courts of Justice, and set up an office for the exchange of money. After receiving the money for a sack of twenty-five roubles, they would throw the bag out of the window. The crowd would then surround the buyers and make a rush for the sacks, facing even musket-shots in their delirium of greed.

During these days, three wine-shops were opened in Moscow by Frenchmen, the waiters being Russian. From these places were heard the sounds of quarrelling, fighting, and even fire-arms. Many French soldiers were murdered in the cellars, in the neighbourhood of the city, and bodies were found in the gardens, in the orchards, at the bottom of deep wells.

A pupil of a seminary was told off as servant to a squad of Hussars quartered at the extreme end of the city. He noticed, one evening, an individual who was looking through the lighted windows, watching all that went on inside the house. "What are you doing there?" he cried. The stranger stepped back quickly, then approached and questioned the young man, after taking him into the garden, and showing him the Cossack uniform under his caftan of coarse cloth. He wished to find out whether the Hussars were numerous, whether they all slept in the same room, where they deposited their arms and horses, and enjoined the most absolute secrecy. Two days afterwards the seminarist was awakened by an extraordinary commotion; all the Hussars had been killed.

There were many similar cases, the French recognizing in all, and with good cause, the handiwork of "the cursed Cossacks."

The situation of the troops in Moscow was, indeed, not without danger. Proclamations, in which the wisdom, charity, and magnanimity of Napoleon were vaunted, inviting the inhabitants to return home, and follow their various occupations in peace, produced no effect whatever.

Relations between the French army and the inhabitants of Moscow were never re-established. Those who passed over to the enemy, especially in the higher classes, were very few. But a very small number can be mentioned, among them being the riding-master Zagriajski, who purposely remained in Moscow to please his friend Caulaincourt, and Samsonoff, who entered the service of Davout.

The clergy behaved with great dignity. They rose superior to the weakness that had been shown in Western Russia. Some priests attempted to hold divine service once more, and to celebrate the Mass; they caused the churches to be cleaned, and locked up. But the soldiers smashed the locks, broke in the doors, and cut up the sacred books. A priest of the Convent of Novinski, named Pilaeff, offered, if Napoleon so desired, to say mass in the Cathedral of the Assumption. By order of the Emperor, he celebrated divine service pontifically, wearing, that is to say, the robes of a bishop.

Many were only too glad to take advantage of Napoleon's difficult situation. A Pole, who seemed to be a person of position, came to the Kremlin, declaring that he was sent with a secret mission by the Commander-in-Chief of the Russian army. Napoleon dictated in person the answers which this spy should deliver to the Russian general, paid him well, and never saw him again.

A handsome woman, and a skilful musician, calling herself a German baroness, who offered her services, received several thousand francs—and disappeared.

But the largest number of persons ready to enter into the service of Napoleon was found among the merchants of the three Guilds, and among officials, doctors, and aliens.

The greater part of the notables had been compelled to enter into the service of the municipality. The members wore round their arm a badge of red and white ribbon, and had the right to call out the soldiery in case of necessity.

The merchant Koltchouguine, for example, gave three reasons for not leaving Moscow; first, because the Governor-General had asserted that the city would not voluntarily be evacuated; secondly, because passports were given only to women and children; and, thirdly, on account of family and business matters. Of course the majority of the people might have put forward the same excuses. All the merchants who remained, including Koroboff, Bakinine, Leschakoff, and, above all, Nahodkin, who had been obliged to act as mayor, declared that they refused to do anything against their faith, or the Emperor Alexander. To this the French Governor, de Lesseps, replied that the differences between the two Emperors were outside their province; their only duty was to watch over the security and prosperity of the city. The merchant Ossipov offered Napoleon bread-and-salt on a silver platter. This gift was sufficient to cause his house to be spared, and he himself was appointed provider to the army. But when he asked for carts for the transport service, the Emperor told him that he would hang him if he raised any difficulties.

The Mayor of Moscow, Nahodkin, whom we have already mentioned, received a hundred thousand roubles for his services, but the bank-notes were false. After the evacuation of Moscow, Rostopchin compelled these gentlemen to sweep the snow off the streets, wearing their white and blue badges, and guarded by soldiers.

The conduct of the merchant Jdanov was very different.

On the recommendation of Samsonoff, cited above as an adherent of Davout, the latter made him a proposal to visit Kaluga, find out the movements of the Russian army, inform himself about its officers, discover whether the regiments had been brought up to their full strength since the battle of Borodino, and learn what was being said about the prospects of peace. He was directed to spread the rumour that there was no want of bread in Moscow, and that Napoleon intended to remain there during the winter. If the Russian army was at Smolensk he was to return as quickly as possible without going to Kaluga.

All precautions were taken, and his family in Moscow guaranteed the faithful performance of his mission. On his return he was to receive a thousand ducats, and the freehold of a house. Jdanov did not hesitate. He went directly to Miloradovitch, the head of the Russian advance-guard, and told him his reasons for leaving Moscow, as well as the services which the French expected from him. He remained with his countrymen, and his family was not molested.

Rostopchin is open to severe censure for his inactivity during the stay of the French army in Moscow, and for not having used his influence to organize volunteer corps. He must also be blamed for his ridiculous attempt to save the city by arming a band of ruffians at the last moment, and for the pompous phrases and dubious meanings with which he filled his reports to the Tsar. In a word, he was emphatically not the man for the place.

But in spite of all, the French army was obliged to abandon Moscow. The situation could no longer be disguised. The three hundred pieces of cannon mounted on the walls of the Kremlin with much labour had proved absolutely useless; but the Kremlin itself must be made to suffer, if only because it could not be carried away with other trophies, such as the cross of Ivan Veliki. An order was issued to blow up the towers, the walls, the cathedrals, and the palaces that constituted the celebrated fortress of former Tsars. The destruction of the Kremlin was merely the expression of Napoleon's vengeance, as cruel as it was useless. It cannot be excused on grounds of policy, for, inasmuch as the Kremlin was merely surrounded by a wall, it was of no use as a fortress.

When the evacuation was decided upon, Marshal Mortier was directed to remain behind in Moscow with the Young Guard. He was ordered to deny any rumours relating to the evacuation, and to pretend that Napoleon would return after defeating the Russian troops whom he had gone out to meet. Nobody believed these assertions, and all who had compromised themselves, from French merchants down to Russian girls of loose character, made ready to follow in the wake of the army.

With the exception of the Imperial Guard, the troops left Moscow helter-skelter, got up in ridiculous and wretched garments, giving them the appearance of scarecrows rather than soldiers. It was arranged that the immense quantity of powder stored up in the cellars of the Kremlin should not be fired until the departure of Mortier and the troops under his command. All that they could not carry away was to be given to the flames; and the mines were so laid that the fire should not reach them until the garrison was at a considerable distance from the city.

"It was an excessively dark night," says A. F. de B——. "At midnight the fire caught the arsenal of the Kremlin, and the first explosion was heard, followed at short intervals by six others. Nothing could be more terrible; immense stones were hurled to a distance of five hundred paces. Not a single pane of glass remained, and the broken pieces were driven into the surrounding walls. The towers and a portion of the walls were blown down. The arsenal was almost destroyed. The steeple of Ivan Veliki shook and cracked, but resisted the shock."

The effect of the explosion was, however, insignificant as compared with what had been intended. A cold rain was falling. The first shock had all the effect of an earthquake. Buildings were shaken to their foundations, walls divided, roofs cracked, and threatened to crush all below them, and all furniture was broken or displaced.

"A great number of the wretched inhabitants were wounded by fragments of glass, or the fall of heavy timber. . . . This awful night caused the death of many persons."

Madame Fusil states that the explosion was so tremendous that many women miscarried through fear; others went mad, and children died of fright and excitement. . . . The French wished to blow up the rest of the town, but happily they had not the time to do so.

"On the day the French left," says a Russian woman, "we were awakened in our cellar by a terrific report. The earth shook under our feet, and it seemed to me as if the walls of the cellar must fall in and bury us alive. At the second explosion a hailstorm of stones flew about in all directions; at the third the church was so shaken that it split from top to bottom. The walls of the Kremlin were destroyed, and a pile of ruins and bricks marked the spot where once the palace had stood. Not only the ground of the Kremlin, but the Polianka, and the far side of the river, were covered with plaster, bricks, and sheets of metal torn away from the roofs."

I copy from Ségur's *Mémoires* a description of the

catastrophe—"On October 23, at half-past one in the morning, the air was shaken by a terrific explosion. . . . Mortier had obeyed his orders, the Kremlin existed no longer. Barrels of gunpowder had been placed in all the rooms of the Imperial palace, and one hundred and eighty-three thousand kilogrammes under the vaults that held them up. The Marshal, with three thousand men, remained on this volcano, that might have been exploded by any stray Russian shell. He covered the march of our army on Kaluga, and the retreat of our various convoys towards Mozjaisk. . . .

"He had been ordered to defend the Kremlin, and when retiring, to blow it up, and set fire to the remainder of the town . . .

"The earth was shaken under Mortier's feet by the force of the explosion. Six leagues off, at Fominskoie, the Emperor heard the report, and, with that ferocity with which he at times addressed Europe, issued, the next morning, a proclamation dated from Borawsk—'The Kremlin, arsenal, magazines, all are destroyed. This ancient citadel, dating from the beginning of the monarchy, the first palace of the Tsars, is a thing of the past. Henceforth Moscow will be nothing but a pile of rubbish, an impure and unwholesome sink, of no importance political or military. He leaves it to the Russian beggars and pillagers, to march against Kutuzof, outflank the left wing of that general, hurl him back, and then quietly reach the borders of the Dvina, where he will pitch his winter quarters.' . . . Then, as if he feared to appear to retreat, he adds—'By this step he will be nearer by eighty leagues to Vilna and St. Petersburg, a double advantage—that is to say, twenty marches nearer to his objective.'

"By this proclamation he sought to give his retreat the appearance of an offensive movement."

"Moscow," says Madame Fusil, "had a charm which it will never possess again. It will perhaps become a beautiful city, but it will be like any other, instead of suggesting Pekin, or Ispahan, a typical city of Asia . . ."

III

THE COSSACKS

Napoleon.

ON quitting Moscow, the Grande Armée fell into the hands of the Cossacks, who surrounded and pursued it to the frontier, and even some way beyond. They so harassed the French that the word "Cossack" soon became a synonym for "Terror," not only in France but all over Europe, representing the height of greed, perfidy, and barbarity. But in pursuing and killing the enemy, the Cossacks were after all doing nothing more than their duty. At times they undoubtedly committed atrocities, but they often gave proof of humanity.

"The Cossacks," says Constant, the Emperor's *valet de chambre*, "seem to have been created to be eternally perched on a horse. There is nothing more amusing than to see them try to walk. Their legs, bowed through the habit of gripping the horse's flanks, resemble the arms of tweezers. When he dismounts, the Cossack seems to be on an element to which he does not properly belong.

"The Emperor, on entering Gjatsk, escorted by two of these barbarians on horseback, ordered that vodka should be served out to them. They swallowed it as if it were water, and held out their glasses with a most amusing calmness for a further allowance. Their horses were small, and had long tails. They appeared to be very docile."

On the road to Mozjaisk 300 Cossacks attacked at night a convoy of 350 carts, having a guard of four regiments of cavalry and two battalions of infantry. In a few moments the harness of all the carts was so hacked about that it was impossible for the drivers to proceed.

Baron Fain speaks somewhat ironically of the Cossack tactics. "Although Kutuzof is rather weak in a pitched battle, he is at least unrivalled on the high-road. The audacity of these undisciplined hordes knows no limit. We have them in front of us, behind us, on our flanks. They face us at every turn. Perhaps the road to Viazma may free us of them for some days."

But after the battle of Viazma, the Russian infantry, which had taken a parallel road to cut off the French, disappeared, and Ney's rear-guard was again beset by Cossacks. Importunate insects, to use Ségur's expression, mounted on little horses with roughed shoes, trained to gallop on the snow, they gave the retreating army no peace.

"To complete the disorder of our retreat, which was of itself enough to undo us," says René Bourgeois, "the Cossacks attacked us unceasingly. . . . As soon as our men caught sight of them, they would scatter in every direction. Some fled hurriedly to the front, while others fell back on the guard, or on some of the companies that were still to be found at intervals."

Another witness, A. F. de B——, adds this sketch—"The number of stragglers was so great that the Cossacks picked out their prisoners, taking those who seemed best dressed, and whom they imagined to have loot. They allowed the others to pass on, without seeming even to notice them."

"That wretched cavalry, which makes a vast amount of noise, and is incapable of breaking through a square of voltigeurs, has become formidable through force of circumstances." Such was Napoleon's opinion of the Cossacks as set forth in one of his bulletins. Platoff, however, almost cut up the whole of the Beauharnais division. He killed 1500 men, and took 3500 prisoners, captured 62 pieces of cannon, several flags, and a large quantity of transport.

"Napoleon did not, and above all would not, understand that the Cossack cavalry was unique of its kind, and in no way resembled regular horse." It never risked a regular action unless victory was certain. If, however, he had seen the Cossack who, having put on the uniform of Marshal Ney, "the bravest of the brave," went calmly about his business, he might have appreciated the fearlessness of these simple children of the steppes.

"It is a historical fact," writes Constant, "that the King of Naples impressed these barbarians greatly. The Emperor was told that they wished to name Murat their Hetman. Napoleon, amused at the proposal, said he would be delighted to second the nomination. It must be admitted that the King of Naples had something theatrical in his bearing calculated to appeal to these barbarians. It was said that by simply flourishing his great sabre he had put an entire horde to flight."

The author of the *Journal de la Guerre* relates that in spite of their critical position, the French troops laughed heartily at an incident that occurred during a Cossack attack. One of the enemy seized hold of one end of an enormous roll of fine linen. The other was held fast by a Frenchman, and as the Cossack galloped away, the roll was unwound and continued to extend in a long serpentine strip until "the barbarian" disappeared into a wood close by.

The Cossacks succeeded one day in capturing Napoleon's baggage. What pleased them most in this haul was the discovery of a number of bottles of old "Château Margaux," stamped with the letter N surmounted with the Imperial crown.

Napoleon's camp-beds, taken by the Cossacks, and now exhibited in the Museum of Armour in Moscow, are interesting. They are two in number, one large and the other small. The former was set up when Napoleon intended to make a more or less protracted stay. The covers were of lilac silk, and provided with pockets for the reception of papers, books, and reports to be read during the night.

The relations between the French prisoners and their Cossack captors were at times marked with the utmost cordiality, if we may credit the following statement made by the author of the *Journal de la Guerre*—"Our artillery having been captured, the gunners were disarmed and marched off roped together. In the evening the Cossacks celebrated their victory by a great festivity, in which drinking and dancing played the principal part. In the expansiveness of their hearts they wished every one to participate in their good fortune, and remembering their prisoners, invited them to take part in the general merry-making. The unfortunate artillerymen desired nothing better than rest after their labours, but little by little, restored by the good cheer lavished upon them, they joined in the dances, and took a hearty part in the amusements of their captors. The Cossacks were so much delighted by this display of good-fellowship that they allowed the French to don their tunics and shakos, restored their side-arms, shook hands vigorously with their new friends, who embraced them in turn, and made the best of their way back to their quarters."

An equally pleasing story is told by a marine of the Guard who was taken prisoner by the Cossacks. "While we were warming ourselves round some pine-logs, a Cossack came up—a tall, lean, wiry man, of such a ferocious countenance that we involuntarily drew back. He approached us with a military salute and began talking; but we were unable to understand a word he said. He was probably questioning us about something. Annoyed at our failure to understand him, he showed signs of his displeasure, which caused us some alarm; but when he saw this he at once assumed a kindly expression, and, noticing that my comrade's clothes were stained with blood, he indicated a wish to examine his wound, and signed to us to follow him.

"He took us into the nearest hut. A woman appeared, and he told her to spread some straw and bring some warm water. Then he went away, giving us to understand by signs that he was coming back again. The woman threw down a little straw, but forgot all about the water, and we did not like to bother her about it. When he returned he at once signed to us, asking if we had had anything to eat. We shook our heads. He apparently bade the woman give us some supper, and when she refused, he rated her soundly. Then she showed him a basin containing some sort of broth in it, vowing, to all appearance, that that was all she had. The Cossack stormed and threatened, but in vain—she would do nothing but warm some water. The Cossack left us again, and soon returned with a piece of salt bacon; and we at once fell to, although it was quite raw. While we ate, the Cossack looked on with pleasure and signed to us not to eat too much at once.

"When we had satisfied our hunger, he again spoke to the woman—apparently about bandages for our wounds.

He asked her for some rags, but she refused to give him any, and tried to put him off with the answer—'*Nyema*—I have none.' Then the gallant soldier took hold of her by the arm and made her turn out every corner of the hut, but he found nothing. At last, irritated by her obstinacy, he drew his sword; she began to scream, and we threw ourselves at his feet, thinking that he was going to kill her. He smiled at us, as much as to say—'You don't know me, I only want to frighten her.'

"The woman trembled in every limb, but still refused to give him anything. So he threw away his coat and pulled off his shirt, which he proceeded to cut in strips with his sword, and set to work to re-bandage our wounds. He talked the whole time he was engaged in this task, using a number of Polish and German words in the course of his remarks; but, however unintelligible this running accompaniment was, his actions clearly showed the nobility of his heart. I believe he was trying to make us understand that he had been accustomed to warfare for more than twenty years—he was about forty—that he had been in a number of great battles, and knew that one must learn after victory to be generous to the unfortunate. He pointed to his medals, as much as to say that such tokens of courage imposed upon him certain obligations. We were delighted at his magnanimity, and he could no doubt read in our faces the expression of our gratitude. I should have liked to say to him—'Friend, rest assured that your kindness will never fade from our memory. There are but two witnesses of your humanity, for this woman is incapable of appreciating it. Only tell us your name, that we in turn may tell it to our comrades.' At first he knelt down, but afterwards becoming tired of that attitude he sat on the floor with a leg on either side of my comrade.

He washed the wound in his shoulder and dressed it with the utmost care. Then, looking towards me, as if for advice, he showed me that he intended, if possible, to extract the ball with a rude knife which he now produced. He tried to probe the wound, but my friend screamed so loudly in his agony that he stopped. Laying his cheek on my comrade's head, he seemed to ask pardon for the pain he had caused. At the sight of so much tenderness I could not forbear from seizing his hands and pressing them warmly. Summoning all the resources of my Polish, Russian, and German vocabulary, I tried to speak, but could not—my heart was full, and my eyes were wet with tears.

"'My dear, dear camarade!' said he, making haste to get the wound dressed, for he seemed to fear there would not be time enough.

"When my turn came, the kindly Cossack, having examined my wound, gave me by signs to understand that it was not deep, and would heal up of its own accord. The force of the lance-thrust must have been broken by my clothing.

"He was still attending to our wants when one of his comrades called to him from the street—'Pavlovski'—so that at last I learned his name—and he left us at once, followed by our blessing.

"We thought we should probably never see our gallant Cossack again, but he returned very early the next day and examined the dressing of our wounds. He also brought us a couple of Russian biscuits apiece, and expressed his regret that he could do no more."

IV

THE GRANDE ARMÉE

Napoleon.

THE Russian general Grabbe, who, during the invasion, visited the French camp, was astonished at the disorganized state of the cavalry.

This impression is emphasized by Fezensac.

"From the very first, I was struck by the exhaustion and numerical weakness of the troops. At head-quarters they only judged by results, without weighing the cost, and thus they had no idea of the condition of the army.

"Four regiments of cavalry were reduced to 900 men out of 2800 who had crossed the Rhine. All articles of clothing, but especially boots, were in a wretched condition. We had at first enough flour, and a few herds and flocks, but these resources were soon exhausted, and to renew them we were obliged to move constantly from place to place, for in twenty-four hours we cleared out any locality through which we passed."

In a conversation with M. de Narbonne at Vitebsk, the

Emperor estimated the two combined Russian armies before Smolensk at 130,000 men; with the Guard, the 1st, 3rd, 4th, 5th, and 8th Corps, he calculated his own strength at 170,000 men. If no battle were fought he did not intend to pass Smolensk; if he won a complete victory, he would perhaps march straight to Moscow; but in any case, a battle, even if undecided, seemed to him likely to pave the way for peace.

At Smolensk and at the battle of Valoutina, René Bourgeois and Fezensac agree in estimating the French losses at 6000 to 8000 killed, and over 10,000 wounded. The Russian loss was equal, if not greater. Together with prisoners and stragglers, the Grande Armée lost in these engagements about 20,000 combatants.

The Emperor, however, does not scruple to assert, in Bulletin XIII., that for every dead Frenchman on the field of battle there were eight Russians, and that the soldiers of the Tsar, encouraged by the proximity of their villages, seized every opportunity to desert. He acknowledges that General Sebastiani was beaten and obliged to fall back, but he estimates his loss at only 100 men. As, however, this retreat of one of his best generals might be looked upon as a serious check, and produce a painful impression on the whole army, the Emperor decided to march on Moscow.

Labaume sketches the situation at that moment in a few strokes—"To describe our distress in the midst of our apparent victory, it is sufficient to say that we were utterly worn out by the persistent and systematic retreat of the Russians. Our cavalry was totally disorganized, and the half-starved artillery horses could no longer draw the guns."

All this took place at the beginning of the campaign; but far from showing alarm, Napoleon merely laughed at the Russians, whether sincerely or not it is difficult to say. "In the midst of all the defeats which they look upon as victories," he writes in Bulletin XIX., "the Russians sing *Te Deums* of thanks. In spite of their ignorance and want of culture, this behaviour begins to strike one as unnatural and hideous."

At Borodino the Russian redoubts turned out to be mere sketches of fortifications, and the trenches shallow and unprotected; yet the Russians defended them so obstinately that, according to Labaume's description, the centre of the Great Redoubt presented an inexpressibly terrible picture. The dead were piled upon one another several deep. The Russians were falling on all sides, but they refused to retire; in the space of one square league there was not a spot that was not covered with dead or wounded. Further on were heaps of dead among scattered fragments of guns, lances, helmets, cuirasses, or cannon-balls covering the ground like hailstones after a violent storm. The most awful spectacle of all was to be seen in the trenches—poor wounded wretches, who had fallen one on the top of the other, lay weltering in their blood, groaning in the most heart-rending manner and praying for death. "Not only," says Fezensac, "had the French army never before suffered such losses as at Borodino, but, what was worse, never before had the spirit of the soldiery been so utterly broken as after that battle. The irrepressible gaiety of the French soldiers vanished, and instead of the songs and jokes in which it had been their wont to forget the fatigues of their long marches, a death-like silence reigned in the camp. Even the officers, it appears, utterly lost heart. Such depression is intelligible when it follows defeat, but it was certainly not to be expected after a victory which had thrown open the gates of Moscow."

According to Russian authorities, whose accounts are completely at variance with Napoleon's own assertions, the Emperor lost more than 50,000 men in the attack, including 1200 officers and 49 generals; while the Russian losses, dead and wounded, amounted to 40,000, including 1732 officers and 18 generals. The enemy's losses must have been increased by the fact that during the three days in which they were engaged on the field of battle they had nothing to eat and drink but roots and water. Ségur admits a loss of 40,000 men, and says that the army which entered Moscow numbered 90,000. The division of Cuirassiers, which had comprised 3600 horses all told, numbered but 800 on that day.

The situation in which the French army found itself within the walls of Moscow was not by any means an enviable one. It had neither bread nor meat, although the tables were spread with sweetmeats and syrups. Valuable wine was readily exchanged for blankets; and a fur-coat could be bartered for any quantity of sugar and coffee.

The camp presented the appearance not of a military bivouac, but rather of a market where every soldier, turned tradesman, was busy selling the most valuable articles at the most moderate prices; where all the men, though living in the open field exposed to rain and storm, ate from porcelain plates, drank out of silver goblets, and were surrounded with the costliest luxuries of the period.

During their stay at Moscow, the battalions quartered outside the walls knew no peace. There existed, as Ségur says, a kind of tacit, informal armistice between the opposing armies, but only in the front. On the flanks and in the rear, not a wagon could pass, not an ounce of forage could be brought in unopposed, so that in reality the war still continued.

During the first few days Murat delighted in showing himself to the outposts of the enemy. He was flattered by the respect paid to his appearance, his reputation for courage, and his rank. The Russian officers took good care not to undeceive him. They loaded him with all the tokens of deference calculated to keep up this illusion. He was allowed to order their vedettes about as if they were Frenchmen. If any part of the ground they occupied pleased him, they hastened to surrender it to him.

Cossack chiefs went so far as to pretend enthusiasm, and to say that they only recognized as Emperor the Emperor who reigned in Moscow. Murat even believed for a time that they would not fight against him.

The Emperor, who was not deceived by these professions, complained bitterly of the exasperating guerilla warfare to which he was constantly exposed. "Had not a hundred and fifty dragoons of the Old Guard met, been attacked, and routed by a horde of these barbarians? And this took place but two days after the armistice on the road to Mozjaisk, his principal line of communications, which connected him with his stores, his reserves, his depôts, with Europe itself."

"Every morning," adds Ségur, "our soldiers, especially the cavalry, had to travel great distances to obtain the necessaries of life. And as the environs of Moscow and Winkovo became more and more denuded, they were obliged to range further and further afield. Men and horses returned worn out, some did not return at all. Each measure of oats, each bundle of straw, had to be fought for, dragged out of the enemy. Nothing but surprises, fights, losses. Even the peasantry began to be troublesome.

"We had war on all sides—in front, on our flanks, in our

rear. The army was growing weaker and weaker; the enemy becoming daily more venturesome. . . . At last Murat himself grew anxious. He saw half the remnant of his cavalry melt away in these daily skirmishes."

In Bulletin XXII. Napoleon only says—"The Cossacks attack our scouts. . . . The Turkish flags, as well as some curiosities taken from the Kremlin, and the image of the Holy Virgin studded with diamonds, have been forwarded to Paris. . . . Rostopchin is said to have gone mad. . . . He has set his country-house on fire. . . . The sun is more brilliant and hotter than in Paris, one might fancy oneself in the south. . . . The Russian army does not approve of the burning of Moscow. . . . The Russians look on Rostopchin as a Marat consoling himself in the society of Wilson, the English *attaché*."

Napoleon says not a word about his endeavours to conclude peace.

Winter was advancing. Ségur continues—"The Russians openly expressed their astonishment that we should appear so indifferent to the approach of their terrible winter. It was their natural ally; they grieved for us, and urged us to retreat. 'In another fortnight,' they said, 'your nails will drop off, your weapons will fall out of your stiffened and half-frozen hands.'"

Fain confirms these details—"The cold seems to be the only cause of future anxiety. But the veterans of the army, who have already learned, in the bogs of Pultusk and the ice-fields of Eylau, to brave the climate, hope to escape this time with the same good luck. Moreover, no calculation has been neglected in this matter, and all the probabilities are reassuring. It is usually only in December or January that the Russian winter displays all its severity. During November the thermometer seldom marks six degrees of frost, in a normal year. Observations made during the preceding twenty years confirm this statement."

On October 13 the Emperor saw the first fall of snow. "Let us hurry," he said, "for in twenty days we must be in our winter quarters." Napoleon repeats this sentence in Bulletin XXIV.

Labaume is very emphatic in his remarks—"It is past all comprehension," he says, "that Napoleon could be so blind and so obstinate as to remain in Russia when he saw that the capital on which he had relied was in ruins, and that winter was approaching. . . . Providence no doubt, in punishment of his pride, must have dulled his wits. Could he otherwise have imagined that the very men who had had the courage to destroy their homes would be weak enough to accept his onerous terms, and sign a peace on the flaming ruins of their cities?"

"In proportion as our strength and energy fell," says the same author, "so did the boldness of the Cossacks rise. It increased to such a pitch that they actually attacked an artillery convoy on its road from Viazma, and repeated the experiment on another artillery convoy coming from Italy. These Tartar hordes dashed in whenever they found a gap between our armies, and availed themselves of the advantages of their position to display the most impudent daring."

The King of Naples, whose cavalry had almost reached the vanishing point, daily implored that something should be done; that peace should be concluded or a retreat begun. But the Emperor was both deaf and blind.

"The spell was broken at last!" exclaims Ségur, "and by a mere Cossack. This barbarian fired at Murat as he was visiting an outpost. Murat was highly indignant, and explained to Miloradovitch that an armistice that existed only to be broken was not worth prolonging."

The position of the French army then became intolerable. It was impossible to remain in Moscow, but it was equally impossible to retreat without preparation. The Emperor of the French nevertheless continued to issue the same characteristic bulletins. "Some think," he said, "that the Emperor ought to set fire to the public buildings, march to Tula in order to be near Poland, and spend the winter in a friendly country where he can easily obtain all he requires from the stores of Dantzic, Kovno, Vilna, and Minsk. Others point out that between Moscow and St. Petersburg there are 180 leagues of bad road, while the distance from Vitebsk to St. Petersburg is only 130 leagues, and conclude that Msocow is worthless as a strategic position, while in its ruined condition it must lose its political importance for a century to come. There are a number of Cossacks with the enemy who give our cavalry some trouble. . . . Everything points to the necessity of seeing to our winter quarters. The cavalry especially are in need of rest."

Bivouac Fire.

The battle of Tarutina opened Napoleon's eyes. He now saw that Kutuzof was merely playing with him, and he resolved to retreat. But what a retreat! "From the very first," says Fezensac, "it resembled a rout." Some companies were dying from sheer starvation, whilst others did not know what to do with their provisions. Those soldiers who straggled from the line of march in search of food, fell into the hands of the Cossacks and the armed peasants. The road was filled with caissons which had been blown up, with guns and carts that had been abandoned.

The soldiers were unwilling to sacrifice their loot, and marched heavily laden. One of them gives an inventory of his share—"I had furs, pictures by old masters, rolled up for convenience of transport, and some precious stones. One of my comrades carried a huge case of quinine. Another had a whole library of beautiful books with gilt edges, and bound in red morocco. I had not forgotten the inner man, and had provided myself with rice, sugar, and coffee, besides in reserve three big pots of jam—two cherry and one gooseberry."

Bourgogne gives similar details—"We were obliged to halt and wait for the left column. I took this opportunity to overhaul my knapsack, which seemed too heavy. It was well loaded. I had several pounds of sugar and rice, some biscuits, half a bottle of liqueur, the silk dress of a Chinese woman embroidered in gold and silver thread, several gold and silver ornaments, among them a fragment of the cross of St. Ivan, or rather the cover which surrounded it. I should state that in the middle of the great cross of St. Ivan was a smaller one, in massive gold, a foot in length. I had also my full-dress uniform, a woman's large cape for riding, two silver pictures, a foot wide by eight inches high, the figures in relief, and several medals and stars set in diamonds belonging to a Russian prince. All these I kept to give away. Moreover, I had on my shirt, a waistcoat of yellow silk, embroidered and wadded, which I had cut out of a woman's petticoat, and over that again a large collar, lined with ermine. A game-bag was slung at my side and held up under the collar by a heavy piece of silver braid. This bag held many precious things, among them a figure of Christ in gold and silver, a china porcelain vase, both of which escaped the general wreck as if by a miracle. . . . Then came my cross-belts, my arms, and sixty rounds of cartridges in my pouch."

The Russian witness, A. F. de B., gives the last touch to this picture—"Every French officer had two or three carriages, and each took with him a Russian or French woman ; for a number of women had in one way or another managed to follow the army. Some of them, suspecting the hard fate that awaited them, changed their minds at the gates of the city and returned. Others were robbed on the road of their horses, their provisions, and their furs. These wretched beings lived to see their children buried under the snow, and later on the greater number of them perished miserably. Very few escaped, and not one of them was seen to cross the frontier."

Speaking of the women who accompanied the Grande Armée, Duverger relates a characteristic episode—"We had orders to prevent any carriage from getting between the guns. A magnificent carriage, drawn by four horses, approached us rapidly. I signalled to the coachman to stop, but he refused, and continued to drive on. My comrades and I seized the bridle, and the carriage was close to the edge of a ditch when a young and pretty woman put her head out of the window. Her handsome new clothes, as well as the luxury which surrounded her, plainly showed that she enjoyed the favour of some very important personage. She ordered us in the name of the Emperor, and of the Major-General, to let her pass, but we refused."

After Malo Jaroslavetz the situation of the army became more and more critical. On November 5, hand-mills, and rather heavy ones, too, were served out to the Guard. It seemed like a practical joke, for there was nothing to grind. The troops threw away these cumbersome and useless utensils within twenty-four hours.

On the following day snow began to fall heavily. The men were blinded by the flakes and numbed by the intense cold.

"Within a few nights," writes Baron Fain, "everything is changed. Horses fall by thousands, cavalrymen march on foot, the artillery are without harness, the edge of the road is strewn with our unfortunate comrades. An entire brigade under General Augereau, the brother of the marshal, is surprised on the 9th, by the Cossacks of Orlov-Davidov and Seslavin, and surrenders! Napoleon has still enough natural feeling to be moved by this new misfortune. He sends General Baraguay d'Illiers—an old comrade of the army of Italy, and one of his most distinguished generals—on to France, with orders to remain under arrest in his own house until he can be tried by court-martial."

Prince Eugène reported the loss of all his artillery and ammunition. On the road into Doukovstchina he met with a terrible disaster crossing the little river Vop. The scene is dramatically described by Labaume—"There was a general panic, for in spite of the efforts made to keep the Russians in check, we knew but too surely that they were advancing. The prevailing panic, moreover, increased our danger. The river, being only half frozen, would not bear the weight of the wagons and droshkies which contained our few remaining provisions. Every one then struggled to transfer his most precious possessions from the wagons to the horses' backs. No sooner were the horses out of a cart than a crowd of soldiers, without giving the owners time to rescue their effects, began to plunder it. Their search was particularly keen for flour and wine. . . . The cries of those who were crossing the river, the terror of those who were preparing for the plunge from the steep and slippery bank, the distress of the women, the weeping of children, and the panic of the soldiers themselves, made the passage of this river so harrowing a scene that it is impossible to recall it without a shudder. For a whole league around, on the edge of the road and the banks of the river, lay abandoned guns, caissons and elegant carriages that had come from Moscow. On every side lay articles that had been flung from the wagons; they were of course especially conspicuous on the dazzling snow. There were candelabra, bronze antiques, old masters, and rare and costly porcelain services."

"On every side reigned terror and despair," says Bourgeois. "Safety seemed to lie only in flight, and of course no one wished to be the last. If the crowd jostled you beneath the wheels of the carriages, you might abandon all hope of the horses pulling up and allowing you to extricate yourself. No one would listen to your cries. In the throng it was impossible to distinguish generals from common soldiers; they were dressed like scarecrows, in tattered garments, suffering the pangs of cold and hunger, and reduced to beg favours of the soldiers under their command."

Chambray relates, for instance—"One day when some soldiers were warming themselves round a fire, a general came up half dead with cold, and begged for a place. No one vouchsafed a word in reply, and it was only on his repeating his petition that one of the men answered—'All right, if you'll fetch another log.'

"Lawlessness and insubordination reached their climax; there was no thought of discipline, and obedience was out of the question. All distinctions of rank were levelled—we were a wretched mass of shrunken, decivilized humanity.

When some poor wretch, wearied with the long struggle, fell at last, a prey to his miseries, his neighbours, fully assured that all was over with him, and that he would never rise again, flung themselves upon their wretched comrade, before the breath was out of his body, and stripped him of the remnants of his clothing. In a few moments he would be left naked on the ground, to die a lingering and painful death. One might often see the spectral semblance of a man dragging himself painfully along to reach the halting-place, striving his utmost to put one leg before the other, until he realized at last that his strength was leaving him. A deep groan would be heard, the man's eyes would fill with tears, his legs would begin to fail him, he would totter along for a few yards, swaying from side to side, then fall to the ground, never to rise again. If the poor wretch's body fell across the road, his comrades would step indifferently over it as if nothing had occurred.

"The courage of which the troops had at first afforded so many signal proofs, gave place to the most hopeless cowardice. They had no thought but of flight. The idea of defending themselves never seemed to occur to them. In many instances they refused to raise a hand to save their own lives.

"At the approach of a handful of Cossacks, or a band of peasants with clubs, there was a general stampede. Even those who carried muskets would fling them away in order to run the more quickly. Those who were taken prisoners never dreamed of resistance—a company of Grenadiers would fall an easy prey to these unarmed peasants."

"The Cossacks and the militia," says the author of *The War of 1812*, "were more formidable to the captives than the regular forces." The Russian generals did all that was in their power to restrain their ferocity, but their animosity was such that the officers would have had to be everywhere at once in order to save the prisoners.

"It was like marching over an endless battle-field," says Fezensac. "Some lay in the snow with frost-bitten limbs; others fell asleep and perished in the burning villages. I remember a private in my battalion who acted like a drunken man. He marched at our side without recognizing any of his comrades, asked after his regiment, named the men of his company, and yet conversed with them as if they were complete strangers. He swayed from side to side as he walked, and his expression was dazed and wandering. . . .

"The soldiers, blinded by the whirl of drifting snow, could not even distinguish the road, and often fell into ditches which became their graves. Ill-shod and worse clad, without meat or drink, huddled and shivering, hardly able to move a limb, they pressed forward at all costs, without paying the slightest attention to those who were failing, falling, and dying around them. Alas! what a mass of poor wretches there was upon that road, perishing of sheer exhaustion, yet still struggling to ward off the approach of death! Some cried 'Farewell' to their brethren and comrades, some with their last breath murmured the names of their mothers and their homes. The cold soon stiffened their limbs and struck into the very marrow of their bones. The place where they fell was marked only by little heaps of snow along the wayside, covering their bodies like the hillocks in the churchyard.

"Flocks of carrion rose up from the valleys and hovered in the air above them, uttering cries of ill omen. The innumerable dogs which had followed the army from Moscow, fattening on carrion, slunk around and howled on every side, awaiting fresh prey."

It should be mentioned that when the retreat began most of the men had furs of different kinds, but in the nightly bivouacs, the snow, melted by the heat of the fires, soaked them through and through, and they afterwards froze again into solid blocks of ice. The result of the alternate freezing and thawing was that at last the fur rotted away and dropped off, and nothing was left of the splendid sables and ermines but a few wretched brown rags.

Stragglers who had deserted from their regiments were repulsed wherever they went, and could find no place in the bivouacs. One can imagine the plight of these poor wretches. Tortured with hunger they flung themselves on every horse that fell, and fought like savage dogs over the carcase. Exhausted with long marches and want of sleep, they could find in the snow no rest for their weary limbs. Half dead with cold, they wandered in every direction, searching the snow for fuel, and even when they were successful, the sodden wood was difficult to kindle and the fire was easily extinguished by the wind. "Then they huddled together like cattle," says an eye-witness, "around birches and pines, or under carts. Sometimes they would set fire to the houses in which the officers had taken refuge, and sit motionless through the night around these monster bonfires."

The soldiers' frost-bitten limbs were covered with sores, which turned into black patches when they warmed them at the fire, and he was a lucky man who could boast of having escaped frost-bite altogether.

In their miseries they forgot their booty. "The road was covered," says Duverger, "with useless plunder, which they had flung away. The famous chest of quinine was left to its fate. I tried to sell my pictures, but no one seemed to want them. I gave my furs away for nothing. The man who brought away the library was struck with the happy thought of selling it in lots, but no one would make a bid."

They had even to abandon the famous trophies from Moscow, casting them into Lake Semlefsky, between Gjatsk and Mikhailov. The guns, the various knights' trappings, and the ornaments from the Kremlin were buried close by. Ségur says that the famous cross from the belfry of John the Great was also sunk in the lake, but according to other authorities it was dragged on as far as the first post-house beyond Vilna. "How did it happen," he asks, "that nothing had been provided for before the army left Moscow? How was it that these masses of soldiers who died of cold and starvation, were found laden with gold and silver instead of the food and clothing they required? How was it that during a rest of thirty-three days they never thought of roughing the horses' feet so that they might get along with more speed and safety? How was it that, even if Napoleon himself gave no orders, these obvious precautions did not occur to the other authorities—the kings, princes, and marshals? Were they not aware that even in Russia autumn is followed by winter? Can we suppose that Napoleon relied upon the sagacity of his men, and left them to look after themselves?

"Was he perhaps misled by his experience of campaigning in Poland, where the winter is no more severe than in France? Was he deceived by those sunny October days, which surprised even the Russians themselves? What midsummer madness was it that scattered the wits of

Napoleon and his army? What mist was it that obscured their vision? What was the resource on which they counted? Even if all heads were turned by the notion of concluding a treaty of peace within the walls of Moscow, they had still in any case to march back again. Yet not the slightest preparation was made even for the most peaceful return."

"At last," continues Ségur, "the army cast its eyes once more upon Smolensk. Before them lay the promised land, where the hungry should be filled and the weary be at rest, where they were to lie in warm and comfortable rooms and forget their nightly bivouacs in forty degrees of frost. 'Now,' they thought, 'we can sleep as long as we wish, mend our clothes, and provide ourselves with boots!' But the skeletons of horses lying in the streets show that even here there is a scarcity of provender. Broken doors and window-frames serve as fuel for camp-fires, and the warm houses and promised winter quarters—where are they? The sick and wounded lie neglected in the street, in the vans in which they arrived. This is but another camp, still colder than the forests through which the march has hitherto lain.

"The greatest care was needed to prevent detachments of the different corps from coming to blows at the doors of the store-houses. When the rations were at last served out the soldiers refused to carry them to their various regiments. They sprang eagerly upon the sacks, seized a few pounds of flour and bore it off to gorge themselves. The same thing happened with the brandy. Next day the houses were filled with the bodies of these poor wretches, dead of their surfeit of food and drink. It was evident that Smolensk, which the army had regarded as the end of its sufferings, was but the beginning. An endless vista of misery opened out before it. There remained forty more days of marching—forty more such days as they had already experienced."

The Emperor arrived on November 9, when their despair was at its height. He locked himself in a house in the market-place, and left it on the 14th, to continue his retreat. He had been counting on a fortnight's full rations for a force of 100,000 men, and he found only half that quantity in flour, rice, and brandy—meat there was none.

"Ever since Napoleon arrived," writes the author of *The War of 1812*, "I have been engaged in serving out rations to the troops of the various corps. I am afraid that the seven sentries who keep guard over me day and night will hardly manage to save me from being torn to pieces by the famishing soldiers. . . . Some of the very highest officers broke one of my windows the other night and climbed in."

Every eye-witness speaks of the bitter disappointment of the soldiers at Smolensk.

"Our horror," says Labaume, "was indescribable when we first learned on the outskirts of Smolensk that the 9th Army Corps had already marched on, that the troops were not to stay at Smolensk, and that such provisions as there were had already been exhausted. Had a thunder-bolt fallen at our feet, we could not have been more astounded than at this news; it was so overwhelming that we refused to believe it. We soon found out, however, that downright famine prevailed in the town—the town which we had pictured a veritable Land of Promise."

Those soldiers who could find no quarters lay in the streets; and within a few hours they would be found dead by their fires. The hospitals, the churches, and all the public buildings were crowded with the sick who flocked thither in thousands. Those who could find no room were left to die in the vans and on the caissons and gun-carriages on which they had been brought.

"One Cuirassier," says an eye-witness, "moaning with hunger, flung himself upon the flayed body of a dead horse, thrust his head in between the naked ribs, and began tearing out the entrails with his teeth. So fierce were the pangs they suffered that the Russians found dead bodies of Frenchmen half devoured by their comrades."

They left 5000 sick and wounded in Smolensk without provisions of any kind. The doctors and officials charged with the duty of attending upon them took to flight, in fear of being massacred or taken prisoners.

Chambray is our authority for saying that, contrary to custom, the sick were not even commended to the generosity of the enemy—they were simply abandoned as so much useless rubbish.

"The war now became so barbarous," says the author of *The War of 1812*, "that it is impossible to imagine within what limits an enemy whose wrath has been aroused by wholesale ruin and destruction will confine his vengeance. Before planning the cruel and wanton destruction of Moscow and Smolensk, the French should have remembered that they were leaving 10,000 of their men in the hospitals and on the road as hostages in the hands of the enemy."

"When they found themselves left to perish of starvation," writes René Bourgeois, "compelled to shift for themselves, these poor wretches crawled about the fields digging up roots and picking up the refuse of cabbages and other vegetables. They lay about on rotten grass and straw, on rags and scraps; they were covered with vermin and filth and surrounded by the decomposing bodies of their comrades. For a distance of eighty leagues the road was impassable; one had, so to speak, to cut a way through corpses and *débris* of every kind. At every halting-place were huge cemeteries, miscalled hospitals, which made their presence known for miles around by their nauseating odour due to the heaps of unburied dead, and the filth of every sort that lay weltering in foul pools."

The fugitives, too, were covered with every sort of vermin. The stench that arose from these living corpses was due both to their disorders, and the fact that through dread of the cold they never removed their clothing for any purpose whatever. Their hands were smeared with horses' blood, and their faces and tattered garments reeked with its effluvium. Many whose faces and arms were frost-bitten resembled the rounded figures of ivory chessmen.

"What I dreaded most," says a German writer, "was the approach of night; not so much because our sufferings were greatly intensified at night, as because when we halted all the soldiers collected together and huddled close to one another so as to keep as warm as circumstances would permit. In the general silence one might hear on different sides, sometimes on all sides at once, the dull thud of men and horses falling on to the frozen ground, dead of cold and privation."

"In one encampment," says Bourgogne, "I was horrified to find that all the men and horses were dead and already covered with snow. The men's bodies lay in the most natural manner round the camp-fires, and the horses remained harnessed to the guns. There were five men snarling and fighting like dogs—on one side lay the hind-leg of a horse, the subject of their dispute.

"They had been buoyed up by the expectation of finding food and lodging in Smolensk, but now they had no further hope; they marched along mechanically wherever they were led, and halted when others halted."

"A veteran Chasseur," says the same author, "who had wrapped his frost-bitten extremities in strips of sheep-skin, sat down by our fire. He cursed the name of the Emperor Alexander, and he cursed Russia and all the saints; then he asked whether any brandy had been served out. When he heard the answer—'No, none has been served out, and none will be,' he exclaimed—'Well, there is but one thing left, and that is death!'

"On the road we came upon a Hussar in his death agony, now rising to his feet, now falling to the ground again. We tried to help him along, but he fell again, and for the last time. Further on we came upon three men engaged upon a fallen horse. Two were standing up, reeling so fearfully that they looked like drunken men. The third, a German, lay across the horse—the poor devil, half dead with hunger and too feeble to cut a piece off, was trying to bite out a mouthful, but he died in the endeavour."

The unfortunate women who still managed to drag on a miserable existence suffered, if possible, still more. "Throughout this terrible march," says Madame Fusil, "I said to myself each day that I should probably not see the end of it; but I could not tell by what death I should die. When we halted and camped in the hope of warming ourselves and eating something, we generally sat on the bodies of those who had fallen victims to the cold, settling ourselves upon them with as little concern as if they were so many sofas. All day long one might hear people exclaiming—'Great heavens, my purse has been stolen!' or 'my bag,' or 'my bread,' or 'my horse.' It was just the same with every one, from generals to privates. People were perpetually trying to push their way through the crowd, with—'Room for Marshal So-and-so's carriage!' or 'His Excellency So-and-so's,' or 'General So-and-so's.' When there was a bridge to be crossed, generals and colonels would range themselves on either side, in spite of the general confusion, so as to expedite the passage of their own vehicles as much as possible, for the Cossacks were never far off."

"The Frenchwomen who had fled from Moscow to escape the vengeance of the Russians," says Labaume, "and who had counted on perfect safety in our midst, presented a most pitiable spectacle. Most of them had to go on foot, shod in summer shoes and clad in the flimsiest of silks and satins, in torn fur cloaks and military great-coats taken from the shoulders of the dead. Their plight would have been enough to wring tears from the hardest heart had not every sentiment of sympathy been stifled by each man's individual privations.

"Of all the victims of this war, not one presents such an interesting figure as the young and lovely Fanny. Modest, amiable, and witty, a talented linguist, adorned with qualities calculated to captivate the least impressionable—she was reduced to begging for the slightest services almost upon her knees, and compelled to pay for every crust of bread at the price of her shame. Her benefactors abused their position to demand the most debasing return for the nourishment they afforded her. I saw her at Smolensk unable to walk, clinging to a horse's tail, until she fell at last upon the snow, and there she probably remained, her fate provoking no sign of sympathy or look of pity."

"The unhappy P.," continues Labaume, "still succeeded in keeping up with us, sharing with servile fidelity in our sorrows and privations. The story of this unfortunate girl is worth narrating. Whether she had lost herself, or whether her romantic spirit prompted her to seek for adventure, I do not know, but she was found secreted in the crypt of the Cathedral of St. Michael. They brought her to one of the French generals, who took her under his protection. He afterwards pretended to be in love with her, and made her his mistress under promise of marriage. With the true heroism of virtue she suffered every misery and privation. She was about to become a mother, and was proud of her condition and of her fidelity in following her husband. But when the man on whose promises she relied learned that the army was not to stay at Smolensk, he resolved to sever a tie which he had never regarded otherwise than as a pastime. This black-hearted scoundrel, whose bosom was closed to every sentiment of pity, announced to the innocent girl, under some plausible pretext, that they must part. The unhappy creature uttered a cry of despair. She declared that having sacrificed her home and her good name for one whom she already regarded as her lawful husband, she looked upon it as her duty to follow him to the world's end—that neither fatigue nor danger should deter her in her resolution to cling to the man she loved.

"The general, unmoved by her fidelity, curtly repeated that they must part—in the first place because circumstances rendered it impossible to maintain women on the march; and secondly, because he was already married; in short, she had best return to Moscow, where no doubt a handsome sweetheart awaited her. The wretched girl was stricken dumb with despair at this announcement. Pale as death, paler than when they found her among the vaults of the Cathedral in the Kremlin, she was unable for many minutes to open her lips. Then she began to weep and moan, and, overwhelmed with grief, she fell into a swoon, of which her betrayer availed himself—not to escape a trying farewell, but to fly from the Russians whose cries were drawing nearer and nearer."

"The scarcity of fodder for the horses," says René Bourgeois, "was appalling. Handfuls of decaying straw, the broken and trampled remnants of former bivouacs, or thatch torn from the roofs of what few huts remained, furnished all their provender, and they perished in the camp by thousands. The sheets of ice that covered the roads gave them their *coup de grâce*—in a short time the cavalry was a thing of the past, and dismounted horsemen swelled the ranks of the pedestrians. The regiments became hopelessly mixed up, order and discipline were no longer maintained. The soldiers took no notice of their officers, and the officers took no thought for the soldiers, every one plodded along at his own sweet will.

French Fugitives.

"This disorderly rabble was clad in the most extraordinary garments—in the skins and hides of various animals, in women's petticoats of every conceivable hue, in great shawls, in scraps of blankets, in old horse-cloths with a hole in the middle for the head, and hanging down all round. As their boots were gone, their feet were wrapped in tattered rags and shreds of felt and sheep-skin, tied up with bits of straw. . . . Above these vermin-infested rags were to be seen sunken faces black with the smoke of camp-fires, smeared with all manner of filth—faces on which were imprinted horror, despair, and the haunting terror of hunger, cold, and all their other ills. There was no centre or flank; the whole army was huddled into a heap, with no cavalry or artillery, and moved forward, baggage and all, in indescribable confusion."

* * * * * * *

At last the French army arrived at the Beresina, where it must have been annihilated but for the folly of the Russian General Chichagof, who had been directed to cut off its retreat.

"It must be admitted," says René Bourgeois, "that throughout the campaign the Russians made the most astounding blunders. At the Beresina, in particular, they might have taken the whole French army prisoner without spilling a drop of blood. Our escape was due solely to the incapacity of the Russian commander, Admiral Chichagof, who took over the command of the army of Moldavia from Kutuzof. . . . He was a young courtier, self-confident and vain, who enjoyed the fullest confidence and favour of the Emperor Alexander."

A perusal of the despatches which this youthful favourite wrote, with the pompous French periods, the confident and condescending criticisms of anybody and everybody, not even excepting Kutuzof, enables us to appreciate his fatuity and incompetence.

The French, having hoodwinked the Russian general—or rather, admiral—proceeded to throw bridges over the Beresina.

"*Esprit de corps* in the different arms of the service," says Marbot, "is of course worthy of all honour, but it does no harm now and then to moderate it under certain circumstances. This was a task beyond the powers of those in command of the artillery and engineers at the passage of the Beresina; for sappers and gunners each insisted that they alone, and no others, were going to build the bridges. The result was that the work remained at a complete standstill until the Emperor, who arrived on the 26/14, settled the dispute by ordering the artillery to build one bridge and the engineers the other."

"Who shall number the victims of this passage," says S. U., "or describe the scenes of horror and destruction? Amid inconceivable confusion the Emperor endeavoured to facilitate the passage by ordering a multitude of vehicles to be burned under his own eyes; the Prince of Neuchâtel led several horses over with his own hands."

"One's pen," says Constant, "simply refuses to depict the scenes of horror that were witnessed at the Beresina. Vehicles of all kinds drove up to the bridge literally over heaps of bodies that lay blocking up the road. Whole crowds of wretched soldiers fell into the river and perished among the blocks of ice. Others clung to the planks of the bridge, suspended over the abyss, until the wheels of the carts passed over their fingers and compelled them to relinquish their hold. Caissons, wagons, drivers, and horses went down together."

"One woman was seen," says de B., "caught between the blocks of ice, holding up her baby in the air and imploring the passers-by to save it from a watery grave."

"I saw soldiers," says the author of the *Journal de la Guerre*, "clinging to their neighbours to save themselves from falling. I saw the feeble, tottering as they went, yet still pressing feverishly forward, jostling one another so that whole rows of them fell into the water together, top-

Ney and the Staff.

pling over like houses of cards. If a Cossack showed himself, or any one repeated the word 'Cossack' two or three times, the whole army of fugitives were seized with such panic that they dashed hither and thither, backwards and forwards, slipping and falling headlong into the river."

* * * * * * *

Beyond the Beresina the cold became even more severe. The whole country round was covered with snow. Even the villages, buried in the drifts, no longer broke the monotony of the horizon, and they could only be distinguished by the smoke and flame of burning houses fired by the inhabitants or by fugitives from the French army.

"The soldiers," says Ségur, "were perpetually burning down whole houses, merely for the sake of warming themselves for a few minutes at the blaze. The glare would attract some poor creatures who had partly lost their wits through cold and privation. Grinding their teeth, and yelling with unearthly laughter, they would leap into and perish in the flames, while their comrades looked on with calm unconcerned countenances. The bystanders sometimes pulled out their burnt and disfigured bodies and, horrible to relate, devoured them."

"The road was so thickly covered with dead and dying," says the author of the *Journal de la Guerre*, "that one had to exercise the greatest care to avoid treading on them. Marching, as we were, in a compact mass, one had no choice but to step on or over these poor wretches who lay writhing in their death agony. One could hear the death rattle in their throats, but it was useless to think of giving them any assistance."

"In the sheds by the roadside," says Ségur, "were to be seen spectacles of indescribable horror. Many of our men who sheltered there for the night found their comrades in the morning frozen by scores around the remains of the fires. In order to get out of these charnel-houses one had to clamber over heaps of poor wretches, many of whom were still breathing."

"I could never understand," says Constant, "why in our wretched plight we must needs continue to play the *rôle* of conquerors, and drag captives along with us, to the infinite discomfort of our own men. The unfortunate Russians, half dead with fatigue and famine, were herded together in a large open space like cattle. A multitude of them died in the night; the rest sat huddled together for the sake of warmth. Those who died of the cold continued to sit cheek by jowl with the living. Some of the prisoners ate the bodies of their dead comrades."

It is interesting to note that all this went on within a few yards of Napoleon's head-quarters—a wooden house, the windows of which had to be stuffed with hay and straw.

When Napoleon left the troops, their confusion, and consequently their misery, became, if possible, worse than before. The army needed the arm of a giant to help it to bear its miseries, but meanwhile the giant abandoned it. On the very first night one of the generals refused to obey orders, and the Marshal in command of the rear-guard had to attend the King's head-quarters almost alone. Round these head-quarters lay all that was left of the Grande Armée, 3000 files of the Old and Young Guard. When Napoleon's departure became known, discipline suffered a severe blow, even among these seasoned veterans.

"There were some among them who had covered two hundred leagues without daring to look back; *sauve qui peut* was the order of the day.

"All that were left of the baggage-wagons after the

passage of the Beresina, including the Emperor's, had to be finally abandoned near the Tamari post-house at the foot of an ice-covered declivity on the further side of Vilna. The continual arrival of more vehicles behind those that had been abandoned intensified the prevailing lawlessness and disorder. Russians and French were soon mingled in an inextinguishable crowd round the wagon-loads of French treasure."

"Every one," says the author of the *Journal de la Guerre*, "took what he pleased from the contents of the carriages and carts. I saw wagons full of gold and silver looted in the middle of the road, partly by Frenchmen, partly by Cossacks, without any display of hostility between them. I made my way into the midst of them, and not one of the Russians attempted to molest me."

At the Russian frontier, two kings, one prince, eight marshals, a few generals and officers, roaming aimlessly about, together with a few men of the Old Guard who still carried muskets, were all that remained of the Grande Armée.

V

THE MARSHALS

Marshal Ney.

THE lack of discipline in the army must in great measure be ascribed to the fact that the kings, marshals, princes, and dukes who held the chief command were wanting in self-restraint and in the virtue of unmurmuring obedience to the Emperor.

As is well known, at the beginning of the campaign the King of Westphalia took umbrage at a well-deserved rebuke which his lack of energy had drawn upon him, and went home, leaving his army corps without even transferring the command, or communicating to any one the orders he had received.

The relations between Marshal Berthier, the chief of the staff, and Marshal Davout, between the latter and Murat, and, indeed, between many of the other commanders, were so strained that they distinctly hindered the progress of the campaign. In 1809 Berthier had been for some days Davout's superior officer. Disregarding his orders, Davout won a battle and saved the army from annihilation; but he incurred the bitter hatred of his chief. When they met again at the opening of the last campaign they had a fierce altercation in the presence of the Emperor. Davout went so far as to say that Berthier must be "either a fool or a traitor," and they threatened one another with personal violence. Berthier, as is well known, was incapable of initiative. He merely served as an echo of Napoleon's wishes; but he was very docile and industrious. A firm believer in the Emperor's maxim—"Never attempt two things at the same time; concentrate all your efforts on one," he did not approve of the war of 1812, but bowed to necessity. He entered upon the campaign without conviction or enthusiasm, deeply disquieted by the position of the French armies in Spain.

In the campaign of 1812 the Duke of Neufchâtel displayed, to say the least, very little foresight. Davout was no doubt the best strategist in the whole galaxy of Napoleon's satellites, but he was of a quarrelsome, envious, and vindictive disposition. The methodical and patient genius of Davout formed a striking contrast to the impulsiveness of Murat. This was the cause of many misunderstandings between these two commanders, old comrades though they were, and almost of the same age, who had risen side by side through the various grades. They were accustomed to obey Napoleon, but were wanting in command over themselves. This was especially the case with Murat. The relations of Murat and Davout throw so interesting a light on the system of command in the Grande Armée that they are worthy of some attention.

Davout was put at one time under Murat's command. He submitted to his orders, but most unwillingly, and although he swallowed his wrath, he ceased all direct communication with the Emperor. Napoleon, however, ordered him to send in his reports as before, for Murat's despatches were hopeless. This was just what Davout wanted, and from that time forth he ceased to recognize the authority of the King of Naples. The extent of their jealousy may be judged from the fact that in an engagement one of Davout's batteries refused to fire on the orders of Murat. The commander of the battery urged the Marshal's own orders in justification of his refusal; he had been told to take orders from no one but Davout under pain of losing his command.

The next day the two rivals had a lively altercation in Napoleon's presence. The King accused the Duke of obstinate resistance to his wishes, and with secret enmity towards himself, an enmity, he averred, that had its origin in Egypt. He went so far as to propose a settlement of the quarrel man to man, urging that the army should not be allowed to suffer through their private differences. Davout, on the other hand, attacked the King furiously for his wanton recklessness, and painted a lively picture of the disorder that reigned in the advance-guard of the army. "I must admit," said he, according to Ségur, "that the Russians are effecting their retreat in the most admirable order. They halt wherever they find it convenient instead of consulting the wishes of our boastful friend Murat. They select their positions so well, and defend them so skilfully, with an eye to the forces at their disposal, and the time they wish to gain, that their tactics must have been carefully thought out long ago.

Marshal Davout.

"They never abandon a position until it becomes untenable. At night they turn in early and leave only as many troops under arms as are absolutely necessary for the defence of their positions and for allowing the rest of the troops an opportunity for sleep and refreshment.

"But the King, instead of profiting by this excellent example, takes no account of time or of the position and strength of the enemy. He is always appearing in the skirmishing line, prancing up and down in front of the enemy or trying to worry them on the flanks, losing his temper, yelling himself hoarse with orders, wasting cartridges and ammunition, men and horses, for no reason whatever, and keeping all the troops under arms until late into the night.

"It wrings my heart to see the wretched men jostling one another in the dark, and groping for fodder and water, firewood and eatables, unable to find their own quarters, and spending the night shouting to one another. It is not only the advance-guard that suffers by this—the whole of our cavalry is visibly worn out. Let Murat do what he likes with his own cavalry, but so long as Davout is in command of the infantry of the 1st Army Corps, he will not let him worry them to death."

"The King in reply hit as hard as his opponent. The Emperor heard them out, rolling a Russian cannon-ball about with his foot. It seemed as if he enjoyed the differences between his officers," says Ségur.

When he dismissed them he cautiously remarked to Davout that "no one man could combine all the virtues; that even if the Duke of Eckmühl—Davout—knew how to win battles, it did not follow that he could lead an advance-guard; and that if Murat had been told off to pursue Bagration in Lithuania he would very likely have prevented his escape."

Napoleon subsequently advised the two rivals to do their best to pull better together for the future; but how much they profited by this recommendation may be gathered from Belliard's despatch to the Emperor on the battle of Viazma. "On the far side of the town the enemy appeared in a convenient position behind a trench, apparently quite prepared for an engagement. The cavalry at once went into action on either flank; but when the time came for the infantry, and the King in person was heading one of Davout's divisions, the Marshal galloped up and ordered the men to halt. He then expressed loud disapproval of the intended movement, and had high words with the King, flatly forbidding the generals to obey his orders. Murat endeavoured to insist, and reminded Davout of his position, but his protests were useless. Meanwhile the chance was gone. The King had to content himself with sending word to the Emperor that it was absolutely impossible to carry on the command under the circumstances, and asking him to choose between him and Davout.

"Napoleon was very angry. He sided with Murat against Davout, but the former could not forget the insult to which his old enemy had given public expression. The longer he considered the matter the fiercer grew his indignation. The affront, he determined, was one that his sword alone could avenge. What mattered the Emperor's decision, or the Emperor's anger? He must wipe out the insult with his own hand!

"He was about to demand satisfaction of Davout, when Belliard stopped him, and represented the consequences of such an act, and the bad example it would set."

On the whole, Davout's accusations were fully justified. In the course of the campaign Murat's precipitation was on more than one occasion the cause of serious loss to the invading army. The repeated attacks of the cavalry on the square formed by Neverofsky's retreating division, when the Russians coolly and successfully sustained forty charges led by the King of Naples in person, is an example in point. When he had sacrificed the whole of his cavalry Murat practically took no further part in the campaign. He merely drove about in the carriage with Napoleon, or followed him on foot, with a stick in his hand and a fur-coat buttoned up to his chin.

The order and discipline of Davout's own division were not, however, proof against the miseries of the retreat, and after the battle of Viazma Napoleon received a very clear report from Ney informing him of the disastrous result of the battle.

"If better order had been maintained," said Ney, "the result would probably have been very different. The most appalling feature of the whole business was the disorganization of Davout's division, which unfortunately spread to the other troops. I feel obliged to tell your Majesty the whole truth, and however unpleasant it is to have to find fault with any of my fellow-officers, I am compelled to state that under the circumstances I cannot answer for the safety of the retreat."

Napoleon himself had occasion to complain of Davout's dilatoriness. He had fallen behind five days' march when he should, at the most, have been only three days in the rear. These complaints were repeated in all quarters, and it was said that his movements against the Cossacks had no other effect than to detain the army.

"*Mon cousin*," wrote Napoleon to Berthier, losing all patience, "tell the Duke of Elchingen—Ney—to take command of the rear-guard and to move as quickly as possible—the Duke of Eckmühl keeps the Regent and Prince Poniatowski waiting every time a Cossack shouts 'Hurrah.'"

Napoleon could not have found a better person than the Duke of Eckmühl to carry out his plan of taking vengeance on the Russians by burning everything on the line of march. When he was in charge of the rear-guard he distinguished himself by the zeal and completeness with which he burned every manor and village within reach.

When snow and frost appeared Davout was utterly unable to meet the altered conditions. Thrown out of his ordinary routine, he was driven to despair by the disorder that prevailed, and was among the first to lose heart.

"Davout," says Ségur, "entered Orcha with 4000 men, all that remained of 70,000! The Marshal lost all his personal belongings; he had no linen, and was literally dying of hunger. When he was offered a piece of bread he positively leaped upon it; when they gave him a handkerchief and he wiped his face for the first time for many days, it was covered with hoar-frost. 'A man must be made of iron,' cried the Marshal, 'to stand such privations! There are such things as physical impossibilities; there is a limit to human endurance, and that limit we have long since passed!'"

Ney was made of very different metal. When Napoleon refused to let him have the Guards for a final attack in the plains of Borodino, he did not hesitate to proclaim aloud, that "if the Emperor is tired of fighting, let him take his d——d way to the Tuileries, and leave us to do what is necessary."

Amid the universal despair and confusion of the retreat,

Ney proved himself not only the "bravest of the brave," as he had always been, but an obedient and efficient officer —he was the true hero of the retreat of the Grande Armée. Of a remarkably strong constitution, Ney was a man of action, not of sentiment. Highly characteristic was his answer to a wounded man who besought him to save him. "What would you have me do?" said he. "You are but one of the victims of the war—*voilà tout!*" When Ney was told of the death of the young de Noailles, he answered, without moving a muscle—"Well, well, his turn has come; it is better that we should lament his death than that he should lament ours." The following incident is equally characteristic of the man. At Smolensk Ney was abandoned by Marshal Davout, and lost almost all his troops, artillery, and baggage. When, by circuitous roads, through bogs and forests, he overtook Napoleon with a handful of men, and the Duke of Eckmühl began to excuse his conduct, Ney merely replied—"I have not accused your Grace of anything. God sees us, and He is your Judge."

"Ney saw," says Ségur, "that some one must bear the brunt of the retreat, and of his own free will he accepted the post of danger, undertaking to cover the rear of the army."

"The Russians were advancing," says an eye-witness of one engagement, "under cover of the forest and of the wagons we had abandoned, and firing on Ney's troops with great effect. The latter were on the point of taking to flight when the Marshal seized a rifle, rushed up, and led them into action. He replied to the Russian fire with as little concern for his own safety as if he did not know what it was to be a father and a husband, wealthy, noble, and respected. Although playing the part of a private soldier he did not cease to be a general. Taking advantage of the ground, he made full use of the cover afforded by hills and houses. In this way he secured for the army a respite of twenty-four hours. On the two following days he displayed the same heroism ; from Viazma to Smolensk he was fighting for ten days without a break."

Military history probably furnishes few instances in which a commander has extricated himself from so difficult a position as that in which Ney found himself when, as we have already said, he was abandoned by Davout on the road from Smolensk to Krasnoye. The rear-guard of the Grande Armée was caught in a trap ; Miloradovitch's forces lay across the road and on either flank, so that it was absolutely impossible to pass. Ney, however, could not bring himself to yield, and did his best to cut his way through. Again and again he led his exhausted troops against the enemy's bayonets; but musketry volleys and the fire of 40 guns at a range of 250 paces could not fail of their effect. At last the greater portion of the French division, consisting of 12,000 men, surrendered, and all their artillery, 27 guns, baggage, etc., passed into the hands of the enemy. Marshal Ney, however, was not one of the prisoners. He took advantage of the darkness to escape with 3000 men, who readily followed him.

The means which he employed to effect his escape were perhaps not quite legitimate. The Marshal detained the officer who came from General Miloradovitch with an offer of surrender, and while he was awaiting a final answer, slipped away, first in the direction of Smolensk, and then by a circuitous flank march to Orcha.

The details of this retreat and final escape have an air rather of romance than of stern fact. The boldness with which the operation was conceived and executed is nothing less than astounding. "The eyes of every man in the little detachment that slipped so quietly out of the hands of the Russians," says Fezensac, "were turned towards the Marshal. He showed no trace of anxiety or irresolution, but no one dared to question him. Ney said to one of his staff-officers who was standing by—

"*Nous ne sommes pas bien.*"

"*Qu' allez vous faire?*" asked the officer.

"*Passer le Dniéper.*"

"*Où est le chemin?*"

"*Nous le trouverons.*"

"*Et s'il n'est pas gelé?*"

"*Il le sera.*"

It was as he said. The fugitives came upon a lame peasant who served them as a guide. The ice was only just strong enough to bear. Nevertheless, most of the troops got across safely after abandoning all their baggage. The Cossacks started in pursuit the following day, but in forty-eight hours Ney made his way by river and forest, after much fighting, to the town of Orcha.

It is said that when Napoleon heard of Ney's arrival, he exclaimed with delight—"I have 200,000,000 francs stored in the cellars of the Tuileries. I would willingly give them all to save such a man as Ney."

However brilliant Ney's movements at the battle of Krasnoye may have been, it is impossible to read Napoleon's account of the engagement, in Despatch XXIX., without a smile. With the most ludicrous perversity Napoleon represents the Marshal as victorious.

General Dumas says that after crossing the frontier, he was one day taking coffee at an hotel in Gumbinen, when a stranger entered. He was dressed in a dark overcoat, and wore a long beard. His face was blackened as if it had been burned, and his eyes were bloodshot. "Here I am at last!" he said. "Why, General Dumas, don't you know me?"

"No. Who are you?"

"I am the rear-guard of the Grande Armée—Marshal Ney."

THE END

Richard Clay & Sons, Limited, London & Bungay.

21 BEDFORD STREET, W.C.

Telegraphic Address,
Sunlocks, London

A List of Mr. William Heinemann's Publications and Announcements

August 1898.

The Books mentioned in this List can be obtained to order *by any Bookseller if not in stock, or will be sent by the Publisher on receipt of the published price and postage.*

Index of Authors.

THE WORKS OF LORD BYRON.

EDITED BY WILLIAM ERNEST HENLEY.

TO BE COMPLETED IN TWELVE VOLUMES.

The Letters, Diaries, Controversies, Speeches, &c., in Four, and the Verse in Eight.

Small Crown 8vo, price 5s. net each.

VOLUME I. IS NOW READY.

Vol. I.—LETTERS, 1804–1813. With a Portrait after PHILLIPS.

To be followed by

Vol. V.—VERSE VOLUME I. Containing "Hours of Idleness," "English Bards and Scotch Reviewers," and "Childe Harold." With a Portrait by HOLMES.

"Mr. W. E. Henley is not only steeped to the lips in Byronic poetry, but he has also a very familiar acquaintance with the remarkable characters who formed 'the Byronic set,' and he knows the manners and customs of the Regency epoch to an extent that gives him full mastery of his subject. There is originality in the very form of this edition.

"He manages to give in a few vigorous sentences vivid sketches of the wide circle of Byron's friends and enemies."—*Pall Mall Gazette.*

"The first volume is delightfully handy and the type excellent."
ANDREW LANG.

"These Byron Letters (Vol. I.) Mr. Henley has annotated as never surely were letters annotated before. His notes provide simply a complete series of little biographies—miniature biographies with such vital selection, such concise completion without dry-as-dustness—such interest as no other writer but Mr. Henley could compass. It may fairly be said that he has discovered a new art, the art of biographic cameos. . . . It is safe to say that henceforth the typical edition of Byron can never be separated from these notes. In conclusion, if Byron has waited long for a heaven-sent editor, he has him at last."
Academy.

"Mr. Henley, so far as elucidation and illustration are concerned, is fully equipped."—*Athenæum.*

There will also be an Edition, limited to 150 sets for sale in Great Britain, printed on Van Gelder's hand-made paper, price Six Guineas net, subscriptions for which are now being received.

Art and Decoration.

AN ALMANAC OF TWELVE SPORTS FOR 1898. By WILLIAM NICHOLSON. Twelve Coloured Plates, each illustrating a sport for the month. With accompanying Rhymes by RUDYARD KIPLING. 4to. In Three Editions. *The Library Edition* all sold.

The Popular Edition. Lithographed in Colours on stout Cartridge Paper. Price 2s. 6d.

The Edition de Luxe (Limited). Printed from the Original Woodblocks. Hand-coloured, and signed by the Artist. In Vellum Portfolio. Price £12 12s. net.

AN ALPHABET. By WILLIAM NICHOLSON. 4to. In Three Editions.

The Popular Edition 5s.

The Library Edition (Limited). Lithographed in Colours on Dutch Handmade Paper, mounted on brown paper and bound in cloth, Gilt Edges. Price 12s. 6d. net.

The Edition de Luxe (Limited). Printed from the Original Woodblocks. Hand-coloured, and signed by the Artist. In Vellum Portfolio. Price £21 net.

PORTRAITS BY MR. NICHOLSON of HER MAJESTY THE QUEEN, MADAME SARAH BERNHARDT, LORD ROBERTS, MR. WHISTLER, MR. RUDYARD KIPLING, MR. CECIL RHODES, and PRINCE BISMARCK, are now supplied separately, mounted on card for framing, price 2s. 6d. net each.

⁂ *A few copies of each Portrait printed from the Original Woodblocks, Hand-coloured, and signed by the Artist, are still obtainable. Price £2 2s. each net.*

A HISTORY OF DANCING: From the Earliest Ages to Our Own Times. From the French of GASTON VUILLIER. With 24 Plates in Photogravure and 409 Illustrations in the Text. In One Volume, 4to. Price 36s. net.

⁂ *Also 35 copies printed on Japanese vellum (containing 3 additional Plates), with a duplicate set of the Plates on India paper for framing. Each copy numbered and signed, price £12 12s. net.*

MEISSONIER. His Life, and His Art. By VALLERY C. O. GREARD, de l'Académie Française. Translated from the French by LADY MARY LOYD and FLORENCE SIMMONDS. With 38 full-page plates, 20 in Photogravure and 18 in Colour, and 200 Text Illustrations. Imperial 8vo, £1 16s. net.

ANTONIO ALLEGRI DA CORREGGIO: His Life, his Friends, and his Time. By CORRADO RICCI, Director of the Royal Gallery, Parma. Translated by FLORENCE SIMMONDS. With 16 Photogravure Plates, 21 full-page Plates in Tint, and 190 ustrations in the Text. Imperial 8vo, £2 2s. net. Also in 14 parts, price 2s. 6d. each net.

⁂ *Also a special edition printed on Japanese vellum, limited to 100 copies with duplicate plates on India paper. Price £12 12s. net.*

REMBRANDT: His Life, his Work, and his Time. By EMILE MICHEL, Member of the Institute of France. Translated by FLORENCE SIMMONDS. Edited and Prefaced by FREDERICK WEDMORE. Second Edition, Enlarged, with 76 full-page Plates, and 250 Illustrations in the Text. In One Volume, Gilt top, or in Two Volumes, imperial 8vo £2 2s. net.

*** *A few copies of the* EDITION DE LUXE *of the First Edition, printed on Japanese vellum with India proof duplicates of the photogravures, are still on sale, price £12 12s. net.*

REMBRANDT. Seventeen of his Masterpieces from the collection of his Pictures in the Cassel Gallery. Reproduced in Photogravure by the Berlin Photographic Company. With an Essay by FREDERICK WEDMORE. In large portfolio 27½ inches × 20 inches.

The first twenty-five impressions of each plate are numbered and signed, and of these only fourteen are for sale in England at the net price of Twenty Guineas *the set. The price of the impressions after the first twenty-five is* Twelve Guineas *net, per set.*

MASTERPIECES OF GREEK SCULPTURE. A Series of Essays on the History of Art. By ADOLF FURTWÄNGLER. Authorised Translation. Edited by EUGENIE SELLERS. With 19 full page and 200 text Illustrations. Imperial 8vo, £3 3s. net.

*** *Also an* EDITION DE LUXE *on Japanese vellum, limited to* 50 *numbered copies in Two Volumes, price* £10 10s. *net.*

THE HOURS OF RAPHAEL, IN OUTLINE. Together with the Ceiling of the Hall where they were originally painted. By MARY E. WILLIAMS. Folio, cloth. £2 2s. net.

BEAUTY AND ART. By ALDAM HEATON. Crown 8vo, cloth, 6s.

A CATALOGUE OF THE ACCADEMIA DELLE BELLE ARTI AT VENICE. With Biographical Notices of the Painters and Reproductions of some of their Works. Edited by E. M. KEARY. Crown 8vo, cloth, 2s. 6d. net; paper, 2s. net.

A CATALOGUE OF THE MUSEO DEL PRADO AT MADRID. Compiled by E. LAWSON. Crown 8vo, cloth, 3s. net; paper, 2s. 6d. net.

ANIMAL SYMBOLISM IN ECCLESIASTICAL ARCHITECTURE. By E. P. EVANS. With a Bibliography and Seventy-eight Illustrations, crown 8vo, 9s.

Biography, Correspondence, and History.

NEW LETTERS OF NAPOLEON I. Omitted from the Edition published under the auspices of Napoleon III. Translated from the French by LADY MARY LOYD. In One Volume, demy 8vo, with Frontispiece, price 15*s*. net.

THE PAGET PAPERS. Diplomatic and other Correspondence of THE RIGHT HON. SIR ARTHUR PAGET, G.C.B., 1794–1807. With two Appendices, 1808 and 1828–1829. Arranged and Edited by his son, The Right Hon. SIR AUGUSTUS B. PAGET, G.C.B., late Her Majesty's Ambassador in Vienna. With Notes by Mrs. J. R. GREEN. New Edition with Index. In Two Volumes, demy 8vo, with Portraits, 32*s*. net.

DE QUINCEY MEMORIALS. Being Letters and other Records here first Published, with Communications from COLERIDGE, the WORDSWORTHS, HANNAH MORE, PROFESSOR WILSON, and others. Edited with Introduction, Notes, and Narrative, by ALEXANDER H. JAPP, LL.D., F.R.S.E. In Two Volumes, demy 8vo, cloth, with Portraits, 30*s*. net.

LETTERS OF SAMUEL TAYLOR COLERIDGE. Edited by ERNEST HARTLEY COLERIDGE. With 16 Portraits and Illustrations. In Two Volumes, demy 8vo, £1 12*s*.

THE LIFE OF NELSON. By ROBERT SOUTHEY. A New Edition. Edited by DAVID HANNAY. Crown 8vo, gilt, with Portraits of Lord Nelson after HOPPNER and Lady Hamilton after ROMNEY, price 6*s*.

ROBERT, EARL NUGENT. A Memoir. By CLAUD NUGENT. Demy 8vo, with a number of Portraits and other Illustrations. [*In preparation.*

THE LIFE OF JUDGE JEFFREYS. By H. B. IRVING, M.A. Oxon. Demy 8vo, with Three Portraits and a Facsimile, 12*s*. 6*d*. net.

PETER THE GREAT. By K. WALISZEWSKI, Author of "The Romance of an Empress," "The Story of a Throne." Translated from the French by Lady MARY LOYD. With a Portrait. 8vo, cloth, 6*s*.; or Library Edition, in Two Volumes, 8vo, 28*s*.

CARDINAL MANNING. From the French of FRANCIS DE PRESSENSÉ by E. INGALL. Crown 8vo, 5*s*.

THE PALMY DAYS OF NANCE OLDFIELD. By EDWARD ROBINS. With Twelve Illustrations, 8vo.

AS OTHERS SAW HIM. A Retrospect, A.D. 54. Crown 8vo, gilt top 6*s*.

BROTHER AND SISTER. A Memoir and the Letters of ERNEST and HENRIETTE RENAN. Translated by Lady MARY LOYD. Demy 8vo, with Two Portraits in Photogravure, and Four Illustrations, 14*s*.

CHARLES GOUNOD. Autobiographical Reminiscences with Family Letters and Notes on Music. Translated by the Hon. W. HELY HUTCHINSON. Demy 8vo, with Portrait, 10*s*. 6*d*.

MEMOIRS. By CHARLES GODFREY LELAND (HANS BREITMANN). Second Edition. 8vo, with Portrait, price 7*s*. 6*d*.

EDMOND AND JULES DE GONCOURT. Letters and Leaves from their Journals. Selected. In Two Volumes, 8vo, with Eight Portraits, 32*s*.

ALEXANDER III. OF RUSSIA. By CHARLES LOWE, M.A., Author of "Prince Bismarck: an Historical Biography." Crown 8vo, with Portrait in Photogravure, 6*s*.

PRINCE BISMARCK. An Historical Biography. By CHARLES LOWE, M.A. With Portraits. Crown 8vo, 6*s*.

CATHERINE SFORZA. A Study. By COUNT PASOLINI. Adapted from the Italian by PAUL SYLVESTER. Demy 8vo, with many Illustrations. [*In preparation.*

VILLIERS DE L'ISLE ADAM: His Life and Works. From the French of VICOMTE ROBERT DU PONTAVICE DE HEUSSEY. By Lady MARY LOYD. With Portrait and Facsimile. Crown 8vo, cloth, 10*s*. 6*d*.

THE LIFE OF HENRIK IBSEN. By HENRIK JÆGER. Translated by CLARA BELL. With the Verse done into English from the Norwegian Original by EDMUND GOSSE. Crown 8vo, cloth, 6*s*.

RECOLLECTIONS OF MIDDLE LIFE. By FRANCISQUE SARCEY. Translated by E. L. CAREY. 8vo, with Portrait, 10*s*. 6*d*.

TWENTY-FIVE YEARS IN THE SECRET SERVICE. The Recollections of a Spy. By Major HENRI LE CARON. With New Preface. 8vo, boards, price 2*s*. 6*d*., or cloth, 3*s*. 6*d*.

*** *The Library Edition, with Portraits and Facsimiles, 8vo, 14s., is still on sale.*

STUDIES IN FRANKNESS. By CHARLES WHIBLEY. Crown 8vo, with Frontispiece, price 7*s*. 6*d*.

A BOOK OF SCOUNDRELS. By CHARLES WHIBLEY. Crown 8vo, with Frontispiece, price *7s. 6d.*

GREAT LIVES AND EVENTS.

Uniformly bound in cloth, 6s. each volume.

SIXTY YEARS OF EMPIRE: 1837-1897. A Review of the Period. With over 70 Portraits and Diagrams.

RECOLLECTIONS OF COUNT LEO TOLSTOY. Together with a Letter to the Women of France on the "Kreutzer Sonata." By C. A. BEHRS. Translated from the Russian by C. E. TURNER, English Lecturer in the University of St. Petersburg. With Portrait.

THE FAMILY LIFE OF HEINRICH HEINE. Illustrated by one hundred and twenty-two hitherto unpublished letters addressed by him to different members of his family. Edited by his nephew, Baron LUDWIG VON EMBDEN, and translated by CHARLES GODFREY LELAND. With 4 Portraits.

THE NATURALIST OF THE SEA-SHORE. The Life of Philip Henry Gosse. By his son, EDMUND GOSSE, Hon. M.A., Trinity College, Cambridge. With a Portrait.

MEMOIRS OF THE PRINCE DE JOINVILLE. Translated from the French by Lady MARY LOYD. With 78 Illustrations from drawings by the Author.

ALFRED, LORD TENNYSON. A Study of His Life and Work. By ARTHUR WAUGH, B.A. Oxon. With Twenty Illustrations from Photographs specially taken for this Work. Five Portraits, and Facsimile of Tennyson's MS.

NAPOLEON AND THE FAIR SEX. From the French of FRÉDÉRIC MASSON. With a Portrait.

PETER THE GREAT. By K. WALISZEWSKI. Translated from the French by Lady MARY LOYD. With a Portrait.

THE STORY OF A THRONE. Catherine II. of Russia. From the French of K. WALISZEWSKI. With a Portrait.

THE ROMANCE OF AN EMPRESS. Catherine II. of Russia. From the French of K. WALISZEWSKI. With a Portrait.

A FRIEND OF THE QUEEN. Marie Antoinette and Count Fersen. From the French of PAUL GAULOT. Two Portraits.

THE WOMEN OF HOMER. By WALTER COPLAND PERRY. With numerous Illustrations, large crown 8vo, 6*s*.

THE LOVE LETTERS OF MR. H. AND MISS R. 1775-1779. Edited by GILBERT BURGESS. Square crown 8vo, 5*s*.

LETTERS OF A BARITONE. By FRANCIS WALKER. Square crown 8vo, 5*s*.

LETTERS OF A COUNTRY VICAR. Translated from the French of YVES LE QUERDEC. By M. GORDON HOLMES. Crown 8vo, 5*s*.

ISRAEL AMONG THE NATIONS. Translated from the French of ANATOLE LEROY-BEAULIEU, Member of the Institute of France. Crown 8vo, 7*s*. 6*d*.

THE JEW AT HOME. Impressions of a Summer and Autumn Spent with Him in Austria and Russia. By JOSEPH PENNELL. With Illustrations by the Author. 4to, cloth, 5*s*

THE NEW EXODUS. A Study of Israel in Russia. By HAROLD FREDERIC. Demy 8vo, Illustrated, 16*s*.

SPANISH PROTESTANTS IN THE SIXTEENTH CENTURY, Compiled from Dr. Wilken's German Work. By RACHEL CHALLICE. With an Introduction by the Most Rev. LORD PLUNKET, late Archbishop of Dublin, and a Preface by the Rev. Canon FLEMING. Crown 8vo, 4*s*. 6*d*. net.

QUEEN JOANNA I. OF NAPLES, SICILY, AND JERUSALEM; Countess of Provence, Forcalquier, and Piedmont. An Essay on her Times. By ST. CLAIR BADDELEY. Imperial 8vo, with numerous Illustrations, 16*s*.

CHARLES III. OF NAPLES AND URBAN VI.; also **CECCO D'ASCOLI**, Poet, Astrologer, Physican. Two Historical Essays. By ST. CLAIR BADDELEY. With Illustrations, 8vo, cloth, 10*s*. 6*d*.

ROBERT THE WISE AND HIS HEIRS, 1278-1352. By ST. CLAIR BADDELEY. 8vo, 21*s*.

MY PARIS NOTE-BOOK. By ALBERT D. VANDAM, Author of "An Englishman in Paris." Demy 8vo, price 6*s*.

UNDERCURRENTS OF THE SECOND EMPIRE. By ALBERT D. VANDAM. Demy 8vo, cloth, 7*s*. 6*d*. net.

STUDIES IN DIPLOMACY. By Count BENEDETTI, French Ambassador at the Court of Berlin. Demy 8vo, with a Portrait, 10*s.* 6*d.*

AN AMBASSADOR OF THE VANQUISHED: Viscount Elie De Gontaut-Biron's Mission to Berlin, 1871–1877. From his Diaries and Memoranda. By the DUKE DE BROGLIE. Translated with Notes by ALBERT D. VANDAM. In One Volume, 8vo, 10*s.* 6*d.*

A HISTORY OF THE LIVERPOOL PRIVATEERS, and Letters of Marque; with an account of the Liverpool Slave Trade. By GOMER WILLIAMS. In One Volume, demy 8vo, price 12*s.* net.

THE CASTLES OF ENGLAND: their Story and Structure, By Sir JAMES D. MACKENZIE, Bart. Dedicated by gracious permission to H.M. the Queen. In Two Volumes, Imperial 8vo, with 40 full-page Plates, and over 150 Illustrations in the Text and many Plans. Price £3 3*s.* net.

KRUPP'S STEEL WORKS. By Professor F. C. G. MÜLLER. With 88 Illustrations. Authorised Translation. 4to, price 25*s.* net.

THE LITTLE MANX NATION. (Lectures delivered at the Royal Institution, 1891.) By HALL CAINE, Author of "The Bondman," "The Scapegoat," &c. Crown 8vo, cloth, 3*s.* 6*d.*; paper, 2*s.* 6*d.*

DENMARK: its History, Topography, Language, Literature. Fine Arts, Social Life, and Finance. Edited by H. WEITEMEYER. Demy 8vo, cloth, with Map, 12*s.* 6*d.*

*** *Dedicated, by permission, to H.R.H. the Princess of Wales.*

THE REALM OF THE HABSBURGS. By SIDNEY WHITMAN, Author of "Imperial Germany." Crown 8vo, 7*s.* 6*d.*

IMPERIAL GERMANY. A Critical Study of Fact and Character. By SIDNEY WHITMAN. New Edition, Revised and Enlarged. Crown 8vo, cloth, 2*s.* 6*d.*; paper, 2*s.*

THE GENESIS OF THE UNITED STATES. A Narrative of the Movement in England, 1605–1616, which resulted in the Plantation of North America by Englishmen, disclosing the Contest between England and Spain for the Possession of the Soil now occupied by the United States of America; set forth through a series of Historical Manuscripts now first printed, together with a Re-issue of Rare Contemporaneous Tracts, accompanied by Bibliographical Memoranda, Notes, and Brief Biographies. Collected, Arranged, and Edited by ALEXANDER BROWN, F.R.H.S. With 100 Portraits, Maps, and Plans. In Two Volumes, royal 8vo, buckram, £3 13*s.* 6*d.* net.

Travel and Adventure.

THE INDIAN FRONTIER WAR. Being an Account of the Mohmund and Tirah Expeditions, 1897. By LIONEL JAMES, Special Correspondent for Reuter's Agency and Artist for the *Graphic*. With 32 full-page Illustrations from Drawings by the Author, and Photographs. and 10 Plans and Maps. 8vo, price *7s. 6d.*

CUBA IN WARTIME. By RICHARD HARDING DAVIS, Author of "Soldiers of Fortune." With numerous Illustrations by FREDERIC REMINGTON. Crown 8vo, price *3s. 6d.*

UNDER THE DRAGON FLAG. My Experiences in the Chino-Japanese War. By JAMES ALLAN. Crown 8vo, *2s.*

MY FOURTH TOUR IN WESTERN AUSTRALIA. By ALBERT F. CALVERT, F.R.G.S. 4to, with many Illustrations and Photographs, price *21s.* net.

ROMANTIC INDIA. By ANDRÉ CHEVRILLON. Translated from the French by WILLIAM MARCHANT. 8vo, *7s. 6d.* net.

THE OUTGOING TURK. Impressions of a Journey through the Western Balkans. By H. C. THOMSON, Author of "The Chitral Campaign." Demy 8vo, with Illustrations from Original Photographs. Price *14s.* net.

THE CHITRAL CAMPAIGN. A Narrative of Events in Chitral, Swat, and Bajour. By H. C. THOMSON. With over 50 Illustrations reproduced from Photographs, and important Diagrams and Map. Second Edition, demy 8vo, *14s. net.*

WITH THE ZHOB FIELD FORCE, 1890. By Captain CRAWFORD MCFALL, K.O.Y.L.I. Demy 8vo, with Illustrations, *18s.*

THE LAND OF THE MUSKEG. By H. SOMERS SOMERSET. Second Edition. Demy 8vo, with Maps and over 100 Illustrations, 280 pp., *14s. net.*

TIMBUCTOO THE MYSTERIOUS. By FELIX DUBOIS. Translated from the French by DIANA WHITE. With 153 Illustrations from Photographs and Drawings made on the spot, and Eleven Maps and Plans. Demy 8vo, *12s. 6d.*

RHODESIA PAST AND PRESENT. By S. J. DU TOIT. In One Volume, 8vo, with Sixteen full-page Illustrations, *7s. 6d.*

THE NEW AFRICA. A Journey up the Chobé and down the Okovanga Rivers. By AUREL SCHULZ, M.D., and AUGUST HAMMAR, C.E. In One Volume, Demy 8vo, with Illustrations, *28s.*

ACTUAL AFRICA; or, The Coming Continent. A Tour of Exploration. By FRANK VINCENT, Author of "The Land of the White Elephant." With Map and over 100 Illustrations, demy 8vo, cloth, price 24*s.*

COREA, OR CHO-SEN, THE LAND OF THE MORNING CALM. By A. HENRY SAVAGE-LANDOR. With 38 Illustrations from Drawings by the Author, and a Portrait, demy 8vo, 18*s.*

NOTES FOR THE NILE. Together with a Metrical Rendering of the Hymns of Ancient Egypt and of the Precepts of Ptah-hotep (the oldest book in the world). By HARDWICKE D. RAWNSLEY, M.A. Imperial 16mo, cloth, 5*s.*

IN THE TRACK OF THE SUN. Readings from the Diary of a Globe-Trotter. By FREDERICK DIODATI THOMPSON. With many Illustrations by Mr. HARRY FENN and from Photographs. 4to, 25*s.*

THE WORKERS. An Experiment in Reality. The East. By WALTER A. WYCKOFF. Crown 8vo, price 3*s.* 6*d.*

THE CANADIAN GUIDE-BOOK. Part I. The Tourist's and Sportsman's Guide to Eastern Canada and Newfoundland, including full descriptions of Routes, Cities, Points of Interest, Summer Resorts, Fishing Places, &c., in Eastern Ontario, The Muskoka District, The St. Lawrence Region, The Lake St. John Country, The Maritime Provinces, Prince Edward Island, and Newfoundland. With an Appendix giving Fish and Game Laws, and Official Lists of Trout and Salmon Rivers and their Lessees. By CHARLES G. D. ROBERTS, Professor of English Literature in King's College, Windsor, N.S. With Maps and many Illustrations. Crown 8vo, limp cloth, 6*s.*

THE CANADIAN GUIDE-BOOK. Part II. WESTERN CANADA. Including the Peninsula and Northern Regions of Ontario, the Canadian Shores of the Great Lakes, the Lake of the Woods Region, Manitoba and "The Great North-West," The Canadian Rocky Mountains and National Park, British Columbia, and Vancouver Island. By ERNEST INGERSOLL. With Maps and many Illustrations. Crown 8vo, limp cloth, 6*s.*

THE GUIDE-BOOK TO ALASKA AND THE NORTH-WEST COAST, including the Shores of Washington, British Columbia, South-Eastern Alaska, the Aleutian and the Sea Islands, the Behring and the Arctic Coasts. By E. R. SCIDMORE. With Maps and many Illustrations. Crown 8vo, limp cloth, 6*s.*

Essays and Belles Lettres, &c.

WILLIAM SHAKESPEARE. A Critical Study. By GEORGE BRANDES, Ph.D. Translated from the Danish by WILLIAM ARCHER, DIANA WHITE, and MARY MORISON. In Two Volumes, roxburgh, gilt top, or buckram uncut, demy 8vo, 24*s*.

SEVENTEENTH-CENTURY STUDIES. A Contribution to the History of English Poetry. By EDMUND GOSSE, Clark Lecturer on English Literature at the University of Cambridge; Hon. M.A. of Trinity College, Cambridge. A New Edition. Crown 8vo, buckram, gilt top, 7*s*. 6*d*.

CRITICAL KIT-KATS. By EDMUND GOSSE. Crown 8vo, buckram, gilt top, 7*s*. 6*d*.

QUESTIONS AT ISSUE. Essays. By EDMUND GOSSE. Crown 8vo, buckram, gilt top, 7*s*. 6*d*.

*** *A Limited Edition on Large Paper*, 25*s*. *net*.

GOSSIP IN A LIBRARY. By EDMUND GOSSE. Third Edition. Crown 8vo, buckram, gilt top, 7*s*. 6*d*.

*** *A Limited Edition on Large Paper*, 25*s*. *net*.

CORRECTED IMPRESSIONS. Essays on Victorian Writers. By GEORGE SAINTSBURY. Crown 8vo, gilt top, 7*s*. 6*d*.

ANIMA POETÆ. From the unpublished note-books of SAMUEL TAYLOR COLERIDGE. Edited by ERNEST HARTLEY COLERIDGE. Crown 8vo, 7*s*. 6*d*.

ESSAYS. By ARTHUR CHRISTOPHER BENSON, of Eton College. Crown 8vo, buckram, 7*s*. 6*d*.

A COMMENTARY ON THE WORKS OF HENRIK IBSEN. By HJALMAR HJORTH BOYESEN. Crown 8vo, cloth, 7*s*. 6*d*. net.

THE POSTHUMOUS WORKS OF THOMAS DE QUINCEY. Edited, with Introduction and Notes from the Author's Original MSS., by ALEXANDER H. JAPP, LL.D., F.R.S.E., &c. Crown 8vo, cloth, 6*s*. each.

I. SUSPIRIA DE PROFUNDIS. With other Essays.

II. CONVERSATION AND COLERIDGE. With other Essays.

THE PROSE WORKS OF HEINRICH HEINE. Translated by CHARLES GODFREY LELAND, M.A., F.R.L.S. (HANS BREITMANN). In Eight Volumes.

The Library Edition, in crown 8vo, cloth, at 5*s.* per Volume. Each Volume of this edition is sold separately. The Cabinet Edition, in special binding, boxed, price £2 10*s.* the set. The Large Paper Edition, limited to 50 Numbered Copies, price 15*s.* per Volume net, will only be supplied to subscribers for the Complete Work.

I. FLORENTINE NIGHTS, SCHNABELEWOPSKI, THE RABBI OF BACHARACH, and SHAKESPEARE'S MAIDENS AND WOMEN.

II., III. PICTURES OF TRAVEL. 1823-1828.

IV. THE SALON. Letters on Art, Music, Popular Life, and Politics.

V., VI. GERMANY.

VII., VIII. FRENCH AFFAIRS. Letters from Paris 1832, and Lutetia.

THE COMING TERROR. And other Essays and Letters. By ROBERT BUCHANAN. Second Edition. Demy 8vo, cloth, 12*s.* 6*d.*

THE GENTLE ART OF MAKING ENEMIES. As pleasingly exemplified in many instances, wherein the serious ones of this earth, carefully exasperated, have been prettily spurred on to indiscretions and unseemliness, while overcome by an undue sense of right. By J. M'NEILL WHISTLER. *A New Edition.*

[*In preparation.*

*** A few copies of the large paper issue of the first edition remain, price £1 11*s.* 6*d. net.*

AMERICA AND THE AMERICANS. From a French Point of View. In one volume. Crown 8vo, 3*s.* 6*d.*

"MADE IN GERMANY." Reprinted with Additions from *The New Review.* By ERNEST E. WILLIAMS. Crown 8vo, cloth, 2*s.* 6*d.* Also Popular Edition, paper covers, 1*s.*

THE FOREIGNER IN THE FARMYARD. By ERNEST E. WILLIAMS, Author of "Made in Germany." Crown 8vo, 2*s.* 6*d.*

THE LABOUR MOVEMENT IN AMERICA. By RICHARD T. ELY, Ph.D., Associate in Political Economy, Johns Hopkins University. Crown 8vo, cloth, 5*s.*

PARADOXES. By MAX NORDAU, Author of "Degeneration," "Conventional Lies of our Civilisation," &c. Translated by J. R. McILRAITH. With an Introduction by the Author written for this Edition. Demy 8vo, 17*s.* *net.*

CONVENTIONAL LIES OF OUR CIVILIZATION. By MAX NORDAU, author of "Degeneration." Second English Edition. Demy 8vo, 17*s.* net.

DEGENERATION. By MAX NORDAU. Ninth English Edition. Demy 8vo, 17*s.* net.

GENIUS AND DEGENERATION: A Psychological Study. By Dr. WILLIAM HIRSCH. Translated from the Second German Edition. Demy 8vo, 17*s.* net.

THE NON-RELIGION OF THE FUTURE. From the French of MARIE JEAN GUYAU. In One Volume, demy 8vo, 17*s.* net.

STUDIES OF RELIGIOUS HISTORY. By ERNEST RENAN, late of the French Academy. 8vo, 7*s.* 6*d.*

THE PASSION PLAY AT OBERAMMERGAU, 1890. By F. W. FARRAR, D.D., F.R.S., Dean of Canterbury, &c. &c. 4to, cloth, 2*s.* 6*d.*

THE WORD OF THE LORD UPON THE WATERS. Sermons read by His Imperial Majesty the Emperor of Germany, while at Sea on his Voyages to the Land of the Midnight Sun. Composed by Dr. RICHTER, Army Chaplain, and Translated from the German by JOHN R. McILRAITH. 4to, cloth, 2*s.* 6*d.*

THE KINGDOM OF GOD IS WITHIN YOU. Christianity not as a Mystic Religion but as a New Theory of Life. By Count LEO TOLSTOY. Translated from the Russian by CONSTANCE GARNETT. Popular Edition cloth, 2*s.* 6*d.*

THE SPINSTER'S SCRIP. As Compiled by CECIL RAYNOR. Narrow crown 8vo, limp cloth, 2s. 6d.

THE PINERO BIRTHDAY BOOK. Selected and arranged by MYRA HAMILTON. With a Portrait. 16mo, cloth, 2*s.* 6*d.*

THE POCKET IBSEN. A Collection of some of the Master's best known Dramas, condensed, revised, and slightly rearranged for the benefit of the Earnest Student. By F. ANSTEY, Author of "Vice Versa," "Voces Populi," &c. With Illustrations reproduced, by permission, from *Punch*, and a new Frontispiece by BERNARD PARTRIDGE. New Edition. 16mo, cloth, 3*s.* 6*d.*; or paper, 2*s.* 6*d.*

FROM WISDOM COURT. By HENRY SETON MERRIMAN and STEPHEN GRAHAM TALLENTYRE. With 30 Illustrations by E. COURBOIN. Crown 8vo, cloth, 3*s*. 6*d*.; or picture boards, 2*s*.

WOMAN—THROUGH A MAN'S EYEGLASS. By MALCOLM C. SALAMAN. With Illustrations by DUDLEY HARDY. Crown 8vo, cloth, 3*s*. 6*d*.; or picture boards, 2*s*.

STORIES OF GOLF. Collected by WILLIAM KNIGHT and T. T. OLIPHANT. With Rhymes on Golf by various hands; also Shakespeare on Golf, &c. *Enlarged Edition.* Fcap. 8vo, cloth, 2*s*. 6*d*.

THE ROSE: A Treatise on the Cultivation, History, Family Characteristics, &c., of the various Groups of Roses. With Accurate Description of the Varieties now Generally Grown. By H. B. ELLWANGER. With an Introduction by GEORGE H. ELLWANGER. 12mo, cloth, 5*s*.

THE GARDEN'S STORY; or, Pleasures and Trials of an Amateur Gardener. By G. H. ELLWANGER. With an Introduction by the Rev. C. WOLLEY DOD. 12mo, cloth, with Illustrations, 5*s*.

GIRLS AND WOMEN. By E. CHESTER. Pot 8vo, cloth, 2*s*. 6*d*., or gilt extra, 3*s*. 6*d*.

DRIVING FOR PLEASURE; or, The Harness Stable and its Appointments. By FRANCIS T. UNDERHILL. Illustrated with One Hundred and Twenty-four full page Plates. Imperial 8vo, buckram sides, leather back, price 28*s*. net.

CONTENTS.—What Constitutes Good Form in Equipage—General Appointments—Coaching—Four-in-hand—Tandem—Horses—Coachmen—Harness and Harnessing—Driving—Liveries, Horse Clothing, etc.—The Stable—Suggestions to the Inexperienced—Bits and Bitting—The Use of Bearing Reins—Carriages.

MANNERS, CUSTOMS, AND OBSERVANCES: Their Origin and Signification. By LEOPOLD WAGNER. Crown 8vo, 6*s*.

THE GREAT WAR OF 189—. A Forecast. By Rear-Admiral COLOMB, Col. MAURICE, R.A., Captain MAUDE, ARCHIBALD FORBES, CHARLES LOWE, D. CHRISTIE MURRAY, and F. SCUDAMORE. Second Edition. In One Volume, large 8vo, with numerous Illustrations, 6*s*.

THE DRAMA: ADDRESSES. By HENRY IRVING. With Portrait by J. McN. WHISTLER. Second Edition. Fcap. 8vo, 3*s.* 6*d.*

SOME INTERESTING FALLACIES OF THE Modern Stage. An Address delivered to the Playgoers' Club at St. James's Hall, on Sunday, 6th December, 1891. By HERBERT BEERBOHM TREE. Crown 8vo, sewed, 6*d.* net.

Poetry.

POEMS FROM THE DIVAN OF HAFIZ. Translated from the Persian by GERTRUDE LOWTHIAN BELL. Small crown 8vo price 6*s.*

THE POETRY OF WILFRID BLUNT. Selected and arranged by W. E. HENLEY and GEORGE WYNDHAM. With an Introduction by W. E. HENLEY. Crown 8vo, price 6*s.*

ON VIOL AND FLUTE. By EDMUND GOSSE. Fcap. 8vo, with Frontispiece and Tailpiece, price 3*s.* 6*d.* net.

FIRDAUSI IN EXILE, and other Poems. By EDMUND GOSSE. Fcap. 8vo, with Frontispiece, price 3*s.* 6*d.* net.

IN RUSSET AND SILVER. POEMS. By EDMUND GOSSE. Author of "Gossip in a Library," etc. Fcap 8vo, price 3*s.* 6*d.* net.

THE POETRY OF PATHOS AND DELIGHT. From the Works of COVENTRY PATMORE. Passages selected by ALICE MEYNELL. With a Photogravure Portrait from an Oil Painting by JOHN SARGENT, A.R.A. Fcap. 8vo, 5*s.*

A CENTURY OF GERMAN LYRICS. Translated from the German by KATE FREILIGRATH KROEKER. Fcap. 8vo, rough edges, 3*s.* 6*d.*

LOVE SONGS OF ENGLISH POETS, 1500–1800. With Notes by RALPH H. CAINE. Fcap. 8vo, rough edges, 3*s.* 6*d.*

*** *Large Paper Edition, limited to 100 Copies, 10s. 6d. net.*

IN CAP AND GOWN. Three Centuries of Cambridge Wit. Edited by CHARLES WHIBLEY. Third Edition, with a New Introduction, and a Frontispiece, crown 8vo, 3*s.* 6*d.* net.

IVY AND PASSION FLOWER: Poems. By GERARD BENDALL, Author of "Estelle," &c. &c. 12mo, cloth, 3*s.* 6*d.*

VERSES. By GERTRUDE HALL. 12mo, cloth, 3*s.* 6*d.*

IDYLLS OF WOMANHOOD. By C. AMY DAWSON. Fcap. 8vo, gilt top, 5*s.*

TENNYSON'S GRAVE. By ST. CLAIR BADDELEY. 8vo paper, 1*s.*

THE BLACK RIDERS. And Other Lines. By STEPHEN CRANE, Author of "The Red Badge of Courage." 16mo, leather, gilt top, 3*s.* net.

Education and Science:

LITERATURES OF THE WORLD.

A SERIES OF SHORT HISTORIES.

EDITED BY EDMUND GOSSE.

Each Volume Large Crown 8vo, Cloth 6*s*.

A HISTORY OF ANCIENT GREEK LITERATURE. By GILBERT MURRAY, M.A., Professor of Greek in the University of Glasgow.

A HISTORY OF FRENCH LITERATURE. By EDWARD DOWDEN, D.C.L., LL.D., Professor of Oratory and English Literature in the University of Dublin.

A HISTORY OF MODERN ENGLISH LITERATURE. By the EDITOR, Hon. M.A. of Trinity College, Cambridge.

A HISTORY OF ITALIAN LITERATURE. By RICHARD GARNETT, C.B., LL.D., Keeper of Printed Books in the British Museum.

A HISTORY OF SPANISH LITERATURE. By J. FITZ-MAURICE-KELLY, Corresponding Member of the Spanish Academy.

The following are already arranged for :—

A HISTORY OF JAPANESE LITERATURE. By WILLIAM GEORGE ASTON, C.M.G., M.A., late Acting Secretary at the British Legation at Tokio.

A HISTORY OF MODERN SCANDINAVIAN LITERATURE. By GEORGE BRANDES, of Copenhagen.

A HISTORY OF SANSKRIT LITERATURE. By A. A. MACDONELL, M.A., Deputy Boden Professor of Sanskrit at the University of Oxford.

A HISTORY OF HUNGARIAN LITERATURE. By Dr. ZOLTAN BEÖTHY, Professor of Hungarian Literature at the University of Budapest, and Secretary of the Kisfaludy Society.

A HISTORY OF AMERICAN LITERATURE. By Professor MOSES COIT TYLER.

A HISTORY OF GERMAN LITERATURE. By Dr. C. H. HERFORD, Professor of English Literature in the University of Wales.

A HISTORY OF LATIN LITERATURE. By Dr. A. W. VERRALL, Fellow and Senior Tutor of Trinity College, Cambridge.

A HISTORY OF BOHEMIAN LITERATURE. By FRANCIS COUNT LUTZOW.

Volumes dealing with RUSSIAN, ARABIC, DUTCH, MODERN GREEK, *and other Literatures will follow in due course.*

The Great Educators.

A Series of Volumes by Eminent Writers, presenting in their entirety "A Biographical History of Education."

Each subject will form a complete volume, crown 8vo, 5*s*.

Now ready.

ARISTOTLE, and the Ancient Educational Ideals. By THOMAS DAVIDSON, M.A., LL.D.

The Times.—"A very readable sketch of a very interesting subject."

LOYOLA, and the Educational System of the Jesuits. By Rev. THOMAS HUGHES, S.J.

ALCUIN, and the Rise of the Christian Schools. By Professor ANDREW F. WEST, Ph.D.

FROEBEL, and Education by Self-Activity. By H. COURTHOPE BOWEN, M.A.

ABELARD, and the Origin and Early History of Universities. By JULES GABRIEL COMPAYRÉ, Professor in the Faculty of Toulouse.

HERBART AND THE HERBARTIANS. By CHARLES DE GARMO, Ph.D.

THOMAS AND MATTHEW ARNOLD, and their Influence on English Education. By Sir JOSHUA FITCH, M.A., LL.D., formerly Her Majesty's Inspector of Training Colleges.

HORACE MANN, and the Common School Revival in the United States. By B. A. HINSDALE, Ph.D., LL.D.

ROUSSEAU; and, Education according to Nature. By THOMAS DAVIDSON, M.A., LL.D.

In preparation.

PESTALOZZI; and the Modern Elementary School. By M. A. PINLOCHE, Professor in the University of Lille.

THE STORY OF THE GREEKS. By H. A. GUERBER. Crown 8vo, with Illustrations. 3s. 6d.

THE STORY OF THE ROMANS. By H. A. GUERBER. Crown 8vo.

ARABIC AUTHORS: A Manual of Arabian History and Literature. By F. F. ARBUTHNOT, M.R.A.S., Author of "Early Ideas," "Persian Portraits," &c. 8vo, cloth, 5*s*.

OUTLINES OF THE EARTH'S HISTORY. A Popular Study in Physiography. By NATHANIEL SOUTHGATE SHALER. 8vo, with Ten full-page Illustrations. *7s. 6d.*

EVOLUTIONAL ETHICS AND ANIMAL PSYCHOLOGY. By E. P. EVANS. Crown 8vo, *9s.*

MOVEMENT. Translated from the French of E. MAREY. By ERIC PRITCHARD, M.A., M.B., Oxon. In One Volume, crown 8vo, with 170 Illustrations, *7s. 6d.*

LUMEN. By CAMILLE FLAMMARION. Authorised Translation from the French by A. A. M. and R. M. With portions of the last chapter written specially for this edition. Crown 8vo, *3s. 6d.*

THE SPEECH OF MONKEYS. By Professor R. L. GARNER. Crown 8vo, *7s. 6d*

HEINEMANN'S SCIENTIFIC HANDBOOKS.

THE BIOLOGICAL PROBLEM OF TO-DAY: Preformation or Epigenesis? Authorised Translation from the German of Prof. Dr. OSCAR HERTWIG, of the University of Berlin. By P. CHALMERS MITCHELL, M.A., Oxon. With a Preface by the Translator. Crown 8vo. *3s. 6d.*

MANUAL OF BACTERIOLOGY. By A. B. GRIFFITHS, Ph.D., F.R.S. (Edin.), F.C.S. Crown 8vo, cloth, Illustrated. *7s. 6d.*

Pharmaceutical Journal.—"The subject is treated more thoroughly and completely than in any similar work published in this country."

MANUAL OF ASSAYING GOLD, SILVER, COPPER, Tin, and Lead Ores. By WALTER LEE BROWN, B.Sc. Revised, Corrected, and considerably Enlarged, and with chapters on the Assaying of Fuels, Iron and Zinc Ores, &c. By A. B. GRIFFITHS, Ph.D., F.R.S. (Edin.), F.C.S. Crown 8vo, cloth. Illustrated, *7s. 6d.*

GEODESY. By J. HOWARD GORE. Crown 8vo, cloth, Illustrated, *5s.*

THE PHYSICAL PROPERTIES OF GASES. By ARTHUR L. KIMBALL, of the Johns Hopkins University. Crown 8vo, cloth, Illustrated, *5s.*

HEAT AS A FORM OF ENERGY. By Professor R. H. THURSTON, of Cornell University. Crown 8vo, cloth, Illustrated, *5s.*

Law.

A SHORT TREATISE OF BELGIAN LAW AND Legal Procedure. From a Practical Standpoint, for the Guidance of British Traders, Patentees, and Bankers, and British Residents in Belgium. By GASTON DE LEVAL. Fcap. 8vo, paper, *1s. 6d.*

PRISONERS ON OATH, PRESENT AND FUTURE. By Sir HERBERT STEPHEN, Bart. 8vo, boards, *1s. net.*

THE ARBITRATOR'S MANUAL. Under the London Chamber of Arbitration. Being a Practical Treatise on the Power and Duties of an Arbitrator, with the Rules and Procedure of the Court of Arbitration, and the Forms. By JOSEPH SEYMOUR SALAMAN, Author of "Trade Marks," &c. Fcap. 8vo, *3s. 6d.*

Fiction—Popular 6s. Novels.

THE TERROR; a Romance of the French Revolution. By FÉLIX GRAS.

VIA LUCIS. By KASSANDRA VIVARIA.

THE SCOURGE-STICK. By Mrs. CAMPBELL PRAED.

THE TRIUMPH OF DEATH. By GABRIELE D'ANNUNZIO.

THE CHILD OF PLEASURE. By GABRIELE D'ANNUNZIO.

THE DULL MISS ARCHINARD. By ANNE DOUGLAS SEDGWICK.

THE BROOM OF THE WAR-GOD. By H. N. BRAILSFORD.

GOD'S FOUNDLING. By A. J. DAWSON.

THE NIGGER OF THE "NARCISSUS." By JOSEPH CONRAD.

EQUALITY. By EDWARD BELLAMY, Author of "Looking Backward."

SOLDIERS OF FORTUNE. By RICHARD HARDING DAVIS.

THE THIRD VIOLET. By STEPHEN CRANE.

THE OPEN BOAT. By STEPHEN CRANE.

PICTURES OF WAR. (The Red Badge of Courage, The Little Regiment, &c.). By STEPHEN CRANE

A ROMANCE OF THE FIRST CONSUL. By MATILDA MALLING.

THE MINISTER OF STATE. By J. A. STEUART.

THE LAKE OF WINE. By BERNARD CAPES.

EZEKIEL'S SIN. By J. H. PEARCE.

A CHAMPION IN THE SEVENTIES. By Edith A. BARNETT.

THE FOURTH NAPOLEON. By CHARLES BENHAM.

THE GADFLY. By E. L. VOYNICH.

THE CAPTAIN OF THE PARISH. By JOHN QUINE.

THE LONDONERS: An Absurdity. By ROBERT HICHENS.

FLAMES. By ROBERT HICHENS.

THE FOLLY OF EUSTACE. By ROBERT HICHENS.

AN IMAGINATIVE MAN. By ROBERT HICHENS.

THE ELEVENTH COMMANDMENT. By HALLIWELL SUTCLIFFE.

Fiction.—Popular 6s. Novels.

PHASES OF AN INFERIOR PLANET. By ELLEN GLASGOW.

GLORIA MUNDI. By HAROLD FREDERIC. [*In preparation.*

ILLUMINATION. By HAROLD FREDERIC.

HERBERT VANLENNERT. By C. F. KEARY.

ANDREA. By PERCY WHITE.

CORRUPTION. By PERCY WHITE.

MR. BAILEY-MARTIN. By PERCY WHITE. With Portrait.

THE FREEDOM OF HENRY MEREDYTH. By M. HAMILTON.

McLEOD OF THE CAMERONS. By M. HAMILTON.

A SELF-DENYING ORDINANCE. By M. HAMILTON.

THE DRONES MUST DIE. By MAX NORDAU.

THE MALADY OF THE CENTURY. By MAX NORDAU.

A COMEDY OF SENTIMENT. By MAX NORDAU.

THE WAR OF THE WORLDS. By H. G. WELLS.

THE ISLAND OF DOCTOR MOREAU. By H. G. WELLS.

THE GODS ARRIVE. By ANNIE E. HOLDSWORTH.

THE YEARS THAT THE LOCUST HATH EATEN. By ANNIE E. HOLDSWORTH.

IN HASTE AND AT LEISURE. By MRS. LYNN LINTON, Author of "Joshua Davidson," &c.

CLEO THE MAGNIFICENT. By Z. Z.

THE WORLD AND A MAN. By Z. Z.

A DRAMA IN DUTCH. By Z. Z.

BENEFITS FORGOT. By WOLCOTT BALESTIER.

A PASTORAL PLAYED OUT. By M. L. PENDERED.

CHIMÆRA. By F. MABEL ROBINSON.

MISS GRACE OF ALL SOULS'. By W. EDWARDS TIREBUCK.

Fiction.—Popular 6s. Novels.

A SUPERFLUOUS WOMAN. By EMMA BROOKE.

TRANSITION. By the Author of "A Superfluous Woman."

LIFE THE ACCUSER. The Author of "A Superfluous Woman."

COTTAGE FOLK. By Mrs. COMYNS CARR.

WITHOUT SIN. By MARTIN J. PRITCHARD.

THE TWO MAGICS. By HENRY JAMES.

WHAT MAISIE KNEW. By HENRY JAMES.

THE OTHER HOUSE. By HENRY JAMES.

THE SPOILS OF POYNTON. By HENRY JAMES.

EMBARRASSMENTS. By HENRY JAMES.

TERMINATIONS. By HENRY JAMES.

THE FAILURE OF SIBYL FLETCHER. By ADELINE SERGEANT.

OUT OF DUE SEASON. By ADELINE SERGEANT.

LAST STUDIES. By HUBERT CRACKANTHORPE. With an Introduction by Mr. HENRY JAMES, and a Portrait.

SENTIMENTAL STUDIES. By HUBERT CRACKANTHORPE.

SAINT IVES. By ROBERT LOUIS STEVENSON.

THE EBB-TIDE. By ROBERT LOUIS STEVENSON and LLOYD OSBOURNE.

THE CHRISTIAN. By HALL CAINE.

THE MANXMAN. By HALL CAINE.

THE BONDMAN. A New Saga. By HALL CAINE.

THE SCAPEGOAT. By HALL CAINE.

ELDER CONKLIN; and other Stories. By FRANK HARRIS.

Fiction.—Popular 6s. Novels.

THE HOUSE OF HIDDEN TREASURE. By MAXWELL GRAY.

THE LAST SENTENCE. By MAXWELL GRAY, Author of "The Silence of Dean Maitland," &c.

THE BETH BOOK. By SARAH GRAND.

THE HEAVENLY TWINS. By SARAH GRAND.

IDEALA. By SARAH GRAND.

OUR MANIFOLD NATURE. By SARAH GRAND. With a Portrait of the Author.

THE STORY OF A MODERN WOMAN. By ELLA HEPWORTH DIXON.

AT THE GATE OF SAMARIA. By W. J. LOCKE.

A DAUGHTER OF THIS WORLD. By F. BATTERSHALL.

ON THE FACE OF THE WATERS. By FLORA ANNIE STEEL.

THE POTTER'S THUMB. By FLORA ANNIE STEEL.

FROM THE FIVE RIVERS. By FLORA ANNIE STEEL.

IN THE PERMANENT WAY. By FLORA ANNIE STEEL.

RELICS. Fragments of a Life. By FRANCES MACNAB.

THE MASTER. By I. ZANGWILL. With Portrait.

CHILDREN OF THE GHETTO. By I. ZANGWILL,

THE PREMIER AND THE PAINTER. A Fantastic Romance. By I. ZANGWILL and LOUIS COWEN.

DREAMERS OF THE GHETTO. By I. ZANGWILL.

THE KING OF SCHNORRERS, GROTESQUES AND FANTASIES. By I. ZANGWILL. With Ninety-eight Illustrations.

THE CELIBATES' CLUB. By I. ZANGWILL.

THE RECIPE FOR DIAMONDS. By C. J. CUTCLIFFE HYNE.

MARIETTA'S MARRIAGE. By W. E. NORRIS.

THE DANCER IN YELLOW. By W. E. NORRIS.

A VICTIM OF GOOD LUCK. By W. E. NORRIS.

THE COUNTESS RADNA. By W. E. NORRIS.

THE WIDOWER. By W. E. NORRIS. [*In the Autumn.*

Fiction.—Popular 6s. Novels.

THE NAULAHKA. A Tale of West and East. By RUDYARD KIPLING and WOLCOTT BALESTIER.

A COURT INTRIGUE. By BASIL THOMSON.

KING CIRCUMSTANCE. By EDWIN PUGH.

THE MAN OF STRAW. By EDWIN PUGH.

TONY DRUM. By EDWIN PUGH. [*In preparation.*

CHUN-TI-KUNG. By CLAUDE REES.

BELOW THE SALT. By C. E. RAIMOND.

A BATTLE AND A BOY. By BLANCHE WILLIS HOWARD. With Thirty-nine Illustrations by A. MAC-NIELL-BARBOUR.

Popular 5s. Novels.

THE SECRET OF NARCISSE. By EDMUND GOSSE. Crown 8vo, buckram, 5*s.*

VANITAS. By VERNON LEE, Author of "Hauntings," &c. Crown 8vo, cloth, 5*s.*

THE ATTACK ON THE MILL. By ÉMILE ZOLA. With Twenty-one Illustrations, and Five exquisitely printed Coloured Plates, from Original Drawings by E. COURBOIN. In One Volume, 4to, 5*s.*

Popular 3s. 6d. Novels.

HER LADYSHIP'S ELEPHANT. By DAVID DWIGHT WELLS.

THE KING OF THE MOUNTAINS. By EDMOND ABOUT.

MRS. JOHN FOSTER. By CHARLES GRANVILLE.

IN SUMMER ISLES. By BURTON DIBBS.

MR. BLAKE OF NEWMARKET. By E. H. COOPER.

A PINCHBECK GODDESS. By Mrs. FLEMING (Alice M. Kipling).

THE OUTSPAN. Tales of South Africa. By J. PERCY FITZPATRICK.

THE REDS OF THE MIDI, an Episode of the French Revolution. Translated from the Provençal of Félix Gras. By Mrs. CATHERINE A. JANVIER.

ELI'S DAUGHTER. By J. H. PEARCE,

INCONSEQUENT LIVES. A Village Chronicle. By J. H. PEARCE.

Fiction.—Popular 3s. 6d. Novels.

THE KING'S JACKAL. By RICHARD HARDING DAVIES. With Four Illustrations by CHARLES DANA GIBSON.

HER OWN FOLK. (En Famille.) By HECTOR MALOT, Author of "No Relations." Translated by Lady MARY LOYD.

CAPT'N DAVY'S HONEYMOON, The Blind Mother, and The Last Confession. By HALL CAINE.

A MARKED MAN: Some Episodes in his Life. By ADA CAMBRIDGE.

THE THREE MISS KINGS. By ADA CAMBRIDGE.

A LITTLE MINX. By ADA CAMBRIDGE.

NOT ALL IN VAIN. By ADA CAMBRIDGE.

A KNIGHT OF THE WHITE FEATHER. By TASMA.

UNCLE PIPER OF PIPER'S HILL. By TASMA.

THE PENANCE OF PORTIA JAMES. By TASMA.

THE COPPERHEAD; and other Stories of the North during the American War. By HAROLD FREDERIC.

THE RETURN OF THE O'MAHONY. By HAROLD FREDERIC. With Illustrations.

IN THE VALLEY. By HAROLD FREDERIC. With Illustrations.

THE SURRENDER OF MARGARET BELLARMINE. By ADELINE SERGEANT.

THE STORY OF A PENITENT SOUL. Being the Private Papers of Mr. Stephen Dart, late Minister at Lynnbridge, in the County of Lincoln. By ADELINE SERGEANT.

THE O'CONNORS OF BALLINAHINCH. By Mrs. HUNGERFORD.

NOR WIFE, NOR MAID. By Mrs. HUNGERFORD.

THE HOYDEN. By Mrs. HUNGERFORD.

MAMMON. A Novel. By Mrs. ALEXANDER.

DAUGHTERS OF MEN. By HANNAH LYNCH.

STORIES FOR NINON. By ÉMILE ZOLA. With a Portrait by Will Rothenstein.

THE TOWER OF TADDEO. By OUIDA.

AVENGED ON SOCIETY. By H. F. WOOD.

APPASSIONATA: A Musician's Story. By ELSA D'ESTERRE KEELING.

A COMEDY OF MASKS. By ERNEST DOWSON and ARTHUR MOORE.

Fiction.—Popular 3s. 6d. Novels.

A ROMANCE OF THE CAPE FRONTIER. By BERTRAM MITFORD.

'TWEEN SNOW AND FIRE. A Tale of the Kafir War of 1877. By BERTRAM MITFORD.

ORIOLE'S DAUGHTER. By JESSIE FOTHERGILL.

THE MASTER OF THE MAGICIANS. By ELIZABETH STUART PHELPS and HERBERT D. WARD.

DONALD MARCY. By ELIZABETH STUART PHELPS.

THE HEAD OF THE FIRM. By MRS. RIDDELL.

A CONSPIRACY OF SILENCE. By G. COLMORE.

A DAUGHTER OF MUSIC. By G. COLMORE.

ACCORDING TO ST. JOHN. By AMÉLIE RIVES.

KITTY'S FATHER. By FRANK BARRETT.

THE JUSTIFICATION OF ANDREW LEBRUN. By F. BARRETT.

A QUESTION OF TASTE. By MAARTEN MAARTENS.

COME LIVE WITH ME AND BE MY LOVE. By ROBERT BUCHANAN.

IN THE DWELLINGS OF SILENCE. A Romance of Russia. By WALKER KENNEDY.

LOS CERRITOS. A Romance of the Modern Time. By GERTRUDE FRANKLIN ATHERTON.

WRECKAGE, and other Stories. By HUBERT CRACKANTHORPE.

MADEMOISELLE MISS, and other Stories. By HENRY HARLAND.

THE ATTACK ON THE MILL, and other Sketches of War. By EMILE ZOLA. With an Essay on the short stories of M. Zola by EDMUND GOSSE.

THE AVERAGE WOMAN. By WOLCOTT BALESTIER. With an Introduction by HENRY JAMES.

BLESSED ARE THE POOR. By FRANÇOIS COPPÉE. With an Introduction by T. P. O'CONNOR.

PERCHANCE TO DREAM, and other Stories. By MARGARET S. BRISCOE.

WRECKERS AND METHODISTS. Cornish Stories. By H. D. LOWRY

Fiction—Heinemann's International Library.

New Review.—"If you have any pernicious remnants of literary chauvinism I hope it will not survive the series of foreign classics of which Mr. William Heinemann, aided by Mr. Edmund Gosse, is publishing translations to the great contentment of all lovers of literature."

Each Volume has an Introduction specially written by the Editor, MR. EDMUND GOSSE.

Cloth, 3s. 6d.; Paper Covers, 2s. 6d.

IN GOD'S WAY. From the Norwegian of BJÖRNSTJERNE BJÖRNSON.

PIERRE AND JEAN. From the French of GUY DE MAUPASSANT.

THE CHIEF JUSTICE. From the German of KARL EMIL FRANZOS, Author of "For the Right," &c.

WORK WHILE YE HAVE THE LIGHT. From the Russian of Count LEO TOLSTOY.

FANTASY. From the Italian of MATILDE SERAO.

FROTH. From the Spanish of Don ARMANDO PALACIO-VALDÉS.

FOOTSTEPS OF FATE. From the Dutch of LOUIS COUPERUS.

PEPITA JIMÉNEZ. From the Spanish of JUAN VALERA.

THE COMMODORE'S DAUGHTERS. From the Norwegian of JONAS LIE.

THE HERITAGE OF THE KURTS. From the Norwegian of BJÖRNSTJERNE BJÖRNSON.

LOU. From the German of BARON ALEXANDER VON ROBERTS.

DOÑA LUZ. From the Spanish of JUAN VALERA.

THE JEW. From the Polish of JOSEPH IGNATIUS KRASZEWSKI.

UNDER THE YOKE. From the Bulgarian of IVAN VAZOFF.

FAREWELL LOVE! From the Italian of MATILDE SERAO.

THE GRANDEE. From the Spanish of Don ARMANDO PALACIO-VALDÉS.

A COMMON STORY. From the Russian of IVAN GONTCHAROFF.

WOMAN'S FOLLY. From the Italian of GEMMA FERRUGGIA.

SIREN VOICES (NIELS LYHNE). From the Danish of J. P. JACOBSEN.

NIOBE. From the Norwegian of JONAS LIE.

THE OLD ADAM AND THE NEW EVE. From the German of RUDOLF GOLM.

Fiction.—The Pioneer Series.

Cloth, 3s. net.; Paper Covers, 2s. 6d. net.

The Athenæum.—"If this series keeps up to the present high level of interest, novel readers will have fresh cause for gratitude to Mr. Heinemann."

The Daily Telegraph.—"Mr. Heinemann's genial nursery of up-to-date romance."

The Observer.—"The smart Pioneer Series."

The Manchester Courier.—"The Pioneer Series promises to be as original as many other of Mr. Heinemann's ventures."

The Glasgow Herald.—"This very clever series."

The Sheffield Telegraph.—"The refreshingly original Pioneer Series."

Black and White.—"The brilliant Pioneer Series."

The Liverpool Mercury.—"Each succeeding issue of the Pioneer Series has a character of its own and a special attractiveness."

JOANNA TRAILL, SPINSTER. By ANNIE E. HOLDSWORTH.

GEORGE MANDEVILLE'S HUSBAND. By C. E. RAIMOND.

THE WINGS OF ICARUS. By LAURENCE ALMA-TADEMA.

THE GREEN CARNATION. By ROBERT HICHENS.

AN ALTAR OF EARTH. By THYMOL MONK.

A STREET IN SUBURBIA. By E. W. PUGH.

THE NEW MOON. By C. E. RAIMOND.

MILLY'S STORY. By Mrs. MONTAGUE CRACKANTHORPE.

MRS. MUSGRAVE—AND HER HUSBAND. By RICHARD MARSH.

THE RED BADGE OF COURAGE. By STEPHEN CRANE.

THE DEMAGOGUE AND LADY PHAYRE. By WILLIAM J. LOCKE.

HER OWN DEVICES. By C. G. COMPTON.

PAPIER MACHE. By CHARLES ALLEN.

THE NEW VIRTUE. By Mrs. OSCAR BERINGER.

ACROSS AN ULSTER BOG. By M. HAMILTON.

ONE OF GOD'S DILEMMAS. By ALLEN UPWARD.

THE LITTLE REGIMENT. By STEPHEN CRANE.

LOVE FOR A KEY. By G. COLMORE.

YEKL. A Tale of the New York Ghetto. By A. CAHAN.

A MAN WITH A MAID. By Mrs. HENRY DUDENEY

Fiction.—Price 3s. net.

LITTLE JOHANNES. By F. VAN EEDEN. Translated from the Dutch by CLARA BELL. With an Introduction by ANDREW LANG. 16mo, cloth, silver top, 3s. net.

THE NOVELS OF BJÖRNSTJERNE BJÖRNSON. Uniform Edition. Edited by EDMUND GOSSE. Fcap. 8vo, cloth, 3s. net each volume.

I. SYNNÖVÉ SOLBAKKEN. With Introductory Essay by EDMUND GOSSE, and a Portrait of the Author.

II. ARNE.

III. A HAPPY BOY.

IV. THE FISHER LASS.

V. THE BRIDAL MARCH AND A DAY.

VI. MAGNHILD AND DUST.

VII. CAPTAIN MANSANA, AND MOTHER'S HANDS.

VIII. ABSALOM'S HAIR, AND A PAINFUL MEMORY.

THE NOVELS OF IVAN TURGENEV. Uniform Edition. Translated by CONSTANCE GARNETT. Fcap. 8vo, cloth, 3s. net. each volume.

I. RUDIN. With a Portrait of the Author and an Introduction by STEPNIAK.

II. A HOUSE OF GENTLEFOLK.

III. ON THE EVE.

IV. FATHERS AND CHILDREN.

V. SMOKE.

VI., VII. VIRGIN SOIL. (Two Volumes.)

VIII., IX. A SPORTSMAN'S SKETCHES. (Two Volumes).

X. DREAM TALES AND OTHER FANTASIES.

XI. THE TORRENTS OF SPRING.

XII. A LEAR OF THE STEPPES.

Fiction.—Popular 2s. 6d. Novels.

THE TIME MACHINE. By H. G. WELLS.
*** Also in paper, 1s. 6d.

THE DOMINANT SEVENTH: A Musical Story. By KATE ELIZABETH CLARKE.

Price 2s.

MAGGIE. By STEPHEN CRANE.

Popular Shilling Books.

PRETTY MISS SMITH. By FLORENCE WARDEN, Author of "The House on the Marsh," "A Witch of the Hills," &c.

THE MOMENT AFTER: A Tale of the Unseen. By ROBERT BUCHANAN.

CLUES; or, Leaves from a Chief Constable's Note-Book. By WILLIAM HENDERSON, Chief Constable of Edinburgh.

THE NORTH AMERICAN REVIEW.

Edited by DAVID A. MUNRO.

Published monthly. Price 2s. 6d.

LONDON: WILLIAM HEINEMANN, 21 BEDFORD STREET, W.C.

CPSIA information can be obtained at www.ICGtesting.com
Printed in the USA
BVOW022233210512

290782BV00007B/66/P

9 781241 447496